Vet School

Preparation, Application, Admission

YOUR JOURNEY, YOUR FUTURE

Rachel A. Winston, Ph.D.

Lizard Publishing is not sponsored by any college. While data was derived by school, state, or nationally published sources, some statistics may be out of date as published sources vary widely based upon the date of submission and currency of numbers.

Attempts were made to obtain the best information during the writing of this book from American Veterinary Medical Association, American Association of Veterinary Medical College Application Service, Veterinary Information Network, Student American Veterinary Medical Association, American Association of Equine Practitioners, World Veterinary Association, The Student Doctor Network, NCES, U.S. Census Bureau, U.S. Department of Education, Common Data Set, College Board, U.S. News & World Report, college, and other organizational sites. Descriptions of colleges are a compilation of college website information as well as student, faculty, and staff interviews with individuals and often from unique experiences and impressions.

Attempts were made to triangulate multiple points of light. If you would like to share program information, data, or an impression of a specific college, please write to Lizard Publishing at the address below or at the e-mail address: *info@mylizard.org.*

ISBN 978-1946432315 (hardback); 978-1946432308 (paperback); 978-1946432322 (e-book)

LCCN: 2021916817

Lizard Publishing* 7700 Irvine Center Drive, Suite 800 Irvine, CA 92618 *www.lizard-publishing.com*

Lizard Publishing creates, designs, produces, and distributes books and resources to provide academic, admissions, and career information. Our mental process is fueled by three tenets:

- Ignite the hunger to learn and the passion to make a difference

- Illuminate the expanse of knowledge by sharing cutting edge thinking

- Innovate to create a world that makes the transition from dreams to reality

We work with academic leaders who transform the educational landscape to publish relevant content and advise students of their educational and professional options, with the aim of developing 21st-century learners and leaders. We also work with students to publish their books and present widely diverse ideas to the college/graduate school-bound community. With headquarters in Irvine, California, Lizard Publishing works virtually with authors to edit, publish, and distribute both hard copy and paperback books.

This book was published in the U.S.A. Lizard Publishing is a premium quality provider of educational reference, career guidance, and motivational publications/merchandise for global learners, educators, and stakeholders in education.

Book design by Michelle Tahan *www.michelletahan.com*

Book formatting by Obinna Chinemerem Ozuo

LIZARD PUBLISHING

This book is dedicated to animal lovers everywhere who cannot imagine a day without animals in their lives.

This book was inspired by Bobbie Werner-Hansen, Deb Chian, and Gracie Hare.

Coming from a long line of Wisconsin and Illinois farmers, I appreciate the compassion, care, and disciplined work ethic of those raised on a farm. Long hours and constant attention to animal welfare and nutrition is a labor of love. Surrounded by companion animal lovers has also provided a keen insight into the close relationship individuals have with their pets. I have supported many students in their quest to attend vet school, including numerous students whose youth was spent with show horses, inspiring me further to understand a bigger picture of animal care and dedication.

ACKNOWLEDGMENTS

There is never enough room to acknowledge every person. Many people contributed to my perspective about veterinary medicine, assisted in the development of my knowledge base, or taught me indelible lessons. In a lifetime of experiences working with students, I am wiser and more worldly.

I gratefully acknowledge Michelle Tahan, Jasmine Jhunjhnuwala, and E. Liz Kim, as well as my family, friends, colleagues, and professors. It is with profound gratitude that I mention the many animal owners I have known.

As a faculty member in the UCLA College Counseling Certificate Program, I met many dedicated counselors who spend their life serving and supporting students. Meaningful contributions to the book have been made indirectly by admissions representatives, college counselors, and faculty members who took a special interest in this book's success.

I would also like to thank the thousands of students I have taught, counseled, or supported in my nearly four decades of service.

Isaac Newton once said, "If I see so far, it is because I stand on the shoulders of giants."

A few of those giants whose broad shoulders lifted me higher and helped teach invaluable lessons include: Zenobia Miro, David Waugh, Leonard/Roberta Mirvis, Batzi Heger, Ray Hunter, Stephanie Tahan, Gaby Diller, Catharine Malzahn, Heather Ferrero, Fariba Hemat, Donia Olia, Hyojung Lee, Haven Yang, Chenoa Craver, Ariela Osuna, Mariana Fernandez, Casey Duan, Regina DeBilio, Jacqueline Xu, Zaid Kuba, Linda Dankwa, Julianne Alfe, Tamar Nicherie, Lisa Salvi, James Mayfield, Timothy Garvin, Robert Franklin, Nanaz Manteghi, and James Sullivan.

Finally, there would be no book on vet school and no career college admissions counseling, without the support of Robert Helmer whose tireless efforts support me every single day.

> *"If I see so far, it is because I stand on the shoulders of giants."*
> *Isaac Newton*

ABOUT THE AUTHOR

Dr. Rachel A. Winston is a tireless student advocate. She has served the educational community as a university professor, college advisor, statistician, researcher, author, cryptanalyst, motivational speaker, publishing executive, and lifelong student. As one of the leading experts in college counseling and an award-winning faculty member, Dr. Winston has spent her lifetime learning, teaching, mentoring, and coaching students. Much of her counseling practice is focused on admissions to medical, dental, vet, and engineering schools.

She started college at thirteen and graduated from college programs in such widely ranging disciplines as chemistry, mathematics, computers, liberal arts, international relations, negotiation, conflict resolution, peacebuilding, business administration, higher education leadership, interpreting, college counseling, and publishing. Throughout her education, she attended Harvard, UChicago, NYU, GWU, Syracuse, Maryland, UCLA, UCI, CSUF, CSUDH, Cal Poly, ASU, Claremont Graduate University, Pepperdine, and USC among other colleges.

Her position working in Washington, D.C. on Capitol Hill and with the White House in the 1980s took her to approximately a hundred universities training campaign managers at colleges from Colorado to California, thoroughly dotting the western states. Later, she led college tours with students and their families on road trips throughout the United States. She has taught or counseled thousands of students over her career and speaks at conferences and academic programs throughout the world.

As a professor and avid writer for numerous publications, she won the 2012 McFarland Literary Achievement Award, Bletchley Park Cryptanalyst Award, and numerous other awards, including Faculty Member of the Year, Leadership Tomorrow Leader of the Year, and college service and leadership awards. While studying Human Capital at Claremont Graduate University, she was a scholarship recipient at the Drucker School of Management. She was also elected to the statewide Board of Governors for the Faculty Association for California Community Colleges, where she served on their executive committee.

She served as a faculty member for the UCLA College Counselor Certificate Program, the Director of Mathematics at Brandman University, and Embry Riddle Aeronautical University, Chapman University, Cal State Fullerton, and a handful of California Community Colleges, including Cerro Coso College where she also served as the Academic Senate President and retired in 2016. Over her career, she taught mathematics online, on television, live interactive satellite, telecourses, and in large and small lecture halls.

AUTHOR'S NOTE

You are reading this book because you are considering vet school. Whatever route you took to get to this point, you are in the right place. Right now, you need to gather information to make informed decisions.

While many people offer advice, suggestions differ. Friends will tell you the 'right' way or the way their neighbor was accepted. Graciously accept this anecdotal information while you commit to learning more. This is your future.

Dig deeper to consider both expert and current information from counselors who have worked with hundreds of students. Changes in programs, curricula, requirements, and links happen each year.

Doublecheck each program's specifics yourself. This guide is current as of August 2021 with each school's website information. However, since researching this book, changes may have taken place. There are books on vet school programs written by talented and experienced counselors. We admire and cheer on their efforts.

> "We are what we think. All that we are arises with our thoughts. With our thoughts, we make the world."
> Buddha

This guide is different in that it provides maps, lists, timelines, and unique tidbits. We hope you find this information valuable. Your job is to begin early by assembling information for the schools you are considering. Create a road map and set yourself on a clear path.

If you see an error in this book or even a suggestion for a future edition, please write to Rachel Winston at collegeguide@yahoo.com and we will fix the entry with the next printed version. All of that said, this book was written with you in mind.

There is a wealth of information on the Internet with free downloads, FAQs, testimonials, and offers to help you with your applications. Some of these advisors are knowledgeable and could help you. Students and parents hunt around the web searching for a tremendous number of hours seeking the information they need.

This book was designed to make your search easier. For now, though, we will assume that you are reasonably confident that you want to attend vet school and are exploring this avenue as a possible way to take advantage of a program that will get you on your way toward your goal.

We assume that you are a highly academic candidate who is willing to work very hard. You may have a fascination with the human body, passion for animals, and a commitment to serve others selflessly. These are virtually prerequisites for veterinary medical programs.

As you investigate colleges, you might find that some schools call these VMD or DVM programs; either way this book will help you get to your goal. Applying to and writing essays for each application will require research to determine which is right for you.

While you might believe that vet programs are relatively similar, each program's nuances make them very different. These small differences may seem confusing. Our goal with this book is to demystify the process.

CONTENTS

Part 1

The Vet School Journey

Part 2

Planning, Competencies, And Data

Part 3
Preparation

Part 4
Pre-Application: Testing And Recs

Part 5
Where And How To Apply

Part 6
The Application

Part 7
Decisions, Decisions

Part 8
Veterinary School Lists

Index

VET SCHOOL ACRONYMS

4H: Head, Heart, Hands, and Health

AABP: American Association of Bovine Practitioners

AAEP: American Association of Equine Practitioners

AAFP: American Association of Feline Practitioners

AAFCO: The Association of American Feed Control Officials

AAFHV: American Association of Food Hygiene Veterinarians

AAHA: American Animal Hospital Association

AAPHV: American Association of Public Health Veterinarians

AASP: American Association of Swine Practitioners

AAV: Association of Avian Veterinarians

AAVA: American Association of Veterinary Anatomists

AAVC: American Association of Veterinary Clinicians

AAVI: American Association of Veterinary Immunologists

AAVMC: The American Association of Veterinary Medical Colleges

AAVDM: The American Academy on Veterinary Disaster Medicine

AAWV: American Association of Wildlife Veterinarians

AAZV: American Association of Zoo Veterinarians

Abc or Abx: Antibiotic(s)

Abd: Abdomen

ABVT: American Board of Veterinary Toxicology

Ac: Before Meals

ACAW: American College of Animal Welfare

ACLAM: American College of Laboratory Animal Medicine

ACT: Activated Clotting Time

ACVA: American College of Veterinary Anesthesiologists

ACVCP: American College of Veterinary Clinical Pharmacology

ACVM: American College of Veterinary Microbiologists

ACVO: The American College of Veterinary Ophthalmologists

ACVPM: American College of Veterinary Preventive Medicine

ACVR: American College of Veterinary Radiology

ACVS: American College of Veterinary Surgeons

ACVSMR: American College of Veterinary Sports Medicine and Rehabilitation

ACZM: American College of Zoological Medicine

AD: Auris Dextra for Right Ear

ADH: Antidiuretic Hormone, Vasopressin

Ad Lib: As Desired

ADR: Ain't Doing Right

AEA: American Equestrian Alliance

AF: Atrial Fibrillation

AHC: American Horse Council

AHVMA: American Holistic Veterinary Medical Association

AI: Artificial Insemination

AIHA: Autoimmune Hemolytic Anemia

ALS: Advanced Life Support

AMA: Against Medical Advice

ANS: Autonomic Nervous System

AP: Anterior-Posterior

APHIS: Animal and Plant Health Inspection Service

APPA: American Pet Products Association

AQHA: American Quarter Horse Association

ARF: Acute Renal Failure

ARF: American Rescue Foundation

AS: Auris Sinistra for Left Ear

ASPCA: The American Society for the Prevention of Cruelty to Animals

ASVO: American Society of Veterinary Ophthalmology

AU: Auris Uterque for Both Ears

AVA: Association of Veterinary Anesthetists

AVDC: American Veterinary Dental College

AVMA: American Veterinary Medical Association

BAR: Bright, Alert and Responsive

BARH: Bright, Alert, Responsive and Hydrated

BCS: Body Condition Score

BDLD: Big Dog Little Dog (attack)

BID: Twice Per Day (every 12 hours)

BLS: Basic Life Support

BM: Bowel Movement

BP: Blood Pressure

BPH: Benign Prostatic Hypertrophy

BPM: Beats or Breaths Per Minute

BT: Bleeding Time

Bx: Biopsy
Cap: Capsule
CBC: Complete Blood Count
CC: Chief Complaint
CD: Canine Distemper
CHF: Congestive Heart Failure
CPV: Canine Parvovirus
CNS: Central Nervous System
Code/Code Blue - Emergency Help
COPD: Chronic Obstructive Pulmonary Disease
COR: Care of remains
CRF: Chronic Renal Failure
CRI: Constant Rate Infusion
CRT: Capillary Refill Time
CSVD: Coughing, Sneezing, Vomiting, Diarrhea
CT Scan: Computed Tomography
CV: Cardiovascular
CVM: College of Veterinary Medicine
CVMA: California Veterinary Medical Association
CVPM: Certified Veterinary Practice Manager
CXR: Chest X-ray (radiograph)
D+: Diarrhea
DACVS: Diplomate, American College of Veterinary Surgeons
DACVECC: Emergency & Critical Care Specialty
DACVIM: Internal Medicine Specialty
DACVR: Radiology Specialty
DACVS: Surgical Specialty
DBW: Dog Bite Wound
D/C: Discontinue
DDD: Degenerative Disc Disease
DDL: Dull, Depressed, Lethargic
DDX : Differential Diagnosis
D.E.L.T.A.: Dedication and Everlasting Love to Animals
DFW: Dog Fight Wounds
DJD: Degenerative Joint Disease
DLH: Domestic Long Hair
DMH: Domestic Medium-Haired Cat
DNR: Do Not Resuscitate

DOA: Dead on Arrival
DSH: Domestic Short Hair
DVM: Doctor of Veterinary Medicine
Dx: Diagnosis
ECG or EKG: Electrocardiogram
ED: Every Day
EEG: Electroencephalogram
EENT: Eyes, ears, nose and throat
EHV: Equine Herpes Virus
EIA: Equine Infectious Anemia
EOD: Every Other Day
EPM: Equine Protozoal Myeloencephalitis
ER: Emergency Room
FAD: Flea Allergy Dermatitis
FAO: Food and Agriculture Organization of the United Nations
FBS: Fasting Blood Sugar
FDA: Food and Drug Administration
Fel: Feline
FeLV: Feline Leukemia Virus
FFA: Future Farmers of America
Fl: Fluid
FIA: Feline Infectious Anemia
FIP: Feline Infectious Peritonitis
FIV: Feline Immunodeficiency Virus
F/I: Intact Female
F/S: Spayed Female
FLUTD: Feline Lower Urinary Tract Disease
FNA: Fine Needle Aspirate
FUO: Fever of Unknown Origin
FX: Fracture
GAPFA: The Global Alliance of Pet Food Associations
GDV: Gastric Dilatation-Volvulus (Bloat)
GI: Gastrointestinal
HBC: Hit by Car
HCT: Hematocrit
HD: Hip Dysplasia
HGE: Hemorrhagic Gastroenteritis
HR: Heart Rate

HW: Heartworm

Hx: History

IAAAM: The International Association for Aquatic Animal Medicine

ICU: Intensive Care Unit

IM: Intramuscular

IMHA: Immune-Mediated Hemolytic Anemia

IN: Internasal

Inj: Injection

IRIS: The International Renal Interest Society

ISID: International Society for Infectious Diseases

IV: Intravenous

K9: Canine

M/I: Intact Male

M/N: Neutered Male

MRCVS: Member of the Royal College of Veterinary Surgeons

MRI: Magnetic Resonance Imaging

NAF: No Abnormal Findings

NAVLE: North American Veterinary Licensing Examination

NBVME: The National Board of Veterinary Medical Examiners

NPO: Nothing by Mouth

NSF: No Significant Findings

NSVECCC: National Student Veterinary Emergency and Critical Care Society

NVL: No Visible Lesions

O: Owner

OD: Oculus Dextrus for Right Eye

OIE: International Office of Epizootics

OS: Oculus Sinister for Left Eye

OSI: Owner Stopped In

OU: Oculus Uterque for Both Eyes

OV: Office Visit

OVMA: Ontario Veterinary Medical Association

PAWS: Performing Animal Welfare Society

PCFO: Phone Call from Owner

PCTO: Phone Call to Owner

PCV: Packed Cell Volume

PE: Physical Exam

PETA: People for the Ethical Treatment of Animals

PO: Per

PRN: As Needed

PTS: Put to Sleep (Euthanasia)

PU/PD: Polyuric/Polydipsic (excessive drinking and urine)

Q: Every (q4hrs means every 4 hours)

QAR: Quiet, Alert, Responsive

QD: Every Day

QOL: Quality of Life

rDVM: Referring Veterinarian

REM: Rapid Eye Movement

R/O: Rule Out

ROM: Range of Motion

RR: Respiration Rate

RRT: Renal Replacement Therapy

Rx: Prescription

SADS: Sudden Arrhythmia Death Syndrome

SAPL: Society for Animal Protective Legislation

SC/SQ: Subcutaneous (Under the Skin)

S/R: Suture Removal

SID: Once Daily/ Every 24 hours

SOAP: Subjective, Objective, Assessment, Plan — a method of organizing medical records

STAT: Immediately

SVECCS: Student Veterinary Emergency & Critical Care Society

SX: Surgery

Sz: Seizure

TID: Three Times Daily/Every 8 Hours

TPR: Temperature, Pulse and Respiration Rates

TX: Treatment

TMDSAS: Texas Medical and Dental School Application Service

UA: Urinalysis

UR: Urination

URI: Upper Respiratory Infection

U/S: Ultrasound

USAHA: United States Animal Health Association

USDA: United Sates Department of Agriculture

USEF: United States Equestrian Federation

UTI: Urinary Tract Infection

V+: Vomiting

V/D: Vomiting/Diarrhea

VCS: Veterinary Cancer Society

VECCS: Veterinary Emergency Critical Care Society

VMCAS: Veterinary Medical College Application Service

VMD: Veterinariae Medicinae Doctoris offered at UPenn (equivalent of a DVM)

VMSAR: Veterinary Medical School Admissions Requirements

VTS: Veterinary Technician Specialty

VX: Vaccine

WHO: World Health Organization

WNL: Within Normal Limits

WVA: World Veterinary Association

PART 1

THE VET SCHOOL JOURNEY

"*Personally, I have always felt that the best doctor in the world is the veterinarian. He can't ask his patients what is the matter... he's just got to know.*"

—Will Rogers

CHAPTER 1

THE LANDSCAPE OF VETERINARY EDUCATION: WHY VET SCHOOL?

Most students who apply to vet school know long before college that they want to be a vet. Typically, this pursuit does not arise from an epiphany that emerges in college, though a few decide to pursue vet school during their undergraduate studies. Rather, most pre-vet students grew up around pets, zoos, wildlife, barns, farms, or livestock and had an internal drive that motivates them to care for animals, ensure the safety of strays, and improve the lives of those in the animal kingdom.

Veterinary medicine applies to the gamut of non-human life. Your patients may be domesticated, stray, or used for agricultural harvesting, dairy production, or food supply. Vet schools also cover marine life. Veterinarians need to learn all aspects of medicine, health maintenance, genetics, fertility, and nutrition.

Vet school takes four years to complete. Most vet students have a bachelor's degree, though this is not required for some vet schools. The median pay is not as high as that of a physician, but growth in the field and demand for veterinarians is high. Conventional and alternative therapies are considered.

There are approximately 450 veterinary degree programs worldwide recognized by the World Health Organization (WHO).

IMPORTANCE OF VETERINARY MEDICINE

Veterinary medicine aids in the prevention, control, diagnosis, and treatment of diseases that affect domestic and wild land and aquatic animals. Veterinarians examine animals to assess their health and diagnose problems, treat and dress wounds, perform surgical procedures, vaccinate against diseases, diagnose diseases, prescribe medications to treat the sick, and counsel owners on proper care.[1]

Vets are also concerned with the transmission of diseases from animals to man.[2] Veterinarians, often called animal doctors, maintain health and improve animals' lives. In turn, the work of veterinarians may translate to better health for humans. An essential part of a vet's job is working with pet owners. This relationship is a crucial part of the job because vets provide valuable information on the preventative measures that can keep animals healthy.

Veterinary medicine is also critical to humankind. Veterinarians treat all types of animals, help ensure the health of animals for a constant supply of food, prevent the transmission of diseases from animals to man, and avert the extinction of animal species. Yet, animals live on four times more of the earth's surface than do humans.[3] This dilemma results in a significant challenge for veterinarians who study various species of animals.

PET OWNERSHIP

In June 2021, a study released by the American Pet Products Association (APPA) showed that pet ownership increased to 70%, with millennials as the largest cohort of pet owners.[4] The survey's press release also provided the following information:

- Pet spending increased approximately 35% during the pandemic. Food, health, and pet care topped the list.

1   Truity, "Veterinarian," *Truity*, 2020, https://www.truity.com/career-profile/veterinarian

2   John M. Bowen, "Veterinary Medicine," *Encyclopedia Britannica*, July 25, 2018, https://www.britannica.com/science/veterinary-medicine

3   Hannah Ritchie, "Humans Make Up Just 0.01% of Earth's Life – What's the Rest?," *Our World in Data*, April 24, 2019 https://ourworldindata.org/life-on-earth

4   Peyton Burgess, "American Pet Products Association Releases Newest Edition of National Pet Owners Survey," *American Pet Products Association*, June 22, 2021, https://www.americanpetproducts.org/press_releasedetail.asp?id=1242

- Approximately 14% of the pet and non-pet owner respondents obtained a new pet, including fish, dogs, birds, cats, reptiles, and horses.
- Online shopping increased nearly 20% due to the limited access to brick-and-mortar stores. Meanwhile, in-person shopping dropped 41%.
- Ethically sourced and financially prudent pet products increased in popularity by 51%.
- More non-cat pet owners purchased pet insurance, amounting to nearly double the rate for cat owners.

As a result of the increase in pet ownership, the demand for veterinarians grew significantly in 2021. The U.S. Bureau of Labor Statistics estimates that the profession will grow 16% over this decade.[5] This trend is global, attributed to the rising instances of pet ownership worldwide.

EXTENDED ANIMAL LIFESPAN

Today, veterinarians perform animal surgery and cancer treatment along with pet health repair and maintenance. Due to improved products, vaccinations, and care, this change has improved animals' overall health, allowing them to maintain a better quality of life and life expectancy. Today, studies show that pets such as cats and dogs are living longer than they once did. Improvements in vet medicine forwarded this trend. For example, a study revealed that the life expectancy for both cats and dogs increased by more than 10% after these improved changes in veterinary medicine.[6]

EMPATHY IS A CORE REQUIREMENT

While there is no test for a person's empathy, vet school admissions officers can tell a great deal from interviewing you and intently listening to your responses, watching your body language, and exploring your sensitivities. Some vet schools require a situational judgment test, called CASPer (Computer-Based Assessment for Sampling Personal Characteristics), but this does not test empathy per se. However, people skills are essential, and empathy is necessary.

---

5 U.S. Bureau of Labor Statistics, "Veterinarians," *U.S. Bureau of Labor Statistics*, n.d., https://www.bls.gov/ooh/healthcare/veterinarians.htm

6 Ross University, "What Do Veterinarians Do?," *Ross University*, n.d., https://veterinary.rossu.edu/about/news/what-do-veterinarians-do

COMMUNICATION TAKES NUMEROUS FORMS

As opposed to working with human patients who can tell you how they feel or where it hurts, veterinarians need to communicate in creative, gentle, and sympathetic ways. The diagnosis may require touching different areas and sensing an animal's needs. The owner may intuitively know these intimate understandings. However, the necessary deductive reasoning involved in veterinary medicine requires a certain amount of sleuth work using medical history, utterances, actions, and symptoms. Therefore, working closely and communicating effectively with the owner is essential. The owner can offer clues in many cases, but sometimes the investigation may require building a communication bridge with the animal through trust-building and support.

SPEND TIME AROUND ANIMALS

In vet school, you are likely to be around a wider variety of animals than wherever you were raised. As a result, you may feel comfortable with some types of animals, though awkward with others. However, it would help if you learned more about those with which you are less familiar. Getting a paid or volunteer job at a zoo or pet store will broaden your understanding. A deep, sincere appreciation and understanding of animals' needs is a fundamental requirement.

WORK WITH A VET OR ANIMAL RESEARCHER

Shadowing a vet is an excellent start to understanding a veterinary medical practice. Some people have owned their pets or farm animals for much of their life. Bringing their animal to a vet clinic or hospital is often a personal and emotional experience. While visits to the vet involve grooming, vaccinations, and checkups, occasionally, the visit is for a situation that is more serious. Pet owners often feel great pain, knowing about any illness, disease, or injury to their pet. Unfortunately, some of the animals need to be put down. Procedures of all kinds should be handled with kindness, compassion, and understanding toward the pet and its owners.

DISCIPLINE YOURSELF TO LEARN SCIENCE

You cannot get accepted to vet school without a strong foundation in science. A corollary is that you cannot complete vet school without understanding the intricacies of biochemistry, pharmacology, immunology, anatomy, physiology, microbiology, cell and molecular biology, reproduction, and many other areas of science. Each subject builds upon the other. Thus, a strong foundation in biology, chemistry, and physics is essential. Disciplined, independent thinking also correlates to success in vet school and the practice of veterinary medicine.

VET SCHOOL PREREQUISITES

While the most current information about prerequisites and requirements is on each school's website, this takes considerable time, particularly if you do not know which schools you want to attend. The prerequisite chart in the following URL is extremely helpful as a point of reference: *https://www.aavmc.org/assets/Site_18/ files/VMCAS/VMCASprereqchart.pdf*

ETHICAL MENTALITY

Ethical practices underpin veterinary medicine. Veterinarians have a duty to protect animals and recognize the signs of animals trapped without the ability to walk, not given proper nutrition for long periods of time, and are being abused. Some animals are transported as mules for drug pushers, runners, or cartels.[7]

Cruelty to animals is rampant, including starvation, abandonment, neglect, zoosadism, animal testing, and sponsored animal fights. Unfortunately, since most state and federal agencies do not compile statistics on animal cruelty, most cases are unreported, and few people are prosecuted.

In February 2021, the U.S. government produced statues regarding animals. The "Federal Statutes Protecting Domesticated and Captive Animals" includes[8]

> A number of federal laws aim to protect the health, safety, and well-being of animals under human control. These laws extend to pets, domesticated livestock, service animals, test subjects, and wild animals kept for exhibition, scientific, or educational purposes, among others. Some prohibit specific harmful acts, others prescribe standards for certain types of activities, and others require owners to have permits and meet certain criteria to possess various types of animals.

7   Tom Hays, "US: Vet Implanted Heroin in Puppies for Colombia Drug Ring," *AP News*, May 1, 2018, https:// apnews.com/article/92c76495809840b180d35918bb7a899b

8   Congressional Research Service, "Federal Statutes Protecting Domesticated and Captive Animals," *Congressional Research Service*, February 5, 2021, https://fas.org/sgp/crs/misc/R46672.pdf

RESOURCES FOR YOUR PURSUIT OF VET SCHOOL

You can obtain valuable information from the American Veterinary Medical Association and the Association of American Veterinary Medical Colleges (AAVMC). This book provides the current information about colleges, requirements, admissions processes, tests, costs, etc., about each vet school as of the summer of 2021. However, you can always find additional information through the Veterinary Medical College Application Service (VMCAS) at website *http://www.aavmc.org*

The AAVMC VMCAS College Chart, current as of May 2021, that summarizes vet school data and admissions requirements, is available at *https://admin. applytovetschool.org/wp-content/uploads/2021/05/General-Info-Chart-VMCAS-2022. pdf.* This chart also includes links to each of the vet schools.

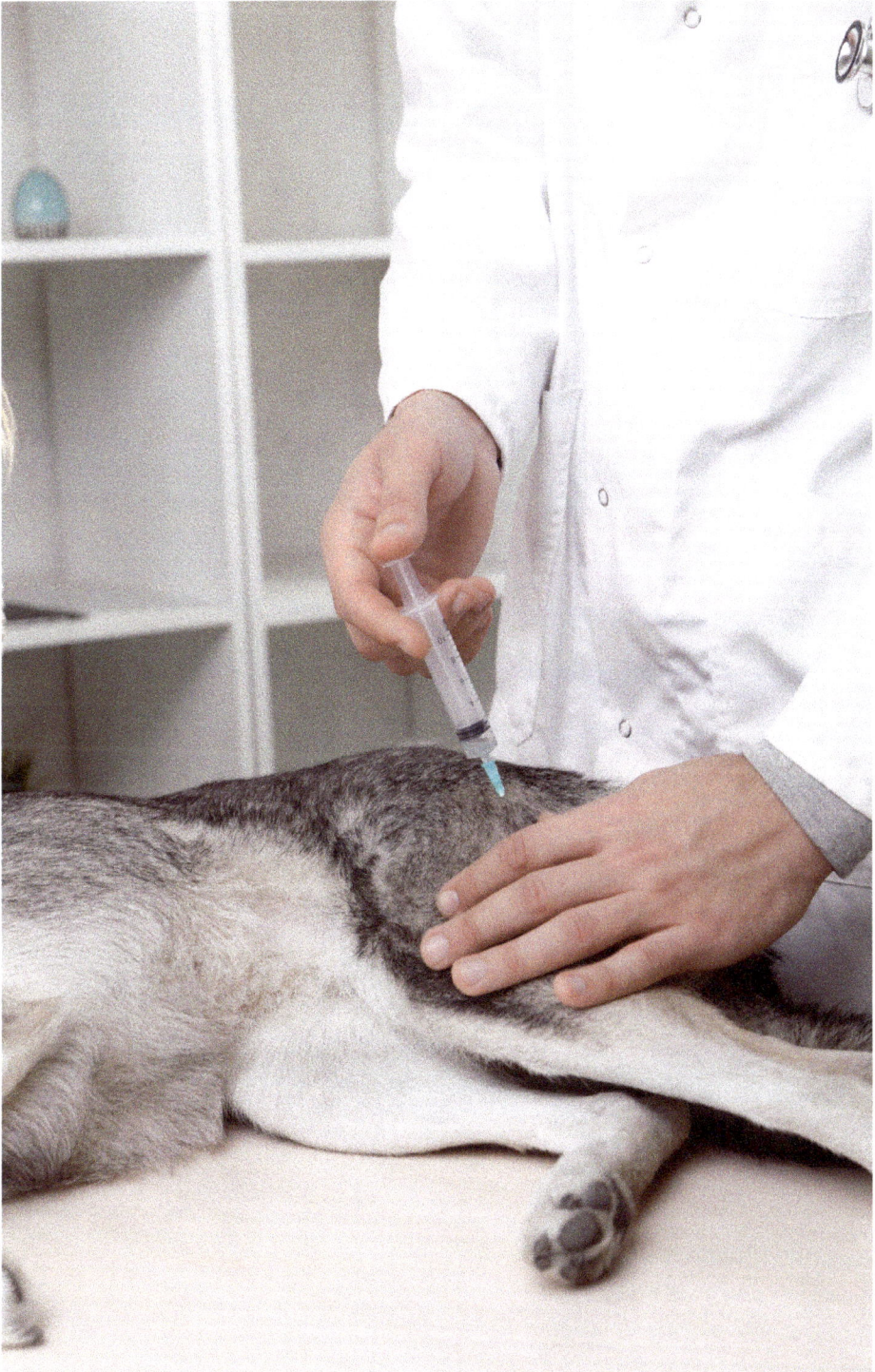

"*Dogs come into our lives to teach us about love, they depart to teach us about loss. A new dog never replaces an old dog; it merely expands the heart. If you have loved many dogs, your heart is very big.*"

– E. Jong

CHAPTER 2

THE PRACTICE OF VETERINARY MEDICINE

Veterinary medicine is the medical discipline encompassing the prevention, diagnosis, and treatment of disease, disorder, and damage in nonhuman living creatures. Veterinary science also deals with animal husbandry, breeding, nutrition, toxicology, environmental exposure, and product development. In addition, veterinary medicine supports and engages with domesticated and wild species, along with a broad spectrum of environments, factors, injuries, and maladies.

SPECIALIZATIONS AND PRACTICES

Veterinary medicine is practiced in emergency situations as well as in long-term care and maintenance. A veterinary surgeon (also known as a veterinarian, veterinary surgeon, or "vet") provides professional treatment, typically with support staff. Paraveterinary personnel such as intake support, groomers, technicians, and veterinary nurses also play a role. Paraprofessionals, surrounding veterinary medicine, offer specific expertise, such as animal physiotherapists, dentists, nutritionists, chiropractors, farriers, even sport-horse specialists as well as species-specific occupations.[1]

---

1   The Editors of Encyclopaedia Britannica, "Veterinary Medicine," *Encyclopaedia Britannica*, July 25, 2018, https://www.britannica.com/science/veterinary-medicine

Some veterinarians are small animal specialists, primarily providing care for dogs and cats. Clinics vary in size and capabilities. Since imaging equipment is costly, most small clinics refer their patients to specialized centers or animal hospitals providing that service. Veterinary assistants may assist with blood draws, vaccine injections, catheter placements, and surgeries. Typical procedures include anesthetic procedures, mass removals, and neutering.

IMPACT OF THE PANDEMIC

Veterinary medicine changed, adapting to the new conditions of quarantine, social distancing, masks, and genuine concerns for their health and the health of their patients. In addition, many employees were unavailable to work or could not work in possibly compromised settings. This required changes in the practice and a re-imagined clinical environment.

As a result, many vets provided "house calls" to locations where they could treat animals on their home premises. Occasionally, this began with a "televisit", where owners relayed the situation, symptoms, and circumstances, allowing the vet to see the animal online, inspect the problem virtually, and follow up with a visit – in the clinic or at the patient's home.

As the pandemic wore on and clinics partially opened, veterinary assistants walked out to cars in parking lots where pet owners discussed the reason for the visit and provided intake at the vehicles. With the owners remaining in the cars, a vet assistant brought the patient into the clinic to take vitals, log pertinent data, and present the information to the veterinarian before seeing the patient.

The vet's next step included analyzing the circumstances, gleaning information from lab results, and making a diagnosis. Using apps, text, and/or e-mail between the veterinary medical staff and the pet owners, consistent communication flowed to those waiting in the car. The situation was not ideal, but veterinarians innovated and adapted to the new environment, consistently improving communication to reduce anxiety and provide comprehensive, holistic care.

Large animal vets also needed to adapt to the pandemic environment. Since large animal veterinarians typically do not have a treatment center or clinic, they work and travel in geographic areas, sometimes in different cities. The vet practice moves and schedules change in the event of an emergency. Since large animals live in larger open spaces and often on farms and ranches, traditional on-site veterinary practices prevailed during the pandemic. That cannot be said for small animal veterinarians, where treatment is usually conducted in a clinical setting. Furthermore, the treatment of marine life would present all-together unique circumstances.

The COVID-19 quarantine and shutdown forced vets to rethink their practices and improve delivery on all levels with all types of nonhuman species. With the goal to provide the best services possible, each step from social distancing and televisits to communication and house calls, changes needed to be made. Some modifications will be permanent for efficiency, while others will be dismissed, like pet owners being in closer contact with the patient during the diagnosis and treatment process.

It is important to note that an increased number of pets, particularly during the pandemic, were adopted as comfort animals for support and therapy given the conditions related to quarantine, isolation, and need for companionship. Animals of all types need care, just as humans do. Yet, in some cases, mainly regarding abuse, nutrition, nurturing, and healthcare are absent. Thus, veterinarians commit to lifelong learning, proper procedures, and compassionate care.

VETERINARY SCIENCE AND RESEARCH COLLABORATION

Veterinary science and clinical practices contribute to animal and human health. By studying, researching, monitoring, and controlling zoonotic disease (infectious diseases transmitted from nonhuman animals to people), veterinary scientists and practitioners continue improving care and treatment. With the growing populations of humans and animals, new ways of thinking need to go hand-in-hand with geographically accessible space, climate change, and alternative therapies.

New diseases have been shown to emanate from animals. Since viruses can jump from animals to humans, research is necessary to prevent widespread pandemics. Within the last decade, society discovered the perils of outbreaks within stocks of pigs, cows, and bats and continued problems related to mosquitos and other insects. Human food supplies could be threatened quickly without mitigation by monitoring and treating livestock and ensuring animals' mental, physical, and nutritional health.

Veterinary scientists frequently collaborate with epidemiologists and scientists in a wide range of fields. Veterinary surgeons, required by law to protect the welfare of animals, aid in serving the animal community. Veterinarians assist by keeping animals safe and healthy, though there are shortages of vet facilities and veterinarians in some parts of the country. This disparity is significant to note, and vet schools are keenly aware of critical needs. By diagnosing, treating, and preventing illness, society can improve health for all living creatures.

"The man who moves a mountain begins by carrying away small stones."

– Confucius

CHAPTER 3

ORIGINS OF VETERINARY MEDICINE

TRANSFORMATION IN THE CARE OF ANIMALS

Over the last 100 years, the field of veterinary medicine witnessed a significant transformation. Now, in the 2020s, it is difficult to recall a time when cats, dogs, cows, and horses did not have access to a veterinarian. However, the widespread practice of veterinary medicine is relatively recent. For centuries, veterinarians mainly treated animals used for transportation like horses, donkeys, mules, goats, sheep, and camels. However, the field of veterinary medicine has grown significantly.

It has been said that necessity is the mother of invention. This proverb, attributed to Plato, rings true with the care and treatment of animals. With millions of animals in our world's food supply, proper nutrition has almost always been a concern. As a result, taking care of livestock grew increasingly important. However, for people to take their pets or livestock to see a medically-trained animal doctor was far less common in the 19th century. Finally, in the early 1900s, animals started to receive more medical attention.

There are many advancements factored into the development of veterinary medicine. One is the advent of new treatments for human diseases, which saves the lives of millions. This occurrence may have inspired the belief that animals could also be spared from outbreaks with more research. The typhoid vaccine came out in 1896. Malaria and yellow fever that plagued the construction of the Panama Canal was overcome at the opening of the 20th century. The polio vaccine emerged in 1955, and immunization for mumps happened in the mid-1900s. With the realization that medical science had answers, farmers could save their herds, zoos could preserve their animals, and pet owners could heal their pets.

Other precipitating events include the first zoo that opened in 1874 in Philadelphia, Pennsylvania. In 1879, Iowa State University, as it is now known, established the first college of veterinary medicine in the United States. Forty-one new vet schools opened in the next few decades, though many closed with the 1929 stock market crash, two world wars, and a change in transportation from horses to motor vehicles. Today, there are 33 vet schools in the United States.

DOMESTICATION OF ANIMALS

Without concrete documentation, little of which remains today, it is hard to determine when or where veterinary medicine originated. Similarly, it is impossible to say when or where animal husbandry began or where dogs were first domesticated. Most likely, veterinary medicine developed rapidly after the initial domestication of animals.

Since humans and wolves competed for food and often killed each other, and since humans stored food and shared their stores with wolves during long ice age winters, they soon relied on each other as wolves became hunting companions and guardians. "Based on paleogenomic analysis, the investigators concluded that Eastern and Western dogs diverged between 17,000 and 24,000 years ago, representing a single origin for domestication, which existed between about 20,000 and 40,000 years ago."[1]

Chickens were domesticated about 10,000 years ago in Southeast Asia. Over time, they were fed and bred to be larger to obtain more meat. While early chickens may have been a couple of pounds and laid a few eggs yearly, now domesticated chickens can weigh over seventeen pounds and lay a couple of hundred eggs.[2] For comparison, the largest turkey was a stag named Tyson who won London's

---

1   Naveed Saleh, "When Did Man First Domesticate Dogs?," *Psychology Today,* March 24, 2021, https://www.psychologytoday.com/us/blog/the-red-light-district/202103/when-did-man-first-domesticate-dogs

2   National Geographic, "Domestication," *National Geographic,* n.d., https://www.nationalgeographic.org/encyclopedia/domestication/

"Heaviest Turkey" competition in 1989, weighing in at 86 pounds.[3] The turkey was auctioned for charity.

Horses are thought to have been domesticated around 6,000 BCE in the Ukraine and Kazakhstan.[4] However, the domestication of goats and sheep began around 10,000 BCE.[5] Historical records trace the growth of veterinary medicine to the ancient civilizations of China, Mesopotamia, Egypt, and India, long before it reached Greece and Rome, where it spread throughout Europe. In early Mesopotamia, goats and sheep were tamed to obtain milk and meat for food and hides for clothing and tents, though oxen were used for plowing fields and horses were used for transportation. Domestication changed the way of life for humans since it eliminated the need to travel by foot and enabled leaving villages to hunt for food, hides, and tools while also forming a stable place to raise livestock.

EARLY PRACTICES OF VETERINARY MEDICINE

Physicians in Asia and the Near East practiced veterinary medicine long before written records attest. Greek and Roman writers who highlighted the pioneers of veterinary medicine, like Gallen or Hippocrates, called them the "Fathers of Veterinary Medicine". In actuality, they only contributed to practices that began thousands of years earlier.[6] Evidence shows that veterinary medicine has existed in China for over 10,000 years.

Emperor Fusi, according to mythology, taught the primordial Chinese society how to domesticate animals and the duties required to care for them. Fusi established training for animal husbandry and veterinary medicine in China. Likewise, shepherds in Middle Eastern countries relied on a "rudimentary understanding" of basic medical techniques and skills to care for their dogs and other livestock.[7]

---

3   Talia Lakritz, "The 10 Wildest Thanksgiving-themed Guinness World Records," *Insider*, November 26, 2020, https://www.insider.com/thanksgiving-guinness-world-records-photos-2019-11

4   Helen Briggs, "Mystery of Horse Taming 'Solved' by Gene Study," *BBC News*, May 8, 2012 https://www.bbc.com/news/science-environment-17943974

5   National Geographic, "Domestication," *National Geographic,* n.d., https://www.nationalgeographic.org/encyclopedia/domestication/

6   Joshua J. Mark, "A Brief History of Veterinary Medicine," *World History Encyclopedia,* April 30, 2020, https://www.worldhistory.org/article/1549/a-brief-history-of-veterinary-medicine/

7   Michigan State University College of Veterinary Medicine, "Hammurabi and Hippocrates: Veterinary Medicine BCE," *Michigan State University College of Veterinary Medicine,* February 6, 2019, https://cvm.msu.edu/vetschool-tails/hammurabi-and-hippocrates-veterinary-medicine-bce

Thousands of years later, in Egypt, though undeveloped as a science, between 4,000 and 3,000 BCE, animal medical therapy grew in importance. Cats, dogs, and poultry were domesticated. Their owners treated them as family, much as many do today. The first written reports of veterinary medicine are written in four sacred Hindu books around 1,900 BC. Two independent texts outlined the domains of human and animal medicine. In 1850, archaeologists uncovered papyrus fragments from an ancient veterinary medical textbook describing diseases affecting birds, cattle, dogs, and fish. Since horses were vital for transportation, agriculture, and trade, they were the primary focus.

Ancient veterinarians employed early types of herbal medicine during the Stone Age. Urlugaledinna, who lived in the Mesopotamia region (modern-day Syria, Iraq, Iran, Turkey, and Kuwait) at the beginning of the Bronze Age (about 3000 BCE), was renowned with extraordinary compassion for animals, adept at healing injuries, and able to cure illnesses. Medical doctors with relatively high social status in Sumeria were known as the a-zu, as found on an excavated tablet dating back to 2700 B.C. One of the Sumerian Lagash physicians, Urlugaledinna (2141-2122 BCE), who also served under Ur-Ningirsu, son of Gudea (r. 2121-2118 BCE), was a doctor of oxen and donkeys.[8]

With the need to care for animals, by 3000 BCE, veterinarians had already established themselves in Mesopotamia. With the work performed by these early veterinarians, the profession had established enough credibility to specify animal-related sicknesses and therapies. In 1930 BCE, the Code of Eshnunna defined rabies, its symptoms, and the fee the owner of a rabid dog that bites someone must pay.

Healing practices were often associated with the divine. Gula (also known as Ninkarrak and Ninisinna) was the Babylonian goddess of health and healing. Her sons Damu and Ninazu were considered the Gods of healing. Ninazu, associated with serpents, symbolizing metamorphosis, healing, and the underworld, was the most influential. Gula's symbol was the staff of intertwined serpents, later associated with Hippocrates, and is now emblematic of the medical profession.[9]

---

8   Samuel Noah Kramer, *The Sumerians: Their History, Culture, and Character* (Chicago: The University of Chicago Press, 1963).

9   OVRS Staff, "Retrospective: A Brief History of Veterinary Medicine," *Oakland Veterinary Referral Services*, September 27, 2019, https://www.ovrs.com/blog/history-of-veterinary-medicine/

Since the practice of veterinary medicine began as early as 2000 BCE in Babylonia and Egypt, it was there that it first became a specialty.[10] Veterinary care was established as a respectable profession in the Code of Hammurabi (1754 BCE), which distinguished veterinarians from other medical practitioners and set their fees.[11] Another record of veterinary medicine is the Egyptian Papyrus of Kahun (12th dynasty of Egypt). The Shalihotra Samhita is an early Indian veterinary treatise, dating back to the time of Ashoka, stating, "King Piyadasi, made provision for two types of medical treatment: medical treatment for humans and medical treatment for animals. Wherever medical herbs suitable for humans or animals are not available, I have had them imported and grown. Wherever medical roots or fruits are not available, I have had them imported and grown. Along roads, I have had wells dug and trees planted for the benefit of humans and animals."[12] The world's first veterinary hospital provided treatments in India during the reign of Ashoka, the great king (r. c. 268 - c. 232 BCE), with its underlying concept based on Shalihotra's work.

It is unknown whether Egyptian veterinary techniques were brought to India or developed independently, but veterinarians were well-established and respected by the Vedic Period (c. 1500-500 BCE). According to R. Somvanshi, the first veterinarians were religious priests responsible for maintaining cattle. Early Vedic hymns mention the healing properties of herbs, using medicinal knowledge to keep livestock healthy.[13]

Sushruta, regarded as the "Father of Indian Medicine," developed medical techniques to treat humans and animals. Sushruta Samhita (Sushruta's Compendium), an Ayurvedic classic, provided the foundation for India's veterinary practice. According to Somvanshi, in ancient India, animals were revered, receiving medical attention as needed. Shalihotra (3rd century BCE) was an animal-loving physician. Sushruta's work on human anatomy, physiology, and surgical methods served as the basis for his veterinary science book, the Shalihotra Samhita.[14]

---

10   Fielding D. O'Niell, "Ancient History of Veterinary Medicine," *Tuckahoe Veterinary Hospital*, n.d., https://www.tuckahoevet.com/post/ancient-history-of-veterinary-medicine

11   Joshua J. Mark, "Code of Hammurabi," *World History Encyclopedia*, June 24, 2021, https://www.worldhistory.org/Code_of_Hammurabi/

12   Joshua J. Mark, "The Edicts of Ashoka the Great," *World History Encyclopedia*, June 29, 2020, https://www.worldhistory.org/Edicts_of_Ashoka/

13   Satish Saroshe, "Sushruta: The Ancient Indian Surgeon," *Hektoen International*, n.d., https://hekint.org/2017/01/22/sushruta-the-ancient-indian-surgeon/

14   Antiquariat Inlibris Gilhofer Nfg. GmbH, "A Manual on Horses, Illustrated with 21 Large Miniatures," *Antiquariat Inlibris Gilhofer Nfg. GmbH*, n.d., https://inlibris.com/item/bn48774/

GREEK AND ROMAN ANIMAL MEDICINE

Greek medical traditions of Hippocrates (460 – 370 BCE), the "Father of Medicine," were transferred to the Romans. Galen (129 – 210), Roman physician and researcher, significantly developed and codified human biology, including anatomy, physiology, pathology, pharmacology, and neurology. In his research, Galen noticed similarities in human and animal physiology. His knowledge of anatomy, gained by working with animals, allowed him to treat his patients.

Galen discovered that injuries to animals were similarly harmful to humans. Thus, the promotion of health in one often promoted health in the other. Nonetheless, Galen's work with animals is often overshadowed by Vegetius, whose Guide to Veterinary Medicine (Digesta Artis Mulomedicinae) became the guidebook for veterinary medical practices. Outside of his works on the diseases and treatment of horses and cattle, little is known about Vegetius.

ARISTOTLE'S STUDIES IN ANIMAL LONGEVITY

The study of animals and their lifespan is not new. Aristotle wrote the following books and treatises.

History of Animals

Parts of Animals

Movement of Animals

Progression of Animals

Generation of Animals

On Plants

On the Soul

On Generation and Corruption

On Breath

Physiognomics

On Sense and Sensible Objects

On Memory and Recollection

On Sleep and Waking

On Dreams

On Prophecy in Sleep

On Length and Shortness of Life

On Youth and Old Age, Life and Death, and Respiration

VETERINARY HISTORY SINCE THE MIDDLE AGES

With the economic importance of horses, associated medical treatments provided the first attempts to systematize the practice of treating animals. In the Middle Ages, farriers merged horseshoeing and "horse doctoring". Concerned about the inadequate standard of care provided to horses in London, the Lord Mayor ordered all farriers operating within a 7-mile (11-km) radius to create an "association" to regulate and improve their methods in 1356.[15]

Veterinary medical schools made their debut in 1761. Claude Bourgelat was chosen to lead in the development of the first veterinary school, located in Lyon, France. In 1764, he established the Alfort Veterinary School near Paris.[16] Following an outbreak of a vicious plague that decimated French cattle herds, Bourgelat devoted his attention to finding a cure.[17] This setback led to his founding of a veterinary school in Lyon in 1761. He sent students to fight the sickness using treatment methods he devised. Shortly thereafter, the plague halted, and livestock health was restored.[18]

In 1783, the Odiham Agricultural Society was founded in England to foster agriculture and industry, which established the profession of veterinary medicine in the United Kingdom. Thomas Burgess, a founding member of the Odiham Agricultural Society, promoted the compassionate care of sick animals. During a 1785 conference, the society resolved to "Promote the study of Farriery upon logical scientific principles." Later, James Clark campaigned for the professionalization of the veterinary field.[19] This effort led to the formation of veterinary institutions, as an outcome of his work, Prevention of Disease.[20]

In 1790, the first veterinary medicine college was established in London. In 1844, the Royal College of Veterinary Surgeons was founded by royal charter. Sir John McFadyean, often regarded as the pioneer of modern veterinary research, made significant contributions to the field in the late nineteenth century.[21] In 1879, the first vet school was established in the United States. Iowa Agricultural College (now Iowa State), a land-grant college, established its professional veterinary program to formalize the American practice of medicine.[22]

While Bourgelat is considered the "Father of Veterinary Medicine", mothers

15 Pamela Hunter, *Veterinary Medicine Historical Sources: A Reference Guide*, (Ashgate Publishing, 2004): 1.

16 Michigan State University College of Veterinary Medicine, "Rinderpest and the First Veterinary School," *Michigan State University College of Veterinary Medicine*, March 11, 2019, https://cvm.msu.edu/vetschool-tails/rinderpest-and-the-first-veterinary-school

17 J. L. Lupton, "Modern Practical Farriery", 1879, in the section: "The Diseases of Cattle Sheep and Pigs," 1.

18 Kit Heintzman, "A Cabinet of the Ordinary: Veterinary Education Becoming More Domesticated, 1766–1799," *The British Journal for the History of Science* 51, no. 2 (2018): 239–260, doi:10.1017/S0007087418000274

19 Cotchen Ernest, *The Royal Veterinary College London, A Bicentenary History* (Barracuda Books, 1990): 11–13.

20 L.P. Pugh, *From Farriery to Veterinary Medicine 1785–1795* (Heffner, Cambridge, 1962): 8–19.

21 Malinda Larkin, "Exacting Researcher Brought Profession into Modern Age," *American Veterinary Medical Association*, April 18, 2021, https://www.avma.org/News/JAVMANews/Pages/110501u.aspx

22 Keith R. Widder, *Michigan Agricultural College: A Land-Grant Philosophy's Evolution*, 1855–1925 (MSU Press, 2005): 107.

of veterinary medicine, like Gula, and other fathers and grandfathers from China, Mesopotamia, Egypt, Greece, and Rome laid the groundwork for the field of study in which you are about to embark.

"**"Veterinary medicine is the perfect example of diversity. The roles in the profession are as diverse as the people who choose it. There are many perspectives and all are equally valid."**

-- James Gaffney

CHAPTER 4
VET SCHOOL TRAINING, CAREER, AND LIFELONG EDUCATION

Veterinarians diagnose and treat diseases in wild and domestic animals.[1] Veterinary medicine is essential to ensuring the supply of much of the protein available to man. Some veterinarians offer animal population control services, serving as advisers to public health officials about animal diseases that threaten human and other animals' existence. Often, vets provide expert advice on controlling disease outbreaks from infected animals and providing a crucial perspective on preventing transmission.[2] Veterinarians work in hospitals, clinics, zoos, and laboratories and are credentialed as a Doctor of Veterinary Medicine (DVM).

VETERINARY MEDICAL SCHOOL TRAINING

Acceptance into a DVM program is highly competitive. Students are typically required to have a minimum number of hours of voluntary or paid work experience before their applications are considered. Admissions representatives advise students to have supervised experience in order to understand the job and its demands. Many schools review student

---

1   Your Free Career Test, "What Does a Veterinarian Do?," *Your Free Career Test,* n.d., https://www.yourfreecareertest.com/veterinarian/

2   Ross University School of Veterinary Medicine, "What Do Veterinarians Do?," *Ross University School of Veterinary Medicine,* n.d., https://veterinary.rossu.edu/about/news/what-do-veterinarians-do

applications holistically. Still, there is no guarantee that students will be admitted during their first attempt.

Becoming a vet requires considerable expertise, competence, and training. Many agree that the veterinary medicine profession is more complicated than human medicine since a vet is expected to be competent in working with hundreds of species. In addition, applicants must possess the willingness to interact with and heal any animal. It typically takes eight years of college to become a veterinarian and ten years to obtain a specialty.[3] Although a B.S. is not necessary for all vet schools, most often, the first four years of undergraduate education lay a foundation before vet school. Successful graduates are required to pass the North American Veterinary Licensing Examination as well as any specific exams for state licensure.

CONSIDERATIONS

Cost: Tuition, Additional Expenses

Scholarships or Alternative Repayment

Prerequisite Courses

Acceptance Rates by GPA and Test Scores

Facilities and Professional Development

Small vs. Large Animal Focus

Location or Multiple Locations

Research Opportunities

Faculty and Quality of Teaching

Dual Programs and Residencies

TYPICAL CURRICULUM IN VET SCHOOL

The entire four years of studying veterinary medicine are divided into two phases. The first phase is the foundational phase, where the students are mainly in the classroom and laboratory. Here, they gain experience by doing internships after classes. Students learn about animal anatomy, physiology, behavior, and diseases. The second phase involves the student performing clinical activities and caring for animal patients. In this phase, students develop proficiency in the diagnosis, prevention, and treatment of animals. During the second phase, students can take care of real-life situations through having real-life experiences in taking care of animals. [4] The curriculum in veterinary medicine school requires perseverance

3   Ross University School of Veterinary Medicine, "What is Vet School Like?," *Ross University School of Veterinary Medicine,* n.d., https://veterinary.rossu.edu/blog/what-is-vet-school-like

4   Texas A&M Veterinary Medicine & Biomedical Sciences, "Curriculum," *Texas A&M Veterinary Medicine & Biomedical Sciences,* n.d., https://vetmed.tamu.edu/dvm/resources/curriculum/

and endurance to complete successfully. The courses are physically taxing and scientifically complex, requiring a thorough understanding if one desires to become a good veterinarian.

The typical vet school curriculum consists of the following content: [5]

- Integrated Animal Care
- Professional and Clinical Skills
- Small and Large Anatomy and Physiology
- Veterinary Immunology
- Histology
- The Veterinarian in Society
- Agents of Disease and Pathophysiology
- Public Health, Epidemiology
- Evidence-Based Medicine
- Pharmacology
- Principles of Surgery and Surgical Techniques
- Introduction to Diagnostic Imaging
- Anesthesia and Analgesia
- Organ Dysfunction
- Diagnostic, Supportive, and Therapeutic Animal Care
- Companion Animal, Equine, Food Animal Careers

Some topics thread through each year's courses; some are repeated with different topics covered. A few are electives chosen by the student. In the third and fourth years, students participate in clinical rotations. In addition, students often take part in field service, clinics, farms, and hospitals.

Courses in the final year often include:[6]

- Equine Neonatology & Intensive Care Medicine
- Clinical Pathology and Laboratory Testing
- Dental Surgery, Including Oral Diseases
- Small and Large Animal Nutrition
- Equine Surgery, Orthopedics, and Lameness:

---

5   Texas A&M Veterinary Medicine & Biomedical Sciences, "Curriculum," *Texas A&M Veterinary Medicine & Biomedical Sciences*, n.d., https://vetmed.tamu.edu/dvm/resources/curriculum/

6   University of Pennsylvania, "Veterinary Clinical Studies - New Bolton Center (VCSN)," *University of Pennsylvania*, n.d., https://catalog.upenn.edu/courses/vcsn/

- Diseases & Management of Sheep & Goats
- Animal Health Economics
- Clinical Biostatistics
- Pet, Equine, & Farm Animal Anesthesia
- Pharmacology
- Animal Production Systems
- Large and Small Animal Welfare Regulations
- Advanced Poultry Medicine
- Large and Small Animal Reproduction
- Large and Small Animal Surgery
- Equine Sports Medicine
- Large Animal Diagnostic Imaging and Radiology
- Advanced Swine Production Medicine
- History Taking, Physical Examination and Animal Management
- Emergency Medicine and Critical Care
- Food Safety, Quality Assurance, Security
- Equine Podology and Ophthalmology
- Large Animal Medicine and Surgery Holiday Emergency Rotation
- Immunology/Infectious Disease[7]

SAMPLE COURSES[8]

Professional and Clinical Skills: Students learn skills and expectations associated with veterinary medicine, including critical thinking, technical work, problem-solving, communication, and others.

1. **Integrated Animal Care:** This course provides a foundation and exposure to the treatment and care of large and companion animals, including husbandry and immunization.

2. **Small Animal Anatomy:** The students learn the anatomy of domestic animals using dogs and cats as models, which provides the basis for radiological and surgical courses.

3. **Physiology:** While learning the physiological structure of mammals,

7   UC Davis Veterinary Medicine, "Curriculum Design," *UC Davis Veterinary Medicine,* n.d., https://www.vetmed.ucdavis.edu/dvm/dvm-curriculum-overview

8   Texas A&M Veterinary Medicine & Biomedical Sciences, "Curriculum," *Texas A&M Veterinary Medicine & Biomedical Sciences,* n.d., https://vetmed.tamu.edu/dvm/resources/curriculum/

laboratory experiments offer hands-on understanding of cardiovascular physiology, neuromuscular, endocrine, skin, and temperature regulation.

4. **Veterinary Immunology:** This course studies the immune system of domestic animals and the interaction with microbes, including the vaccination and immunization necessary to prevent diseases.

5. **Histology:** This course focuses on the cells, tissues, and organs of domestic animals and their clinical applications. The course dives into the microscopic and gross anatomy of common domestic species.

6. **Veterinarians in Society:** Veterinarians play various roles, including shelter medicine, companion animal care, conservation medicine, and public health.

7. **Clinical Anatomy of Large Animals:** This class focuses on the gross and topographical anatomy of livestock, including porcine, avian, equine, and ruminants.

8. **Agents of Disease:** This course considers agents of infectious diseases, including bacteria, fungi, viruses, protozoa, prions, helminths and arthropods, which are important in the diagnosis of infections.

9. **Public Health, Epidemiology & Evidence-Based Medicine:** This class considers public health, determinants of disease, and evidence-based medicine.

10. **Pathology:** This class studies the pathogenesis and morphology of disease, including the structural and functional changes in animal cells, tissues, and organs.

11. **Pharmacology:** This course focuses on drugs affecting the gastrointestinal, cardiovascular, urinary, endocrine, and musculoskeletal systems, including antibiotics, anti-inflammatory, anticancer agents, and those used to treat disease. It considers dosage range, duration, evaluation, and drug interactions.[9]

12. **Principles of Surgery:** This course begins with the management of surgery, equipment, techniques, and procedures, as well as the preparation of both the patient and surgeon for procedures.

13. **Diagnostic Imaging:** Use of radiography and ultrasonic imaging to make a diagnosis.

14. **Principles of Anesthesia & Analgesia:** This course discusses the preparation of patients for anesthesia and the use of analgesics to control and reduce pain.

15. **Organ Dysfunction: Recognition, Diagnostics & Supportive Care:** This course involves the diagnosis of animal ailments and supportive care.

---

9 University of Pennsylvania, "Veterinary Clinical Studies - New Bolton Center (VCSN)," *University of Pennsylvania*, n.d., https://catalog.upenn.edu/courses/vcsn/

16. **Small Animal Diagnostics & Therapeutics:** This course considers the pathophysiology, diagnosis, and management of diseases in domestic animals.

17. **Large Animal Diagnostics & Therapeutics:** This course considers the diagnosis, prevention, and treatment of diseases in large animals such as horses, cattle, sheep, goats, pigs, and poultry.

18. **Career-Focus Tracking:** Students choose their focus either on equine, companion, or food animal and study advanced pathophysiology, diagnosis, surgical procedures, and medical treatment.

19. **Surgery:** Students carry out anesthesia and perform surgery.

20. **Emergency Medicine:** A clinical rotation is undertaken in a Veterinary Medical Teaching Hospital (VMTH).

21. **Cardiology:** Students learn cardiac physical examinations, electrocardiography, radiography, echocardiography, cardiac catheterization, and medical, interventional, and surgical therapy of cardiac disorders [10]

There are differences in small and large animal curricula, though some vet schools offer both.

Small animal veterinary classes will include courses in anatomy, physiology, and animal care.[11] Small animal coursework involves the diagnosis, treatment, and prevention of diseases in typically domestic animals such as cats and dogs, including the science and practice of companion animal medicine.[12] Veterinarians can specialize in small animal veterinary medicine by completing a residency. Small animal veterinarians provide care for domesticated animals and often work in private clinics.[13] Courses learned in the clinical aspect of small animal veterinary medicine are:[14]

- Clinical Neurology
- Emergency and Critical Care

10 UC Davis Veterinary Medicine, "Curriculum Design," *UC Davis Veterinary Medicine*, n.d., https://www.vetmed.ucdavis.edu/dvm/dvm-curriculum-overview

11 Learn.org, "Small Animal Veterinary Schools," *Learn.org*, n.d., https://learn.org/articles/Small_Animal_Veterinary_Schools_Your_Questions_Answered.html

12 University of Georgia College of Veterinary Medicine, "Department of Small Animal Medicine and Surgery," *University of Georgia College of Veterinary Medicine*, n.d., https://vet.uga.edu/education/academic-departments/small-animal-medicine-and-surgery/

13 Study.com, "Small Animal Veterinarian Education Requirements," *Study.com*, June 15, 2021, https://study.com/articles/Small_Animal_Veterinarian_Educational_Requirements_to_be_a_Small_and_Domestic_Animal_Vet.html

14 Cornell University College of Veterinary Medicine, "Clinical Rotations & Pathways," *Cornell University College of Veterinary Medicine*, n.d., https://www.vet.cornell.edu/education/doctor-veterinary-medicine/curriculum/clinical-rotations-pathways

- Cardiology
- Oncology
- Infectious Diseases
- Anesthesiology
- Surgery
- Dermatology
- Radiology[15]

Large animal veterinary care involves providing care to animals such as horses, cattle, goats, and other farm animals as well as counsel to owners of the animals.[16] Large veterinary medicine also includes equine science with courses on the care, management, breeding, and health of horses.[17]

Equine and farm animal courses often include: [18]
- Large Animal Medicine and Surgery
- Anesthesiology and Clinical Neurology
- Large Animal Emergency and Critical Care
- Theriogenology
- Production Animals
- Ambulatory Medicine
- Community Practice Service

15 Study.com, "Small Animal Veterinarian Education Requirements," *Study.com*, June 15, 2021, https://study.com/articles/Small_Animal_Veterinarian_Educational_Requirements_to_be_a_Small_and_Domestic_Animal_Vet.html

16 University of Georgia College of Veterinary Medicine, "Home," *University of Georgia College of Veterinary Medicine*, n.d., https://vet.uga.edu/

17 The University of Vermont, "Undergraduate Program: B.S. in Animal and Veterinary Sciences," *The University of Vermont*, n.d., https://www.uvm.edu/cals/asci/undergraduate-program-bs-animal-and-veterinary-sciences

18 Cornell University College of Veterinary Medicine, "Clinical Rotations & Pathways," *Cornell University College of Veterinary Medicine*, n.d., https://www.vet.cornell.edu/education/doctor-veterinary-medicine/curriculum/clinical-rotations-pathways

"Until one has loved an animal, a part of one's soul remains unawakened."

–Anatole France

CHAPTER 5

THE VET SCHOOL EXPERIENCE

VET SCHOOL LEARNING EXPERIENCE

It takes approximately eight years of advanced training past high school to become a veterinarian. However, some veterinarians may spend ten years or more when they specialize in a particular field.[1] Veterinary studies include two phases; the first phase is concerned with classroom study and laboratory training.

The veterinarian's course of study is similar to the curriculum required by those training to become medical doctors. Undergraduate science courses include biology, chemistry, organic chemistry, and physics (more suggested). Meanwhile, graduate courses typically include anatomy, physiology, pharmacology, immunology, nutrition, microbiology, toxicology, pathology, biochemistry, and surgical techniques.[2] Anatomy and physiology are the two most important classes.[3]

During the first years of vet school, students listen to lectures and participate in laboratory training; they participate in clinical experiences as

---

1   Ross University School of Veterinary Medicine, "What is Vet School Like?," *Ross University School of Veterinary Medicine*, n.d., https://veterinary.rossu.edu/blog/what-is-vet-school-like

2   Texas A&M Veterinary Medicine & Biomedical Sciences, "Curriculum," *Texas A&M Veterinary Medicine & Biological Sciences*, n.d., https://vetmed.tamu.edu/dvm/resources/curriculum/

3   St. George's University, "What is Vet School Like> A Day in the Life of a DVM Student," *St. George's University*, October 19, 2018, https://www.sgu.edu/blog/veterinary/what-is-vet-school-like/

well. Afterward, the bulk of the learning experience focuses on clinical activities and animal patients. Thus, the first phase is compulsory and foundational, providing enough information for students to proceed with in-depth analysis of a range of animals through the clinical years of vet school.

The second phase encompasses the clinical, experimental, and analytical aspects of animal science. This stage involves classroom study of infectious and noninfectious diseases, diagnostic and clinical pathology, obstetrics, radiology, anesthesiology, and surgery. During this period, students carry out evaluations, diagnoses, and procedures in hands-on work with animals. Unlike the first, the second phase allows students to have course choices from the electives offered.[4]

Most students find vet school extraordinarily challenging but also rewarding.[5] To become a successful veterinarian, students must be determined, disciplined, and hardworking. Classes often stretch from the early hours of the day to late into nighttime; a significant number of hours are spent studying as well. Aside from the long hours spent attending classes, students spend considerable time preparing for tedious practical exams. What is most important is that, due to the breadth of veterinary medicine and required skill levels across the spectrum of animals, students of veterinary medicine must acquire sufficient and expert knowledge, surgical skills, and technical expertise.

People aspiring to become veterinarians must have the ability to endure and persevere while staying focused throughout the long years of vet training. Although the time and persistent effort may be grueling, eventually, the career can be gratifying, especially when students sustain a passion for the work.

VETERINARY SCHOOL CURRICULUM

Vet school involves classroom study and other aspects, such as group exercises, laboratory exercises, and discussions that aid in the development and abilities related to clinical care. Foundation courses in vet medicine include lectures on The Animal Body, Neuroanatomy, General Pathology, Cell Biology and Genetics, Function and Dysfunction, Host, Agent, and Defense, Parasitology, Animal

4   Mississippi State University College of Veterinary Medicine, "DVM Curriculum," *Mississippi State University College of Veterinary Medicine,* n.d., https://www.vetmed.msstate.edu/academics/graduate-education/dvm-program/class-selection/dvm-curriculum

5   Mary Hope Kramer, "Things You Should Know About Vet School," *The Balance Careers,* Updated October 30, 2019, https://www.thebalancecareers.com/things-you-should-know-about-vet-school-4020896

Health and Disease, Clinical Rotations, and Veterinary Practice.[6] Schedules change yearly as students progress. In addition, students must learn to employ consistency in studying and understanding the material provided.

EXPERIENCES DURING VET SCHOOL

In vet medicine, experience is vital. Experts suggest that students must have hundreds of hours working with animals during the program. Thus, gaining exposure before starting helps students understand the demands and dimensions of the practice before investing time and money.

To excel as a veterinarian, you must stand out as an authority and professional. This ability will develop over time. Moreover, students should intern with vets to boost their knowledge. Aspiring veterinarians will continue their pre-vet school interests in the profession well before applying. Your experiences might include volunteering in zoos and farms. While you may have had a dog, cat, hamster, or horse in your lifetime, you want to broaden your knowledge to become more familiar with various animals.

Some undergraduate curricula allow students to work on farms, like Virginia Tech, to work with animals. Veterinary experience, however, should include working directly with a veterinarian. Veterinary schools want their students to have at least 400 hours of veterinary or animal health and maintenance experience. For many students, this personal and sometimes lifelong involvement means taking care of horses or pets, but actual work with a vet is essential.

Options for experiences include working in pet stores or animal shelters with domestic animals like dogs, cats, etc., or working alongside a livestock veterinarian, exotic veterinarian, wildlife veterinarian, zoological veterinarian, specialty veterinarians, research, shelters, and humane societies. Students can acquire alternative but extremely valuable experiences by working with the federal government such as USDA, NIH, FDA, and CDC.[7]

Students can also involve themselves in community service, carrying out activities that will portray their passion and interest in working with animals. These activities help show the level of dedication the student has in veterinary work.

---

6   Cornell University College of Veterinary Medicine, "Courses," *Cornell University College of Veterinary Medicine,* n.d., https://www.vet.cornell.edu/education/doctor-veterinary-medicine/curriculum/courses

7   Hamilton College, "Gaining Experience," *Hamilton College,* n.d.,"https://www.hamilton.edu/after/healthprofessions/veterinary/gaining-experience

A career in vet medicine is very promising. Graduates have varied opportunities, particularly with the rise in pet spending and a growing need for professionals who can sustain a safe food supply. Demand for veterinary services is expected to rise significantly in the future. While some veterinarians specialize, this is not a requirement. Instead, some choose to work with a wide variety of animals.

Furthermore, veterinary medicine offers considerable job security. The need for more veterinarians has surged, with surfacing reports showing a significant rise in animal care facilities, companion animals, and pets. According to the US Bureau of Statistics, employment for veterinarians is expected to climb 18 percent by 2026.

Vet medicine provides rewarding opportunities for students. Graduates can use their knowledge to work with agencies to positively impact wildlife and protect endangered, slaughtered, or abused animals. They can also educate people on the importance of wildlife conservation.[8] In addition, a DVM opens the door to numerous careers as animal doctors, farm leadership, corporate management for food companies, advocates, policy analysts.

VETERINARY SCHOOL AND CLINICAL ROTATIONS

The vet school curriculum comprises clinical activities in the last few years of training. In addition, students carry out clinical rotations involving: small animals, equine, general animals, exotic pets, zoo and wildlife, and production animals.[9]

SKILLS REQUIRED IN VETERINARY MEDICINE SCHOOLS

Scientific and technical skills are essential for vet school.
- Vet students must master scientific concepts surrounding anatomy and physiology along with biological and chemical components.
- Veterinarians must exhibit compassion and care when dealing with and caring for animals and people.
- They must have good communication skills when talking to animal owners and caregivers while showing empathy towards their patients.[10]
- Veterinarians must live by high moral and ethical standards and follow the profession's code of conduct.

8 St. George's University, "DVMs Share 8 Benefits of a Being a Veterinarian," *St. George's University*, November 25, 2019, https://www.sgu.edu/blog/veterinary/benefits-of-being-a-veterinarian/

9 Cornell University College of Veterinary Medicine, "Clinical Rotations & Pathways," *Cornell University College of Veterinary Medicine*, n.d., https://www.vet.cornell.edu/education/doctor-veterinary-medicine/curriculum/clinical-rotations-pathways

10 Skills You Need, "5 Key Skills You Need for a Career as a Veterinarian," *Skills You Need,* n.d., https://www.skillsyouneed.com/rhubarb/skills-career-veterinarian.html

- Students aspiring to become excellent veterinarians should possess good observational skills, emotional intelligence, and situational judgment by appropriately using their intellectual, social, and behavioral skills.[11]

Observation: A veterinarian should be able to assess a patient by observation, noting the patient's signs and signals and employing all senses during patient observation. These skills are equally essential when caring for animals. It is also vital to have the ability to assess findings obtained from experiments such as microscopy and animal dissections as well as from journal articles.

Communication: A veterinarian must communicate professionally and effectively with the entire healthcare team. A veterinarian will be expected to offer clear and understandable explanations about an animal's condition.[12]

Motor Function/Manual Dexterity: Animal doctors must be constantly aware, employing quick agility and deliberate movement to escape and evade situations involving animals. Motor skills and lifting are also required to carry out diagnostic procedures like palpation and auscultation as well as adjustment activities in the care of the animals. Percussion is often employed in veterinary medicine and is often required when performing clinical care, surgery, and surgical procedures, especially during emergencies.[13]

Intellectual Skills: This includes conceptual, integrative, and quantitative skills. Vets should be able to apply their intellect in situations where critical thinking and problem-solving are necessary. They should be able to gather and analyze information in making decisions that will benefit the animal's recovery. Often without much time, veterinarians must be able to test hypotheses before making appropriate decisions.

Behavior and Social Skills: Veterinarians must have the ability to work under pressure and communicate effectively without imposing stress on others. Additionally, a veterinarian's good attitude and compassionate behavior are valued during clinical care. Competence, kindness, integrity, and concern for others

---

11   Cornell University College of Veterinary Medicine, "Essential Skills and Abilities," *Cornell University College of Veterinary Medicine*, n.d., https://www.vet.cornell.edu/education/doctor-veterinary-medicine/curriculum/essential-skills-and-abilities

12   Granville College, "Top 5 Skills Needed to Succeed as a Veterinary Assistant," *Granville College*, 2020, https://granvillecollege.ca/blog/top-5-skills-needed-to-succeed-as-a-veterinary-assistant/

13   Indeed, "Veterinarian Skills: Definition and Examples," *Indeed*, March 1, 2021, "https://www.indeed.com/career-advice/resumes-cover-letters/veterinarian-skills

should also be demonstrated.[14]

VET AND HOSPITAL EXPERIENCE

Making clients (owners and their animals) feel happy after visiting the veterinary clinic is paramount in veterinary clinical practice. This attitudinal advantage makes the clinic stand out and ensures future patronage. In addition, allowing an open clinic/hospital policy for animal owners to tour will ease their anxiety, help them feel more comfortable, and know their animals will be safe. This openness can improve communication and transparency while creating value for the clinic.[15]

ELECTRONIC AND EXPERIENTIAL METHODS

Students learn better when they engage with a subject. This hands-on approach, along with digital simulations, allows vet schools to employ innovative and application-oriented methods. Furthermore, observing and doing expands a vet student's understanding and is crucial for mastery. For this reason, creative, experiential learning, whether in education, including in medicine (either animal or human), strengthens learning effectiveness.

Vet practitioners must adjust to changing trends in agricultural practices and domestic animal ownership. This adaptation project requires flexibility and resilience, often posing challenges for practitioners and students. The introduction of e-learning in vet schools, however, has increased. Methods, software, and tools are improving, though innovations in robotics and digital diagnostics require a continual commitment to learning. With e-learning, particularly during the pandemic, vet students and practitioners have taken advantage of alternative experiences.

E-learning in vet medicine has student-centered advantages, offering the ability to visualize anomalies that the student may not otherwise encounter with real-time techniques or recorded events. In addition, if done well, e-learning can encourage student-to-student interaction, fostering knowledge sharing and healthy relationships between students.

---

14 Alice Dusenberry, "What Specific Skills Do You Need to Be a Veterinarian?," *The Good Universities Guide,* June 28, 2018, https://www.gooduniversitiesguide.com.au/careers-guide/veterinarian

15 Alie Volpatti, "The Future of Veterinary Medicine: Open Hospitals?," *Scil Vet,* n.d., https://www.scilvet.ca/company/articles/the-future-of-veterinary-medicine-open-hospitals/

Since veterinary medical training can be very expensive with students paying staggering fees, and with the inclusion of e-learning, training costs may decrease and offer enhanced learning—possibly tailored to meet their needs. In addition, digital textbooks, videos, and innovative experiences will continue to provide alternative education. A recent study revealed that students spend approximately $1,200 per year on textbooks alone, often using growing student loans.[16]

Innovative programs have introduced e-learning in veterinary training institutions, such as The International E-Learning Veterinary School (IEVS), which provides opportunities for students to learn some aspects of veterinary medicine online. Courses also include lectures, discussions, demonstrations, case presentations as well as laboratory work. Students earn certificates when they have completed the curriculum.[17]

Though online veterinary medical education will never take the place of hands-on, experiential methods, the vet school experience is likely to change with new learning methods and technologies. Furthermore, improved imaging techniques, less invasive surgical procedures, and bioengineering technologies are likely to improve medicine in the future and offer these advances to animals so their lives can be improved and lived fully.

16 Elliot Masie, "Advantages of E-Learning," *E-Student.org,* September 13, 2020, https://e-student.org/advantages-of-e-learning/

17 International Veterinary Information Service (IVIS), "IEVS - International E-Learning Veterinary School," *IVIS,* 2020, https://www.ivis.org/library/ievs

"*If you're going to live, leave a legacy. Make a mark on the world that can't be erased.*"

— *Maya Angelou*

CHAPTER 6
ETHICS IN ANIMAL WELFARE

ANIMAL WELFARE

The American Veterinary Medical Association (AVMA) describes animal welfare as the healthy, comfortable, well-nourished, safe condition in which animals live and cope with expressions, feelings, and environment. Furthermore, animal welfare includes physical and mental disease prevention, medical treatment, and both appropriate and well-maintained handling and shelter.[1] Humans have a responsibility to care for animals from birth to death, watching their behavior and ensuring their maintenance and health while minimizing pain and suffering up to and including their humane death.

In many cases, humans establish close bonds with animals. Research shows that 88% to 98% of owners consider their companion animals as family members and that this close relationship is a growing trend in society.[2] During the pandemic, with many people in isolation, emotional support animals (ESA) grew in popularity. An ESA is different from a service dog and does not have the same legal rights, although both may be loved and cherished just the same in a home. Families care for animals – large and small – and there are numerous conditions in which they may need

---

1   American Veterinary Medical Association, "Animal Welfare: What Is It?," *American Veterinary Medical Association*, n.d., https://www.avma.org/resources/animal-health-welfare/animal-welfare-what-it

2   Bernard E. Rollin, "Euthanasia, Moral Stress, and Chronic Illness in Veterinary Medicine," *Vet Clin North Am Small Anim Pract.* 41, no. 3 (2011): 651-659.

treatment and equally as many questions about their ethical care and treatment. Yet, pet owners rarely have insurance, and pet owners must pay for treatment, and thus, some animals, when treatment costs are astronomical, are brought to veterinarians to be euthanized.[3] These and other challenges pose ethical dilemmas for animal owners and veterinarians.

VETERINARIAN'S OATH

Veterinarians vow to ethically and responsibly treat animals. The American Veterinary Medical Association adopted the oath below.[4]

> Being admitted to the profession of veterinary medicine, I solemnly swear to use my scientific knowledge and skills for the benefit of society through the protection of animal health and welfare, the prevention and relief of animal suffering, the conservation of animal resources, the promotion of public health, and the advancement of medical knowledge.

> I will practice my profession conscientiously, with dignity, and in keeping with the principles of veterinary medical ethics.

> I accept as a lifelong obligation the continual improvement of my professional knowledge and competence.

Animal welfare means the way an animal adapts to and copes with the conditions in which it lives. An animal is said to be in a good state if it is comfortable, well-nourished, and secure. On the other hand, the animal is in bad welfare if it suffers from pain, fear, and distress. Protecting an animal's welfare necessitates providing for its physical and mental needs.[5]

Ethics, in general, refers to the rules of behavioral conduct that guide various interactions. It refers to the principles or theories that govern interrelationships and determines proper rules of practice. There are explicit rules that govern ethical conduct in professional and patient interactions. The relationship between humans and animals is one such area where there is ethical conduct. Animal ethics analyzes both human-animal connections and how people ought to treat creatures.[6]

---

3   Bernard E. Rollin, "Euthanasia, Moral Stress, and Chronic Illness in Veterinary Medicine," *Vet Clin North Am Small Anim Pract.* 41, no. 3 (2011): 651-659.

4   American Veterinary Medical Association, "Veterinarian's Oath," *American Veterinary Medical Association,* n.d.,https://www.avma.org/resources-tools/avma-policies/veterinarians-oath

5   American Veterinary Medical Association, "Animal Welfare: What Is It?," *American Veterinary Medical Association,* n.d., https://www.avma.org/resources/animal-health-welfare/animal-welfare-what-it

6   One Welfare, "Animal Ethics," *One Welfare,* n.d., https://onewelfare.sydney.edu.au/animal-ethics/

LEGISLATION AND PROTECTION MECHANISMS

The Animal Welfare Act (AWA), signed into law in 1966, is the only Federal law in the United States that regulates the treatment of animals in research, exhibition, and transport and declares the minimum acceptable standard.[7] Enforced by the United States Department of Agriculture (USDA), the AWA describes animals and regulated activities related to commerce, research, exhibitions, treatment, licensure, and transportation,[8]

1. to ensure that animals intended for use in research facilities, exhibition purposes, or use as pets are provided humane care and treatment;

2. to assure the humane treatment of animals during transportation in commerce; and

3. to protect animal owners from the theft of their animals by preventing the sale or use of stolen animals.

In 1876, the United Kingdom passed the first law regulating animal cruelty. The Cruelty to Animals Act established an overseeing body to review, approve, and regulate animals used in research as well as creating a licensing system for animal experimentation. This law was replaced by the Animals Act of 1986.

Initially, advancements in medicine resulted from experimentation and vivisection on animals, often without anesthesia. With the goal to better understand anatomy and physiology, humans were originally used for experiments. With the preponderance of moral questions asked, early researchers conducted tests on animals. Unregulated surgical experiments on animals continued until a movement questioned the ethics of this type of science. Prevention of cruelty to animals became a moment that expanded worldwide, stemming from unregulated procedures without the use of anesthetics. Throughout the world, groups have attempted to establish the natural rights of all living creatures.

Human vivisection reawakened the consciousness of cruelty during World War II with the infamous Japanese Unit 731, Nazi experimentation on humans, and, more recently, the live organ harvesting conducted in China.

The British government produced the Brambell Report (report of the technical committee to examine the welfare of animals housed under intensive livestock husbandry systems) in 1965, which established animal welfare as a recognized

---

7   U.S. Department of Agriculture, "Animal Welfare Act," U.S. *Department of Agriculture,* n.d., https://www.nal.usda. gov/awic/animal-welfare-act

8   U.S. Government Publishing Office, "Chapter 54 – Transportation, Sale, and Handling of Certain Animals," U.S. Government Publishing Office, 2015, https://www.govinfo.gov/content/pkg/USCODE-2015-title7/html/ USCODE-2015-title7-chap54.htm

discipline.[9] Universally, ethical issues are contentious. Ethical decisions are often debated with animals, and their treatment, mainly since animals are kept for various reasons. Moral discussions regarding animal welfare often involve the handling and managing of these animals, including nourishment, living conditions, and care. Against this backdrop, questions arise regarding animals for companionship, for work, food, skins, and pets. Is it acceptable to keep animals as pets? What responsibilities do owners have to their pets? Furthermore, is it appropriate to keep large aquatic mammals in captivity?[10]

BREEDING AND CONSUMPTION OF ANIMALS FOR FOOD

Food consumption and research on animals are issues that commonly arise in animal welfare. However, regardless of the ethical issue, the main arguments for ethical and moral decisions concerning the welfare of animals are based upon several models. Two are utilitarianism and deontology.[11].

Utilitarianism: This theory, attributed to 18th and 19th century philosophers Jeremy Bentham and John Stuart Mill, explains that the consequence determines the action, and the outcome should be 'for the greater good of the greater number'. For example, "Would you cut off your own leg if it was the only way to save another person's life? Would you torture someone if you thought it would result in information that would prevent a bomb from exploding and killing hundreds of people? Would you politically oppress a people for a limited time if it increased the overall well-being of the citizenry?"[12]

Therefore, in the utilitarian belief system, an individual seeks to give the most pleasure and the least suffering. Relating this to animal welfare, a utilitarian decision would be that the suffering of laboratory rats used in research to find a cure for Parkinson's disease are less compared to the benefits the human population would derive if such a cure were found.

Deontology: This theory, attributed to the 18th century German philosopher Immanuel Kant, is based on the belief that humans have a duty to help other

---

9   Nibeit Priyadarshini Jena, "Animal Welfare and Animal Rights: An Examination of Some Ethical Problems," *Journal of Academic Ethics* 15, no. 4 (2017): 377-395, https://eric.ed.gov/?id=EJ1244185

10 Ibid.

11 ACS Distance Education, "Animal Welfare Ethics," *ACS Distance Education,* n.d., https://www.acsedu.com/info/wildlife/animal-care/animal-welfare-ethics.aspx

12 Michael Shermer, "Does the Philosophy of 'The Greatest Good for the Greatest Number' Have Any Merit?," *Scientific American,* May 1, 2018, https://www.scientificamerican.com/article/does-the-philosophy-of-the-greatest-good-for-the-greatest-number-have-any-merit/

beings and follow basic rules, like do not lie; do not steal; do not cheat; tell the truth. Costs and benefits are not considered, and thus, deontology avoids subjectivity and uncertainty since the objective is merely to follow a set of rules.

Proponents of this theory posit that the act must occur, even if they must suffer as a consequence. Depending on the circumstance, this theory plays out differently. To illustrate, a gamekeeper would shoot at wild animals because he believes that he must protect his livestock from predatory animals. In another instance, a wildlife rescuer would be against the killing of predatory animals because he feels he has a duty to protect them.

EMERGENCY VETERINARY MEDICINE

Genetically, pets are generally hardwired to hide pain and illness. This feature can make discovering a medical condition difficult for even the most observant pet owner or caregiver to notice. Notwithstanding, animals can manifest signs and send signals to indicate the kind of suffering that warrants immediate medical attention.

If an animal bleeds for more than five minutes from the nose, mouth, or rectum, this is a clear sign of an emergency. Additionally, when clawed by another animal, hit by a vehicle, or mauled by a predator, an animal caregiver should not hesitate to bring in the animal for medical attention, particularly if there are visible signs of damage. Finally, refusal to eat or drink for more than 24 hours is an indication of animal discomfort.[13]

Other signs of animal emergency include:[14]

1. Reasonable suspicion that the pet has eaten something poisonous
2. Fractured bones, severe lameness, or inability to move legs
3. Severe vomiting or diarrhea

Outside of routine exams, toenail trims, or vaccinations, any visual clues or concerns about an animal's wellbeing should be considered an emergency. When an emergency veterinarian sees the animal, the specialist provides medical care, often with internal medicine specialists and vet surgeons who work at larger veterinary hospitals. In addition, they take referrals from general veterinarians to treat existing animal patients under duress.[15]

---

13 Lone Tree Veterinary Medical Center, "Lone Tree Veterinary: When Is It a Pet Emergency?," *Lone Tree Veterinary Medical Center*, February 5, 2016, https://www.lonetreevet.com/blog/when-is-it-a-pet-emergency/

14 American Veterinary Medical Association, "Emergency Care," *American Veterinary Medical Association*, n.d., https://www.avma.org/resources/pet-owners/emergencycare

15 Ross University School of Veterinary Medicine, "What Is an Emergency Veterinarian?," *Ross University School of*

Emergency veterinarians are trained in the medical treatment of animals in accidents, injuries, reproduction, and diseases. They are trained to examine the animal to identify, cure and prevent diseases in animals. Essentially, veterinarians play an important role in animal welfare. Many veterinarians agree that certain diseases, some of which are caused by micro-organisms, may be caused by poor welfare in the animal. Ensuring animal welfare is a human responsibility. It includes consideration for all aspects of animal wellbeing such as proper housing, management, nutrition, disease prevention and treatment, responsible care, and humane handling.[16]

COGNIZANCE OF ALTERNATIVE BELIEF SYSTEMS

The use, abuse, research, and consumption of animals are not the same in all countries. The ethical treatment of animals is not codified in some countries and disregarded altogether in others. People for the Ethical Treatment of Animals (PETA) has exposed numerous issues surrounding animal ethics. A quote on the PETA website says, "Animals are not ours to experiment on, eat, wear, use for entertainment, or abuse in any other way.[17] Meanwhile, many other groups are involved too. The problem with ethical care, treatment, and protection of animals has appeal worldwide, and numerous groups are involved with devastating situations involving numerous species.

PROFILE ON THE DONKEY TRADE

In China, a traditional medicine called Ejiao (eh-gee-yow) is a hard gel that can be dissolved in hot water or alcohol. The substance is used in face creams and in other cases to improve blood flow, treat anemia, low blood cell counts, and issues involved with pregnancy.[18] These unproven remedies are obtained by extracting ingredients from donkey hides. Manufacturers of these products boil donkey skins to create a medicinal gelatin. The demand for donkeys is so high that China cannot produce enough. Donkey Sanctuary estimates that China uses 4.8 million hides per year. With a gestation period of a full year, Chinese manufacturers have searched for donkeys worldwide to obtain donkey hides, resulting in massive donkey

---

Veterinary Medicine, n.d., https://veterinary.rossu.edu/blog/veterinary/what-emergency-veterinarians-do

16 American Veterinary Medical Association, "Animal Welfare: What Is It?," *American Veterinary Medical Association,* n.d., https://www.avma.org/resources/animal-health-welfare/animal-welfare-what-it

17 PETA, "The Issues," *PETA,* n.d., https://www.peta.org/issues/

18 The Donkey Sanctuary, "What is Ejiao," *The Donkey Sanctuary,* n.d., https://www.thedonkeysanctuary.org.uk/about-us/our-international-work/issues/donkey-skin-trade/what-is-ejiao

population declines.[19]

In Nigeria, donkeys are bought in large herds or stolen from farms. They are walked to slaughter with no rest, food, or water, while those driven have their legs tied together, slung alive onto piles, strapped to hoods of vehicles, and driven with broken limbs to slaughterhouses. Without other means, they are murdered with hammers, axes, and knives and turned over for $200 per hyde of quick cash.[20] Importing donkey hides for this purpose is not illegal in China.

The condemnation of this horrific practice, decimating the global population of donkeys, is worldwide. Brooke, an international charity committed to protecting and improving the lives of horses, donkeys, and mules, held a conference in June 2021, warning "that almost half of the world's donkeys could be wiped out in the next five years. The trade is believed to be active in Ghana, Nigeria, Botswana, Burkina Faso, Mali, Niger, Senegal, Uganda, Ethiopia, South Sudan, Tanzania, Kenya, and Egypt, as well as outside of Africa in Afghanistan, Pakistan and Brazil. In Kenya, a court lifted a ban on the slaughter of donkeys for their skins, giving the green light for slaughterhouses to begin trading again."[21]

SPANA (Society for the Protection of Animals Abroad), another global agency, has also worked to increase awareness, protect animal welfare, and reach out to help animals abroad.[22] According to SPANA, "The donkey population in Botswana, for example, has decreased 39 percent from 229,000 in 2014 to 142,000 in 2016… In early 2018, SPANA staff in Mali reported that 2,000 donkeys were being sold for slaughter every week at the country's seven major livestock markets."[23]

ETHICS IN VETERINARY MEDICINE

As has been already established, ethics refers to a code of conduct that governs an individual or a group of persons. It sets out what is morally accepted as right or wrong. Every profession has a code of ethical conduct which its members are

---

19 Christa Lesté-Lasserre, "Chinese Trade in Hides has Led to Global Donkey Massacre," *Science Magazine*, December 12, 2019, https://www.sciencemag.org/news/2019/12/chinese-trade-hides-has-led-global-donkey-massacre

20 Ibid.

21 Brooke, "Brooke West Africa Hosts Conference on the Devastating Impact of the Donkey Skin Trade in Africa," Brooke, June 16, 2021, https://www.thebrooke.org/news/brooke-west-africa-hosts-conference-devastating-impact-donkey-skin-trade-africa

22 The Society for the Protection of Animals Abroad is a global charity with the objective and purpose of providing veterinary care to working animals, including donkeys, horses, elephants and camels.

23 Amy Yee, "Donkeys are Dying Because China Wants Their Hides for a Traditional Remedy," *NPR*, April 30, 2019, https://www.npr.org/sections/goatsandsoda/2019/04/30/716732762/donkeys-are-dying-because-china-wants-their-hides-for-a-traditional-remedy

expected to follow. Veterinary ethics refers to a set of moral principles drawn from professional and animal ethics to enable veterinarians to fulfill their professional and moral obligations in their relationships with colleagues, patients, and society.[24] Why are ethics important in veterinary practice? Veterinary medicine's ethical code challenges veterinarians to determine right from wrong, demanding the astuteness of the practitioner to give an informed and wise diagnosis.[25]

The ethical code for veterinary medicine is enshrined in the veterinarian oath. Different countries have their oaths. "As a part of the veterinary medical profession, I solemnly promise that I shall use my scientific knowledge and talents for the benefit of society," says the veterinarian oath in Canada.

I will strive to:

- Promote creature wellbeing and welfare,
- Prevent and calm creature suffering,
- Protect the wellbeing of the open and the environment, and
- Advance comparative therapeutic knowledge.

I will perform my proficient obligations scrupulously, with respect, and in keeping with the standards of veterinary restorative ethics.

I will endeavor ceaselessly to move forward my proficient information and competence and to preserve the most noteworthy proficient and moral measures for myself and the calling."[26]

In the United Kingdom, on admission to the membership of Royal College of Veterinary Surgeons, and in exchange for the right to practice veterinary surgery, every veterinary surgeon makes the following declaration:

> " I PROMISE AND SOLEMNLY DECLARE that I will pursue the work of my profession with integrity and accept my responsibilities to the public, my clients, the profession and the Royal College of Veterinary Surgeons, and that, ABOVE ALL, my constant endeavor will be to ensure the health and

24 E.O Njoga, O.E Ariyo, and J.A Nwata, "Ethics In Veterinary Practice In Nigeria: Challenges And The Way-Forward," *Nigerian Veterinary Journal* 40, no. 1 (2019), https://www.ajol.info/index.php/nvj/article/view/191718

25 American Veterinary Medical Association, "Principles of Veterinary Medical Ethics of the AVMA," *American Veterinary Medical Association*, n.d., https://www.avma.org/resources-tools/avma-policies/principles-veterinary-medical-ethics-avma

26 Canadian Veterinary Medical Association, "The Canadian Veterinary Oath," *Canadian Veterinary Medical Association*, n.d., https://www.canadianveterinarians.net/about/veterinary-oath

welfare of animals committed to my care."[27]

Despite the difference in the use of words contained in the various veterinarian oaths applicable to multiple countries, it is evident that a core responsibility of veterinarians is to ensure the health and welfare of animals. They are saddled with the responsibility to protect the animal's health and to relieve its suffering.

Veterinary oaths and professional codes of conduct highlight the obligations veterinarians owe to animals. However, these principles may be difficult to practice. Veterinarians may find it difficult to know where their responsibilities lie. To illustrate, a veterinarian who receives instructions that cases must be dealt with as far as possible "in-house" may be reluctant to refer patients out of their clinic. Another instance is where an employee works for an employer struggling with an addiction that impairs their performance. Such an employee may be fearful of ramifications for reporting such unprofessional conduct.[28]

Another area of ethical conflict exists between the animal patient's interests and the client who is typically paying for the treatment.[29] This conundrum happens where the choice of treatment chosen by the client differs from what the vet thinks is an appropriate treatment. In most jurisdictions, the animal is the legal property of the owner, and it is the owner that makes decisions regarding the health decisions of the animal. Thus, an owner may decide that the best course of action may be to request a humane killing of an animal with a treatable condition.

The veterinarian's dilemma is whether or not he should proceed with the request even though they disagree. In these situations, the question that arises is this: "to whom does the veterinarian owe a primary obligation; the owner or animal?[30]

Ethical questions are complicated in veterinary medicine because veterinarians serve not only the patients but also the clients. A veterinarian's judgments affect the health and wellbeing of the animal and the humans who deal with those animals on a regular basis.

27 The Royal College of Veterinary Surgeons, "Code of Professional Conduct for Veterinary Surgeons," *The Royal College of Veterinary Surgeons*, https://www.rcvs.org.uk/setting-standards/advice-and-guidance/code-of-professional-conduct-for-veterinary-surgeons/

28 Elein Hernandez, Anne Fawcett, Emily Brouwer, Jeff Rau, and Patricia V. Turner, "Speaking Up: Veterinary Ethical Responsibilities and Animal Welfare Issues in Everyday Practice," *Animals* 8, no. 1 (2018): 15, https://www.ncbi.nlm.nih.gov/pmc/articles/PMC5789310/

29 Ibid.

30 Ibid.

PART 2

PLANNING, COMPETENCIES, AND DATA

"*When you live for a strong purpose, then hard work isn't an option. It's a necessity.*"

– Steve Pavlina

CHAPTER 7

INTELLECTUAL AND BEHAVIORAL COMPETENCIES

B efore you begin the active phase of your clinical career, your life educational experiences, particularly in science and around animals, have already given you a foundation for your future. First, consider what you would want to see in a veterinarian. How do you envision a clean, safe, and friendly office? What would you expect when you go to a veterinarian?

The friendliest and most accommodating veterinarians get to know you, listen to your concerns, and consider your needs while taking the time to explain both preventative care and potential problems. They respect your time, money, and situation while also following up and valuing your long-term relationship. Success as a veterinarian is different from success in vet school. A person who is intellectually capable of mastering biomedical education and quantitative analysis is not necessarily the best individual to support your needs or those of your animal.

Competencies in both are necessary to complete vet school and have a successful vet practice. Vet school coursework is complex and often more demanding than the most challenging undergraduate classes. The comprehensive and detailed nature of the vet school curriculum sharpens the student and prepares them to address stressful clinical experiences in a broad context. It is never just a nail, eye, or stomach ailment; animal tissues are inexorably connected to the rest of its body. As such, every veterinary procedure must be performed to the best of the clinician's ability.

THE CONCEPT OF CULTURAL COMPETENCE

Cultural competence is a concept from psychology referring to the capacity of an individual to create connections with individuals of different cultural backgrounds.[1] Acknowledging and accepting differences in appearance, behavior, and culture, individuals who display cultural competence appreciate social norms of ethnically and geographically diverse regions.[2] Thus, cultural competence is essential in both human and animal relationships and welfare.

During vet school and professional life, veterinarians work in socioculturally and linguistically diverse teams and environments.[3] Moreover, in a veterinary practice, cultural perspectives of animal owners impact the treatment of animals as well as animal health and welfare. It is thus vital for veterinarians to develop the cultural competence to enable them to work effectively.

Before interacting with animals, the veterinarian's (or representative) first interaction is typically with the client, either the animal owner or caregiver. Demonstrating cultural competence when communicating with clients enables a practitioner to promote inclusion and provide services to a more diverse client population.[4] To be culturally competent, a veterinarian needs to attend to the client, respecting their culture and beliefs, understanding their communication, and communicating in a way that respects any differences.

In addressing the issue of providing culturally competent veterinary care, Bob Levoy, board member of *Veterinary Economics*, highlighted four ways to achieve that objective:[5]

1. Speak their language.
2. Listen and learn.
3. Be aware of cultural differences.
4. Do your research.

---

1   Maria Rosario T. de Guzman, Tonia R. Durden, Sarah A. Taylor, Jackie M. Guzman, and Kathy L. Potthoff, "Cultural Competence: An Important Skill Set For The 21st Century," *University of Nebraska – Lincoln Extension,* February 2016, https://extensionpublications.unl.edu/assets/html/g1375/build/g1375.htm

2   Ottawa University, "Why is Cultural Competence Important," *Ottawa University,* August 2020, https://www.ottawa.edu/online-and-evening/blog/august-2020/the-importance-of-cultural-competence

3   Jaime Gongora, Meg Vost, Sanaa Zaki, Steward Sutherland, and Rosanne Taylor, "Fostering Diversity Competence in the Veterinary Curriculum," *Transforming Lives and Systems,* June 3, 2020, 63-73, https://link.springer.com/chapter/10.1007/978-981-15-5351-6_6

4   Virginia Kiefer et al., "Cultural Competence in Veterinary Practice," *Journal of the American Veterinary Medical Association 243,* no. 3 (2013): 326-328, https://avmajournals.avma.org/doi/abs/10.2460/javma.243.3.326?journalCode=javma

5   Bob Levoy, "4 Ways to Provide Culturally Competent Veterinary Care," *DVM360,* January 31, 2012, https://www.dvm360.com/view/4-ways-provide-culturally-competent-veterinary-care

In considering behavioral competencies, Bob Levoy suggested that each veterinarian also consider staff appreciation and recognition, saying,[6] "When is the last time you …

- thanked an employee at the end of the day for a job well done?
- gave a staff member a raise without being asked?
- had fresh flowers delivered to your team after a hectic week at work?
- sent a fruit basket or small gift to an employee's home in appreciation of his or her extra efforts?
- sent an e-mail or thank-you note to a staff member who went above and beyond the call of duty?
- celebrated the achievement of practice goals or the completion of special projects with plenty of public pats on the back?

ACADEMIC, PERSONAL, & PROFESSIONAL COMPETENCIES

Behavioral/Personal	Professional/Ethical	Clinical/Scientific
Self-Awareness	Leadership & Tolerance	Biomedical
Self-Forgiveness	Laws, Rules, & Accounting	Disease Mechanisms
Care & Compassion	Best Practices	Zoonotic Diseases
Persistent	Multicultural Awareness	Clinical Pathology
Respect	Problem Solving	Immunology
Commitment	Critical Thinking	Epidemiology
Trust & Honesty	Active Participation	Environmental Impact
Focus & Attention	Lifelong Learning	Intake & Examination
Empathy & Altruism	Evaluation & Assessment	Emergency Medicine
Balanced & Dependable	Social Accountability	Ophthalmology
Punctual	Social Responsibility	Nutrition & Dentistry
Reliable & Resilient	Business Management	Reproduction & Genetics
Affable & Easy Going	Computer Proficiency	Diagnosis & Surgery
Writing & Speaking	Medical Records	Public Health
Collaboration	Ethical Decision Making	Therapy & Intervention
Teamwork	Ethical Treatment	Visualization
Organization	Research/Assessment	Imaging Interpretation
Prioritization	Data Analysis	Laboratory Techniques

ORGANIZATION

Appreciate and embrace technology while also recognizing and compensating for its limitations. Digital planners may be helpful. However, you might find that the paper versions of the Franklin Planner, Planner Pad, Blue Sky, Erin Condren, or Panda Planner are equally helpful for managing lists, reminders, and appointments. Online calendars and reminders are essential. However, the drawback of various digital systems is that there is little room for notes. Choose the method that works best for you, remembering that organization, planning, punctuality, dependability, and responsibility are as essential in a veterinary medical practice as they are in school.

HIPAA REQUIREMENTS

Competencies are not limited to vet expertise. Knowledge of the laws and responsibilities is essential. Vet students will learn the provisions of HIPAA (Health Insurance Portability and Accountability Act). This bill, signed into law on August 21, 1996, was written to protect patients from the disclosure of personally identifiable information. In modernizing healthcare information flow - presentation, documentation, sharing, and distribution – protection mechanisms are put in place to secure patient information from access, fraud, theft, and abuse. A code of ethics and responsibilities binds veterinarians. As such, veterinarians must put the needs and interests of their patients ahead of their own.

HIPAA statutes and regulations vary by state. The AVMA provided a summary of requirements for the release of veterinary records. Since state veterinary boards have the authority to interpret and enforce provisions at their own determination, contact your state's veterinary medical board for more and current information.[7] Almost all states require authorization for release, though there are some exceptions.

Accreditation for veterinary medical colleges is provided by the Council on Education (COE) and approved by the U.S. Department of Education for all colleges seeking this approval in the U.S. and abroad.

"PRINCIPLES OF VETERINARY MEDICAL ETHICS OF THE AVMA"[8]

The American Veterinary Medical Association (AVMA) published the "Principles of Veterinary Medical Ethics of the AVMA" (PVME) in August 2019. This document provides a guideline to the AVMA rules for ethical behavior and practices.

The basic premise of PVME is that, as a member of the scholarly profession of

---

7   American Veterinary Medical Association, "Confidentiality of Veterinary Patient Records," *American Veterinary Medical Association,* n.d., https://www.avma.org/advocacy/state-local-issues/confidentiality-veterinary-patient-records

8   American Veterinary Medical Association, "Principles of Veterinary Medical Ethics of the AVMA," *American Veterinary Medical Association,* n.d., https://www.avma.org/resources-tools/avma-policies/principles-veterinary-medical-ethics-avma

veterinary medicine, veterinarians must be legally and professionally bound by oath and education and practice medicine ethically. Irrespective of the situation or circumstance, veterinarians represent the profession and are expected to work in a professional and ethical way. The following is adapted from the PVME:

1. A veterinarian shall be influenced only by the welfare of the patient, the needs of the client, the safety of the public, and the need to uphold the public trust while avoiding conflicts of interest or the appearance thereof.

2. A veterinarian shall provide competent veterinary medical clinical care under the terms of a veterinarian-client-patient relationship (VCPR) with compassion and respect for animal welfare and human health.

3. A veterinarian shall uphold the standards of professionalism, be honest in all professional interactions, and report veterinarians who are deficient in character or competence to the appropriate entities.

4. A veterinarian shall respect the law while also recognizing their responsibility to seek changes to laws and regulations contrary to the best interests of the patient and public health.

5. A veterinarian shall respect the rights of clients, colleagues, and other health professionals, safeguarding medical information within the confines of the law.

6. A veterinarian shall continue to study, apply, and advance scientific knowledge, maintain a commitment to veterinary medical education, make relevant information available to clients, colleagues, the public, and obtain consultation or referral when indicated.

7. A veterinarian shall provide appropriate patient care, except in emergencies, be free to choose whom to serve, with whom to associate, and the environment in which to provide veterinary medical care.

8. A veterinarian shall recognize a responsibility to participate in activities contributing to the improvement of the community and the betterment of public health.

9. A veterinarian should view, evaluate, and treat all persons in any professional activity or circumstance based on their abilities, qualifications, and other relevant characteristics.

A more thorough explanation of each of these in addition to valuable terms may be found here: *https://www.avma.org/resources-tools/avma-policies/ principles-veterinary-medical-ethics-avma*

"At the end of the day, you put all the work in, and eventually it'll pay off. It could be in a year, it could be in 30 years."

— Kevin Hart

CHAPTER 8
ACADEMIC PLAN – GPA, AP CREDIT, PACING

A cademic focus, passionate pursuit, and career vision are the mainstays of vet school. The process of planning, applying, and completing vet school is not easy and requires a full dose of dedication. Yet, each step leads to the next. Persistence is a crucial element of success in the hardest of college classes while keeping your sanity. Working in a vet clinic is helpful to put on your resume, but the experience is even more valuable for you to clarify where you are headed and why.

You are on a journey. The destination is just ahead, past the hurdles and roadblocks – financial, academic, social, experiential, and the admissions process. Your life encompasses a bit of purpose and a bit of mystery. The sleepless nights are just as monumental as you take strides toward your goal. The professors you endure in subjects you do not enjoy are as indelible as the dreams you have for your future.

Your journey has a story. That story should be part of your personal statement, complete with the triumphs and pitfalls. Each anecdote is an intriguing problem you resolved, the serendipity that led to your research, and the intentional act of unsuccessfully applying to fifty internships until you succeeded in the last attempt. You do not need to use the word 'persistence' in your story when you can demonstrate its existence in your narrative.

BODY, NUTRITION, MINDFULNESS, AND WELLNESS

Always be mindful of your mental and physical health. Students are often so engrossed in their studies that they miss or ignore signs of exhaustion, anxiety, ulcers, or weight fluctuations. Ironically, a veterinarian is trained to be cognizant of others' mental health challenges while often missing their own. Within that realm of physical awareness, proper nutrition and water consumption are equally important. What goes into your body impacts your mental and physical health. You may consume a dozen energy drinks a week or a pot of coffee a day, but there are long-term effects.

Frequently, a balanced diet is not available or not quickly attainable during very long study sessions when only junk food is offered in vending machines. This note of caution may seem blatantly obvious to students on the road to vet school, but after four hours of study, some students will not take an hour to drive or walk to a store or restaurant, cook or eat a meal then return. As much human science as students know, pizza delivery or chips from a machine may seem most sensible, when a refrigerator with fruit and salad fixings might be more prudent.

Mindfulness and thoughtful self-reflection can aid in your personal wellness. Patience is a skill to be practiced and appreciated. In a jam-packed life, where every moment seems to count, patiently waiting for a book to arrive, an elevator to open, or even a website to upload is not as easy as it sounds. As a veterinarian, you will need to be patient with those who come for your services, but equally important is to be patient with yourself. A certain amount of emotional intelligence is required to process complex situations while also managing your own emotions.

PRIORITIZATION, PROCRASTINATION, AND OVERCOMING STRESS

Stress, anxiety, and overwhelm can be debilitating to a vet med student. With the enormous amount of material to cover, if you are concerned about being engulfed with subject matter you do not know, buy the books ahead of time. Dedicate time to learning the details before you begin your classes. Some students suffer from the elusive 'Imposter Syndrome'. They feel unsure if they are good enough or if the shortcuts they took will be 'discovered'.

Prioritization is a crucial element in the pursuit of a veterinary medical education. Ask yourself, "What is most important today, and how can I squeeze in sports, clubs, service, or spiritual activities that will maintain my sanity and close relationships?"

While some people describe this as balance, compromise, or sacrifice, it is useful to think of your relationships and activities as supportive or helpful for your education, commitment, and attitude. One can aid the other rather than consider the process as a zero-sum concession. You are more humane and more compassionate because you care, laugh, and engage in new experiences. However, you must not lose track of time. Assignments still need to be a high priority. Your work as a veterinarian will demand focus, attention, and time consciousness.

Any number of people or stressors can complicate a given day. Instructors may criticize while patients complain. Vet opportunities may not materialize, and those that do may create anxiety. The vet med student must digest feedback humbly without losing confidence.

Competencies that are often under-acknowledged are trust, loyalty, and honesty. These may become apparent first within the vet school community and later in your career. These go hand-in-hand with respect. By being honest, demonstrating transparency, and building trust, a procedure will be appreciated rather than questioned. Showing that you care, listening attentively, and modulating between very different personalities in a family and with their animals can make all the difference. At this point, academic knowledge takes a backseat to interpersonal relationship building.

Being proactive rather than reactive is essential. If you have assignments that you know must be done, you are better off finishing them ahead of time – well ahead of time. There is an adage, which fits well here.

"THERE'S NO TIME LIKE THE PRESENT."

Finishing a paper, online quiz, or research project in the present moment relieves stress. First, there is one less thing to remember. Second, less brain space is required in trying to remember the task. Third, you can proceed to other projects with a reduced mental burden. Fourth, something may come up at the last minute. Thus, why worry when you can finish what you need to accomplish? Some people are procrastinators and have numerous justifications for delaying projects until the last minute. After all, it worked the last few times, so it should work this time too.

However, emergencies can occur at the last minute, and getting caught off-guard with a professor who is unwilling to give an extension can be detrimental. You would not want your animal patients to see you only for emergencies and not have routine checkups to prevent a problem. Walk-the-walk means that you, too, should be proactive with your assignments.

Finally, be observant and avoid pitfalls. Be keenly aware of challenges and opportunities from those around you. You can learn from other people's mistakes and take advantage of academic and clinical opportunities. Shadowing veterinarians is one of the best ways to learn. See what works best and what does not. Rather than doing your work by trial and error, learn from your classmates who have diverse backgrounds and experiences. Learn from veterinarians who have been in practice for decades. Attend school and gain experiences without regret.

"Success is no accident. It is hard work, perseverence, learning, studying, sacrifice, and most of all, love of what you are doing or learning to do."

– Pele

CHAPTER 9

PLANNING CALENDAR – THE ADMISSIONS CYCLE

PLANNING & APPLICATION CALENDAR - MAY THROUGH FEBRUARY

The 2020-2021 and 2021-2022 vet school admission cycles were novel due to the pandemic. Changes in society required workarounds. In both undergraduate and graduate institutions across the country, professors altered teaching methods. In some cases, course material was left out with the early termination of semesters. Furthermore, with cancelations, delays, and self-study, and the elimination of labs, vet school admissions officers did not know what to expect or variations in academic preparation. As classes moved online, some colleges gave pass/fail grades, and students clamored to earn credit from local community colleges. At the same time, graduate school admissions policies formerly dissuaded students from these options. At present, vet school admissions committees are adjusting by being flexible with each of these pandemic-driven measures given today's uncertain and uncommon circumstances.

Testing delays and cancelations added to student's challenges. Despite the difficulties, a good strategy is to apply early for 2022 and 2023 to help counter delays caused by closed test centers, rescheduled GRE and CASPer tests, and revised admission requirements. Meanwhile, vet school hopefuls searched for shadowing experiences and positions in clinics which were hard to find. The lack of volunteer and experiential opportunities severely impacted many applicants.

The pandemic resulted in unprecedented hurdles for vet school admissions that will probably redefine the admission process for many years.

PLANNING AND ADMISSIONS CONSIDERATIONS

The Veterinary Medical College Application Service (VMCAS) opens in May of the year before you plan to attend. The deadlines for most schools are in September. However, it is advisable to apply early since applications need to undergo a verification process, and a few schools have rolling admissions and have early interviews. Review the VMCAS and American Association of Veterinary Medical Colleges (AAVMC) websites. Note: Texas vet school applications are on the Texas Medical & Dental Schools Application Service (TMDSAS) site.

You will need to write essays about the reasons you are applying to vet school. Typically, you must write a few short and long essays on this topic. Thus, you want to design your life to tell that story by living, working, and caring for animals that you might gain a wide variety of experiences. Also, research the schools since vet schools want to know why you chose their specific school environment and learning experience. They also want to learn more about your personality, including life choices and obstacles you may have had to overcome. Note: if you are asked to submit a secondary application with additional essays, you may have a limited amount of time to return these, so read your e-mail and watch for their deadlines.

PRIOR TO APPLYING

- Volunteer with community service organizations, military, children, and the elderly
- Conduct animal research in school or professional laboratories
- Work in a vet clinic or hospital, learning medical terminology and veterinary practices
- Compile a list of faculty and individuals who will write letters of recommendation
- Create a system that works for you to track letters of recommendation. Interfolio is one option
- Prepare for and take for the GRE; the MCAT is often accepted in lieu of the GRE (not all schools require tests)
- Register for GRE, MCAT, or CASPer if necessary
- Sign up for AAVMC and VMSAR updates and school-specific changes

- Attend workshops for health professionals and vet school fairs
- Obtain official transcripts from ALL schools and universities attended

WHEN APPLYING

- Create a VMCAS account and investigate requirements
- Investigate vet school options and select schools
- Chart VMCAS deadlines, GPA/course/test/recommendation requirements, minimum clinical hours for the schools you chose
- Input personal information, letters, and transcripts
- Work on activity statements, personal statements, and supplemental essays
- Submit applications before the deadlines
- Interview invitations in fall and winter
- Interview
- Decisions are typically rolling
- Decision Day!

VET SCHOOL ADMISSION PROCESS

Studying veterinary medicine in the United States is very attractive, with seven U.S. vet schools ranking among the top twenty in the world. Four of the top twenty schools are in the United Kingdom. The other top-ranking schools are in The Netherlands, Canada, Denmark, Switzerland, Belgium, Scotland, Germany, Australia, New Zealand, Spain, and Japan, depending upon the ranking agencies. UC Davis, Cornell, Ohio State, and NC State are consistently ranked at the top in the United States and abroad.

In addition to the VMCAS admissions site, students applying to Texas A&M or Texas Tech must complete the Texas Medical & Dental Schools Application Service (TMDSAS). VMCAS and TMDSAS standardize the application process and allow students to choose the schools to which they want to apply and then collect, collate, and distribute submitted credentials, including grade point average (GPA), test results, letters of recommendation, essays, personal/demographic data, and experiences.

UNDERGRADUATE COURSEWORK

While the prerequisites for vet school admissions vary, the general requirements for undergraduate coursework typically include each of the following:

● Biology with Lab ● Physics ● English *Statistics

● General Chemistry with Lab ● Organic Chemistry with Lab

Modifications brought about by the pandemic, such as online learning, have affected students' curriculum and performance in some of these required courses. Studies have shown that online learning has many challenges both for learners and faculty. These challenges could be technological, social, or motivational.

As a result of social distancing regulations, a majority of students could not perform in-person laboratory experiments. Instead, many schools transitioned to virtual reality demonstrations, videos, and previously formulated datasheets.

These changes resulted in some schools altering their grading system from letter grades to pass/fail.

PRE-VET ACADEMIC REQUIREMENTS ADJUSTED

Some vet schools agreed to temporarily accept pass/fail grades and online courses taken during the pandemic.

INTERVIEWS

Personal interviews remained part of the admissions process for the 2020-2021 admissions cycle and will continue for 2022 and 2023. However, many schools offered virtual interviews due to COVID-19, although in-person interviews will likely resume in 2022, 2023, and beyond. On-campus interviews allow admissions staff and faculty to get to know students. At the same time, students also had the opportunity to learn more about the campus environment, academic atmosphere, and student life.

Virtual interviews limited the spread of the virus, accounting for social distancing and travel restrictions. While some schools continued in-person interviews, video conferencing offered a reasonable alternative. Those universities that held in-person interviews observed safety protocols, including face masks, hand sanitizers, and social distancing.

CLINICAL EXPERIENCES

Shadowing opportunities, typically expected, were not required for the 2020-2021 cycle. Although many veterinary clinics and hospitals were closed or observing no or limited access to non-essential persons in 2020, for 2021-2022 and beyond, shadowing experiences will be highly recommended, even if the hours are virtual.

OTHER REQUIREMENTS

Applicants to vet schools are required to provide letters of recommendation or letters of evaluation. Letter types include individual letters, committee letters, and composite letters. For the individual letters, schools usually require one or two letters from an applicant's science professor, one from a veterinarian, and one from an advisor.

This requirement remains unaffected by the pandemic.

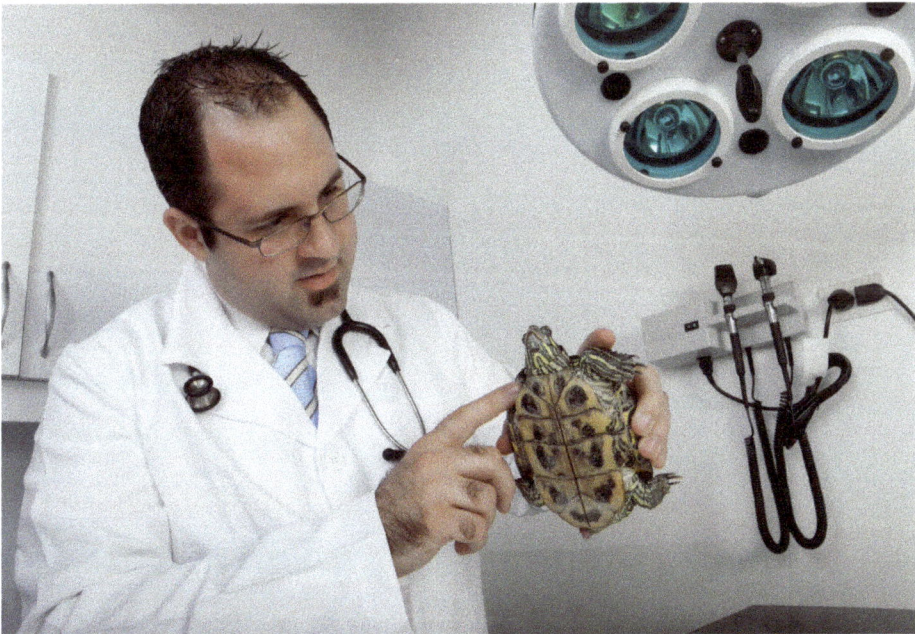

"The more that you read, the more things you will know. The more that you learn, the more places you'll go."

— Dr. Seuss

CHAPTER 10

CONSIDERING A GAP YEAR

GAP YEAR AND THE PANDEMIC

The 2020-2021 pandemic provided significant challenges to vet school applicants whose education was complicated by the change in learning environments, pass-fail grading, and laboratory courses that discontinued traditional, syllabus-described outcomes. As a result, many research projects and volunteer opportunities were curtailed, though some students recalibrated by devising innovative ways to support the underserved in their communities.

With the adjustment to online learning and the use of Zoom, which was unfamiliar to most faculty at the beginning, students and faculty were concerned about the depth of learning in academic courses. This situation was true, especially with science courses with labs (e.g., biology, chemistry, organic chemistry, and physics), raising vet schools' concerns about preparedness. As a result, some students needed to retake these courses.

Many students were unable to take the GRE. The Educational Testing Service (ETS), which offers the GRE, canceled tests as students scrambled to find new sites. This scenario amounted to students spinning in a frustrating runaround of register-study-cancel-reregister and repeat. For students who did take the test and plan to take a gap year, schools will accept test scores taken within two to three years. Check the school to see their requirements.

Alternative testing options were made available in 2021, which improved this predicament. However, many students earned low scores during the pandemic given their frustration, canceled tests, and need to retake the exam. While there is a stigma associated with students who retake the exams, you should retake the test if your score is low. An uncompetitive score is likely to eliminate your chances, and the show of improvement shines a positive light on your capabilities and potential to bounce back.

Shadowing and other clinical experiences were unavailable, and virtual platforms lacked the veracity for HIPAA requirements. With quarantines, COVID-19 concerns, and risks to students, patients, and local residents, most specialized study abroad and overseas medical mission trips were canceled. Students constructed alternative plans of action to complete courses, gain animal care experiences, devise research projects, work on farms, and support the healthcare needs of their community. Some decided to attend graduate school as a gap year option to gain a stronger foundation and await opportunities that had previously been unavailable.

GAP YEAR PLAN

Applying to vet school during a busy junior and senior year is incredibly challenging. Thus, taking a gap year to work at a veterinary medical practice is helpful. Students can finish college, prepare for tests, and apply to school while also gaining skills and experiences. This period between a student's undergraduate and veterinary medical education also improves foundational academic skills and allows more time to study and take the GRE. In addition, some students choose to work for a year in the animal care profession to earn money and immerse themselves in the field.

Most students, particularly during the pandemic, used their gap year to strengthen their application and increase their skills. Whether you work on your personal and mental health, conduct research, serve your community or take additional classes, use this opportunity to become more focused, aware, and prepared. If you work closely with a vet or research advisor, they may be willing to write one of your letters of recommendation. Continue to communicate with your former professors, lab supervisors, and volunteer coordinators who you may ask to write a recommendation. Keep them informed about your current pursuits and that you would like to receive a recommendation from them at a later date.

While you are pursuing your gap year, take the time to volunteer and shadow vets. A year away from the classroom may be necessary. Still, this period is also an excellent opportunity to take advantage of new experiences that deepen your understanding of the veterinary medical profession. Non-vet healthcare experiences, scribing, and animal hospital work are also valuable along your journey to vet school. A paid position in the vet field would also provide you with a broader understanding of the field. Certifications can also be a worthwhile pursuit.

Another option is to build your language and cultural skills by traveling abroad. Do your research to determine the best options for you. However, a few options to consider include:

- Wildlife Conservation Centers
- Aquarium and Marine Life Locations
- Animal Care Services
- Bird Sanctuaries
- Teaching Animal Healthcare
- Organizations that Protect Species
- Zoos
- World Veterinary Association
- Vets without Borders
- Wildlife Vets International
- African Conservation Experience
- Operation Wallacea
- CELA Belize
- Loop Abroad
- Adelante Abroad
- Broadreach
- Eko Tracks
- Ecolife Expeditions

The opportunity to gain these kinds of experiences for extended periods may not happen again. However, if you are interested and want to explore the world, many opportunities are available; the value cannot be quantified.

POST-BACCALAUREATE PROGRAMS

Two predominant types of post-baccalaureate programs serve as intermediaries between undergraduate degree programs and vet school, including a one-year post-bacc foundation-strengthening program. Often, these programs include a component whereby applicants prepare throughout the year for vet school.

The other is a master's program in a scientific area like public health, healthcare administration, human physiology, molecular genetics, or biochemistry. These are typically one to two years and can be completed with or without a thesis and research project. In both cases, students demonstrate continued interest in the sciences, the discipline to continue learning, and a stronger foundation to build upon for vet schools. Needless to say, high grades in either of these types of programs are essential to be a competitive applicant.

ADVICE FROM YOUR PRE-HEALTH ADVISOR

Advice from a pre-health advisor can be invaluable. They typically know about regional jobs, internships, scholarships, honors programs, college activities, leadership development, service organizations, shadowing opportunities, and professors looking for students to assist with research. They can also provide advice on courses, professors, summer programs, and gap year options.

While a gap year may seem like a waste of time or a delay in your long-term plan to attend vet school and become a veterinarian, this is an excellent opportunity to regroup and gain a much-needed break from intense studying. Unsurprisingly, taking a gap year was more common during the pandemic, given the multitude of roadblocks. However, with a renewed spirit and additional animal care experiences, data show that students who begin vet school a year later are more excited to get back to work and eager to learn.

"Study while others are sleeping; work while others are loafing; prepare while others are playing; and dream while others are wishing."

– C. Everett Koop

CHAPTER 11

LOOKING AHEAD: MCAT, LETTERS OF REC, ESSAYS

From the moment you know that you plan to pursue veterinary medical school, set up a plan. Preparation is essential. You do not want to miss required or desirable courses, activities, or considerations along the way. Think about what is needed around the corner before you get there. At some point, you will apply.

To do so, you will need to:
1. Meet with your pre-health advisor

2. Map out your academic curriculum so that you complete the required courses

3. Get involved on campus – student body leadership, admissions ambassador, social groups, academic clubs, science organizations, spiritual fulfillment, athletic teams, artistic practice, musical training/performances, theatrical groups, etc.

4. Gain language skills and basic health certifications (CPR, AED, BLS, EMT, Phlebotomy, etc.)

5. Plan your volunteer work, animal care, tutoring, shadowing vets, clinical experiences, or scribe position

6. Consider summer and school-year research opportunities

7. Consider study abroad, animal care support abroad, or work in a vet clinic in an underserved area

8. Prepare and take the Graduate Record Exam (GRE)

9. Request transcripts; send them to VMCAS
10. Determine those who will write your letters of recommendation
11. Consider and chart out the schools to which you want to apply and determine their requirements
12. Write your personal statement
13. Prepare your application

COURSE PREPARATION AND GRADES

You will need high grades. Sure, some students have lower grades, but the process of admissions is competitive. Vet schools are looking for the best students who will be the best veterinarians. Even if the process is holistic, there are many variables. You need to do the best you can do with your own interests and skills.

Some of your classes will be exceptionally difficult. Most colleges have free tutors. Seek out tutoring assistance even if you are not behind. They are invaluable and may know better ways to study for classes or prepare for specific professors' tests. Tutors can be beneficial to help you get unstuck from a problem or clarify a concept that could take you hours to figure out.

Your GPA is possibly the single best predictor of your academic success in vet school. Focus on being organized and efficient. One technique that helps students feel more confident and prepared is to buy textbooks and begin reading ahead of time. If the book is on an audio file, listen to the books before classes start.

If you are required to memorize large volumes of information, like the nomenclature in organic chemistry, put the information on flashcards, posters, or digital files to learn ahead of time. Make studying more efficient and more manageable. With a plan and determination, success will follow.

GRADUATE RECORD EXAMINATION (GRE)

You will have a hard time mastering the material on the GRE without the knowledge of verbal skills, reading comprehension, and quantitative reasoning. Begin preparing as soon as you can by purchasing a book with practice tests and take one section of the test every week. Get to know the test and feel comfortable with the questions.

There are also numerous private in-person and virtual test prep centers where you can practice in individual and group settings to master the topics on the exam. There are also video prep lessons on YouTube as well as other free sources.

LETTERS OF RECOMMENDATION

In each class you take, you want to think, "Could this professor be one of my recommenders?" Of course, this is not why you should be punctual, responsible, and attentive in class, but literally, any of your professors could be a recommender. Noting this in your mind demands that you show up prepared and ready to be engaged in discussions in every class.

Finish your homework. If you are stuck, get help so you can follow along and not get behind. As you finish a class, consider whether that professor is one of those people you might ask to be a recommender. If so, remain in contact. You may ask that professor to recommend you for a leadership position, scholarship application, or some other opportunity before you apply to vet school.

Of course, it is great to keep in touch with all of your professors, but sometimes doing so is not practical, and the faculty member has shown no real interest in your success. Nevertheless, you may write to them later, even if they are not a recommender, to tell them that you appreciate what you learned or acknowledge that their teaching made a difference in your life. I recently wrote to a few of my undergraduate chemistry and biology professors from many decades ago. They were overwhelmingly appreciative of the notes of thanks and appreciation I sent.

PERSONAL STATEMENT AND OTHER ESSAYS

Your personal statement is an essay about your journey to vet school and how you came to realize that this career is your future. Although there are many ways to tell your story and lots of anecdotes you might include, as you begin your pursuit of vet school, consider the activities you want to have along the way.

Your goal is for the admissions committee to have a robust understanding of who you are, how you made your life choices, and where you envision your journey heading. Looking ahead at what you might write, plan what you will do over the rest of your college experience so that your actions match your intention.

What values do you hold? What is most meaningful to you? Since life is a matter of choices, you will need to decide what pursuits make the most sense and how you want to portray these to vet schools when you write your personal statement.

Benjamin Franklin once said, "If you fail to plan, you are planning to fail."

"The ones who say "You can't" and "You won't", are probably the ones scared that you will."

— Ziad K. Abdelnour

CHAPTER 12

SHOW ME THE DATA!

VETERINARY MEDICAL APPLICANTS

The demand for veterinarians is expected to jump 16 percent by 2029.[1] Meanwhile, 10,273 students applied to veterinary medical programs in the U.S. to start in the 2021-2022 academic year, representing a significant jump from the 8,645 applicants the previous year.[2] These statistics are impressive since they represent the equivalent surge in pet adoptions and student interest.

Nevertheless, applying to vet school is challenging since there are numerous academic, testing, and extracurricular requirements. In addition, students must juggle multiple balls in the air at the same time. Thus, the preparation process can be painstaking for applicants eager to join a vet school and gain their DVM degree.[3] The deadline for applications is September 15th.

The Association of American Veterinary Medical Colleges maintains an application service, Veterinary Medical College Application Service

1   U.S. Bureau of Labor Statistics, "Veterinarians," *U.S. Bureau of Labor Statistics*, n.d., https://www.bls.gov/ooh/healthcare/veterinarians.htm#tab-1

2   Jennifer Fiala, "Number of Veterinary School Applicants Climbs 19%," *Vin News*, October 27, 2020, https://news.vin.com/default.aspx?pid=210&Id=9905318

3   AAVMC, "Admitted Students Statistics," *AAVMC*, n.d., https://www.aavmc.org/becoming-a-veterinarian/what-to-know-before-you-apply/admitted-student-statistics/

(VMCAS), for students applying to vet school. This clearinghouse serves 44 member universities, including 31 of the 33 vet schools in the U.S. The exceptions are Texas A&M and Texas Tech, both of which use the Texas Medical and Dental Schools Application Service (TMDSAS). Overseas colleges served include Australia, Canada, Grenada, Ireland, New Zealand, St. Kitts, and the United Kingdom.

Member institutions of the AAVMC include those in the U.S. (33), Australia/New Zealand (5), the British Isles (3), Canada (5), the Caribbean (2), France, Ireland, Mexico, the Netherlands, and South Korea.

Quick Facts – Veterinary Medicine	
2020 Median Pay	$99,250 yearly; $47.72 per hour
Typical Entry-Level Education	DVM
Work Experience & On-the-Job Training	Gained in Vet School
Number of Jobs in 2019	89,200
Job Prospects (2019 - 2029)	16 percent (faster than other careers)
Change in Employment, (2019 – 2029)	14, 200

Stats about Veterinarians (U.S. Bureau of Labour Statistics)[4]

The application process is only one hurdle. On the other end, you must wait to hear whether you are accepted or denied. The best way is to plan, prepare, and execute, and when you are done with that, move forward with more academic, work, and volunteer experiences.

Applicants frequently submit applications to multiple programs.[5] Applicants can also apply to vet schools abroad in Europe or the Caribbean. As encouraging as this may be, studying abroad is often expensive. Therefore, students seeking to move outside the country must consider, among other things, the high travel costs and living expenses.[6]

Gaining acceptance to a vet college has been largely tied to its available spots and the significant number of applicants seeking admission. It is important to note that schools modified their admissions requirements during COVID-19.

---

4   U.S. Bureau of Labor Statistics, "Veterinarians," *U.S. Bureau of Labor Statistics,* n.d., https://www.bls.gov/ooh/healthcare/veterinarians.htm#tab-1

5   Tufts Cummings School of Veterinary Medicine, "Adventures in Veterinary Medicine: FAQ," *Tufts Cummings School of Veterinary Medicine,* n.d., https://vetsites.tufts.edu/avm/faqs/

6   VeterinarianEDU.org, "Why the Majority of Veterinary School Applicants are Denied," *VeterinarianEDU.org,* March 20, 2017, https://www.veterinarianedu.org/2017/03/why-the-majority-of-veterinary-school-applicants-are-denied/

Check the American Association of Veterinary Medical Colleges website for current information. The link provided here may be a year old but gives an idea of the changes.[7]

IN-STATE VS. OUT-OF-STATE

Nearly half of U.S. states do not have a veterinary medical school. As a result, many applicants apply to vet schools out of state. There are 33 accredited vet schools in the United States.[8] This figure is considerably smaller than the 172 accredited U.S. and Canadian medical schools.[9] Medical colleges are scattered throughout the U.S., though stiff competition exists for medical school admission. However, students applying have a higher chance of securing a spot than applicants to vet schools.

Like medical schools, the competition is high. Acceptance rates hover around 10 and 15 percent.[10] Successful applicants usually reside in the same state as the respective vet schools since public colleges give preference to in-state residents and sometimes even primarily exclude those who live outside.

The average public vet school accepts 50 percent from in-state. However, some cross the norm and accept more than 80 percent of applicants from the same state. As a result, applicants who reside and apply in the same state as a vet school have a higher chance of getting accepted.

Note that Alabama, Tennessee, Texas, and California have two in-state vet schools.

Some states have a Regional Contract Program that allows students in states without a vet school to be considered in-state residents with in-state or reduced out-of-state tuition. This opportunity may be limited since taxpayers typically fund public schools from that state. Neighboring states usually do not contribute to the vet school costs, though some underwrite their students. Furthermore, vet schools want to ensure that enough veterinarians remain to work in-state and serve their communities.

7   AAVMC, "Updated Veterinary Medical School Admissions Policies in Response to COVID-19," *AAVMC*, Updated August 21, 2020, https://www.aavmc.org/wp-content/uploads/2020/09/updates_cvm_admissions_policies__covid-19..pdf

8   AVMA, "Accredited Veterinary Colleges," *AVMA*, n.d., https://www.avma.org/education/accredited-veterinary-colleges

9   AAMC, "Who We Are," *AAMC*, n.d., https://www.aamc.org/who-we-are

10 AAVMC, "Admitted Student Statistics," *AAVMC*, n.d., https://www.aavmc.org/becoming-a-veterinarian/what-to-know-before-you-apply/admitted-student-statistics/

According to the Southern Regional Education Board, Arkansas, Delaware, Kentucky, and South Carolina residents can attend vet schools out-of-state through state-to-state agreements.[11] Since creating a vet school is expensive, states piggyback on other programs to train their residents. Delaware's program, for example, partners with the University of Georgia College of Veterinary Medicine, while Kentucky partners with Auburn University in Alabama. Arkansas pairs with other states through their Arkansas Health Education Grant Program (ARHEG).

PROFILE OF ADMISSION TO VETERINARY MEDICAL SCHOOL

Applicants who lack experience but have an impressive grade point average and test scores may find that their academic credentials are insufficient; it takes more than just good grades to get admitted to a vet school. GPA and test scores are just part of the equation.

According to a December 2020 AVMA article, 63% of the veterinarians in the nation's workforce of 116,000 professionals are female, an increase of 12% in the past decade. Despite this, more males own veterinary medical practices.[12] Female applicants traditionally have a higher chance of securing a spot in vet colleges than males. This statistic is because females dominate veterinary medical practice, comprising around 30 percent of the profession.[13] Furthermore, with the growing demand for vet specialists and a wide variety of animal care needs, applicants looking to specialize improve their chances of gaining admission.

11 Southern Regional Education Board, "Regional Contract Program," *Southern Regional Education Board*, n.d., https://www.sreb.org/regional-contract-program

12 R. Scott Nolen, "women Practice Owners Projected to Overtake Men Within a Decade," *JAVMA News*, Updated January 11, 2021, https://www.avma.org/javma-news/2020-12-15/women-practice-owners-projected-overtake-men-within-decade

13 VeterinarianEDU.org, "Why the Majority of Veterinary School Applicants are Denied," *VeterinarianEDU.org*, March 20, 2017, https://www.veterinarianedu.org/2017/03/why-the-majority-of-veterinary-school-applicants-are-denied/

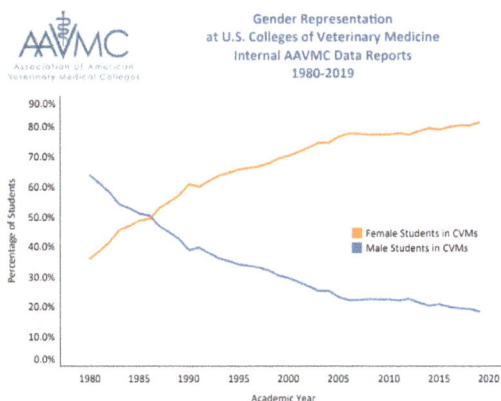

Gender Representation
at U.S. Colleges of Veterinary Medicine
Internal AAVMC Data Reports
1980-2019

**U.S. Veterinary Medicine Gender Representation 1980 - 2020
(2019 AAVMC Annual Data Report)[14]**

NON-U.S. VET SCHOOL CONSIDERATIONS

While seeking admission to vet colleges overseas is an option for those rejected by U.S. vet schools, the journey is challenging. For example, U.S. applicants applying to schools in Canada face the challenge of limited availability. Canada has only five accredited veterinary medical colleges. These schools predominantly pick Canadian applicants first before considering U.S. applicants. Also, applying to vet schools outside the U.S. is costly. Successful applicants suffer a debt arising from tuition, accommodation, transportation, and relocation.

14 AAVMC, "Annual Data Report 2018-2019," *AAVMC*, 2019, https://www.aavmc.org/assets/Site_18/files/Data/2019%20AAVMC%20Annual%20Data%20Report%20(ID%20100175).pdf

"Be so busy improving yourself that you have no time to criticize others."

– Chetan Bhagat

CHAPTER 13

CAREER OUTLOOK AND OPTIONS

MEETING THE NEED FOR VETERINARIANS,

The demand is high for veterinary medical practitioners. This growth is not only seen in the double-digit percentage increases in the need as described by the Bureau of Labor Statistics, but also in the numbers of people who adopted animals throughout the pandemic. As a result, there is a great need for additional support, medical care, vaccinations, and emergency attention for animals. The career outlook for veterinarians is better than most other professions. The demand will only increase in the post-pandemic environment.

However, meeting these needs will be difficult since there are only 33 veterinary medical schools in the United States. Thus, wages are likely to rise as well as the demand for veterinary medical assistants and technicians. If this career pursuit is your life's commitment, then vet school is the way to go.

WHAT MEDICAL PROFESSION IS RIGHT FOR YOU?

Given that pre-vet students have taken all of the prerequisites, there are other options for medical-related careers. Thus, there are numerous rewarding options in healthcare and many roads to arrive at your goal.

There are numerous alternative possibilities for students who find medicine, dentistry, healthcare, and human biology fascinating. Popular choices include: allopathic medicine (MD), osteopathic medicine (DO), podiatrist (DPM), dentist (DDS), veterinarian (DVM), pharmacist (PharmD), psychologist (M.A., Ph.D., Psy.D.), psychiatrist (MD), optometrist (OD), chiropractor (DC), physician's assistant (PA), physical therapist (PT), speech pathologist, nurse practitioner (MSN, DNP), occupational therapist (MSOT, DOT), nurse anesthetist (MSN).

MEETING THE NEED FOR HEALTHCARE WORKERS

According to the Bureau of Labor Statistics (BLS), the healthcare industry is expected to grow faster than the average for all other occupations. With a projected increase of 14 percent from 2018 to 2028, approximately 1.9 million new jobs will be available for those interested in medicine. The demand for healthcare will only increase in the post-pandemic environment. However, increases are also anticipated due to the aging population in a demographic shift sometimes referred to as the "gray tsunami."

According to the U.S. Census Bureau, baby boomers, born between 1946 – 1964, are turning 65 at a rate of about 10,000 per day. By 2030, when the next census is taken, all baby boomers will have crossed that threshold. This information is critical to understanding careers in healthcare and is the key reason why the healthcare profession will have a surge of jobs. Hospitals, emergency services, home healthcare, nursing homes, and mental health services will require professionals to meet the rising need. Wages are likely to rise in this arena during the next decade.

WHAT MEDICAL PROFESSION IS RIGHT FOR YOU?

When students ponder the pursuit of medicine in general, they tend to consider medical school as the quintessential career and life objective. No doubt, medical school is the right pursuit for many students. Yet, there are many rewarding options, and there is more than one road to reach your goal.

In the 1990s, a Harvard interviewer asked one of my very talented Hispanic students why she would want to attend a liberal arts school if she wanted to pursue nursing. My student answered the question without hesitation, explaining that her mom had a DNP but always wished she had started her road with a rigorous liberal arts education. However, I never stopped thinking about that question. Sure, specialized undergraduate nursing education is a more direct pathway and this route would extend her timeline, but she was committed to expanding her knowledge base. After we talked, I came to understand her long-term objective. She did not get accepted to Harvard, but she did attend Columbia, and she is now a nurse practitioner.

There are numerous possibilities for students who find medicine, dentistry, healthcare, and human biology fascinating. Popular choices for those who complete graduate school include the following: allopathic medicine (MD), osteopathic medicine (DO), podiatrist (DPM), dentist (DDS), veterinarian (DVM), pharmacist (PharmD), psychologist (M.A., Ph.D., Psy.D.), psychiatrist (MD), optometrist (OD), chiropractor (DC), physician's assistant (PA), physical therapist (PT), speech pathologist, nurse practitioner (MSN, DNP), occupational therapist (MSOT, DOT), nurse anesthetist (MSN).

OCCUPATION/DEGREE	ASSOCIATIONS, CERTIFICATION ORGANIZATIONS	BUREAU OF LABOR STATISTICS DATA (2018)
Medical Doctor (MD) Allopathic Medicine – AMCAS - 154 accredited colleges in the U.S.; 17 in Canada	*American Association of Medical Colleges (AAMC) *American Medical Association (MDs & DOs)	Median Annual Salary – $208,000 Number of Physicians & Surgeons (2018) – 756,800 Projected Job Change (2018 – 2028) – 7% inc. Job Openings (2018 – 2028) – 55,400
Physician (DO) Osteopathic Medicine – AACOMAS - 36 accredited colleges in the U.S.	* American Association of Colleges of Osteopathic Medicine (AACOM) *American Osteopathic Association (AOA) *Bureau of Osteopathic Specialists (BOS) *Certifying Board Services (CBS)	Median Annual Salary – $208,000 Number of Physicians & Surgeons (2018) – 756,800 Projected Job Change (2018 – 2028) – 7% inc. Job Openings (2018 – 2028) – 55,400
Podiatrist (DPM) – CPME - 9 accredited colleges in the U.S.	*American Association of Colleges of Podiatry Medicine (AACPM) * Council on Podiatric Medical Education (CPME)	Median Annual Salary – $129.550 Number of Podiatrists (2018) – 10,500 Projected Job Change (2018 – 2028) – 6% inc. Job Openings (2018 – 2028) – 600
Dentistry (DDS) – ADEA AADSAS – 67 ADA accredited dental schools in the U.S.; 10 in Canada	*American Dental Education Association (ADEA) *American Dental Association (ADA)	Median Annual Salary – $156,240 Number of Dentists (2018) – 155,000 Projected Job Change (2018 – 2028) – 7% inc. Job Openings (2018 – 2028) – 11,600

OCCUPATION/DEGREE	ASSOCIATIONS, CERTIFICATION ORGANIZATIONS	BUREAU OF LABOR STATISTICS DATA (2018)
Veterinary Medicine (DVM) – VMCAS - 30 accredited veterinary medical schools in the U.S.; 5 in Canada	*Association of American Veterinary Medical Colleges (AAVMC) *American Veterinary Medical Association (AVMA)	Median Annual Salary – $93,830 Number of Veterinarians (2018) – 84,500 Projected Job Change (2018 – 2028) – 18% inc. Job Openings (2018 – 2028) – 15,600
Pharmacist (PharmD) – PharmCAS - 144 full or candidate accredited pharmacy schools in the U.S.	*Accreditation Council for Pharmacy Education (ACPE) *American Pharmacists Association (APhA)	Median Annual Salary – $126,120 Number of Pharmacists (2018) – 314,300 Projected Job Change (2018 – 2028) – 0% inc. Job Openings (2018 – 2028) – (-100)
Psychologist (MA, Ph.D., Psy.D) – numbers vary by type	*American Psychological Association (APA)	Median Annual Salary – $79,010 Number of Psychologists (2018) – 181,700 Projected Job Change (2018 – 2028) – 14% inc. Job Openings (2018 – 2028) – 26,100
Psychiatrist (MD)	See MD	Median Annual Salary – $208,000 Number of Physicians & Surgeons (2018) – 756,800 Projected Job Change (2018 – 2028) – 7% inc. Job Openings (2018 – 2028) – 55,400
Optometrist (OD) - 23 accredited optometry schools in the U.S. and 2 in pre-accreditation	*Association of Schools and Colleges of Optometry (ASCO) *Association of Optometrists (AOP)	Median Annual Salary – $111,790 Number of Optometrists (2018) – 42,100 Projected Job Change (2018 – 2028) – 10% inc. Job Openings (2018 – 2028) – 4,000
Chiropractor (DC) - 20 chiropractic schools in the U.S.	*Association of Chiropractic Colleges (ACC) *American Chiropractic Association (ACA) *Council on Chiropractic Education	Median Annual Salary – $71,410 Number of Chiropractors (2018) – 50,300 Projected Job Change (2018 – 2028) – 7% inc. Job Openings (2018 – 2028) – 3,700
Physician's Assistant (PA) - 254 ARC-PA accredited PA programs in the U.S.	*Accreditation Review Commission on Education for the Physician Assistant (ARC-PA) *American Academy of Physician Assistants (AAPA)	Median Annual Salary – $108,610 Number of PAs (2018) – 118,800 Projected Job Change (2018 – 2028) – 31% inc. Job Openings (2018 – 2028) – 37,000

OCCUPATION/DEGREE	ASSOCIATIONS, CERTIFICATION ORGANIZATIONS	BUREAU OF LABOR STATISTICS DATA (2018)
Physical Therapist (PT) - Over 400 CAPTE accredited PT schools	*American Physical Therapy Association (APTA) *Commission on Accreditation in Physical Therapy Education (CAPTE)	Median Annual Salary – $87,930 Number of PTs (2018) – 247,700 Projected Job Change (2018 – 2028) – 22% inc. Job Openings (2018 – 2028) – 54,200
Speech Pathologist – 230 accredited programs	*American Speech–Language– Hearing Association (ASHA)	Median Annual Salary – $77,510 Number of Speech Pathologists (2018) – 153,700 Projected Job Change (2018 – 2028) – 27% inc. Job Openings (2018 – 2028) – 41,900
Nurse Practitioner (NP) MSN, DNP - Approximately 400 NP programs	*American Association of Colleges of Nursing (AACN) *American Association of Nurse Practitioners (AANP)	Median Annual Salary – $113,930 Number of NPs (2018) – 240,700 Projected Job Change (2018 – 2028) – 26% inc. Job Openings (2018 – 2028) – 62,000
Occupational Therapist (MSOT, DOT) - 37 fully accredited DOT programs	*American Occupational Therapy Association (AOTA) * Accreditation Council for Occupational Therapy Education (ACOTE)	Median Annual Salary – $84,270 Number of Occupational Therapists (2018) – 113,000 Projected Job Change (2018 – 2028) – 18% inc. Job Openings (2018 – 2028) – 23,700
Nurse Anesthetist (MSN)	See NP	Median Annual Salary – $113,930 Number of NPs (2018) – 240,700 Projected Job Change (2018 – 2028) – 26% inc. Job Openings (2018 – 2028) – 62,000

ALLIED HEALTH PROFESSIONS

The medical profession would not be able to serve the public without the talented and dedicated service of allied health professionals who support, assist, record, evaluate, and rehabilitate patients. From intake and testing to nutrition and maintenance, if it 'takes a village', the village that is needed to treat patients is multifaceted, multilingual, and multitalented. These careers often require interpersonal skills in communication and listening along with recordkeeping, problem-solving, and critical thinking. In addition to healthcare administrators, managers, and insurance professionals, the following presents a list of some of the many professionals in the medical support community.

- *Athletic Trainer*
- *Audiologist*
- *Cardiovascular Technologist*
- *Clinical Laboratory Technician*
- *Clinical Laboratory Technologist*
- *Diagnostic Medical Sonographer*
- *Emergency Medical Technician*
- *Exercise Physiologists*
- *Dental Assistant »*
- *Dietician (RD, RDN)*
- *Dispensing Optician*
- *Genetics Counselors*
- *Health Information Technician*
- *Home Health Aide*
- *Kinesiologist*
- *Massage Therapist*
- *Medical Assistant*
- *Medical Records Assistant*
- *Medical Transcriptionist*
- *Midwife*
- *MRI Technologist*
- *Nuclear Medicine Technologists*
- *Nursing Assistant (CNA)*
- *Nutritionist*
- *Occupational Therapy Assistant*
- *Orderly*
- *Orthodontists*
- *Orthotists*
- *Paramedics*
- *Pharmacy Technician*
- *Phlebotomist*
- *Physical Therapy Assistant*
- *Prosthetists*
- *Psychiatric Aide*
- *Recreational Therapist*
- *Radiation Therapists*
- *Radiologic Technologist*
- *Registered Nurse (RN, BSN)*
- *Respiratory Therapist*
- *Ultrasound Technician*
- *Veterinary Assistant*
- *Veterinary Technologist*

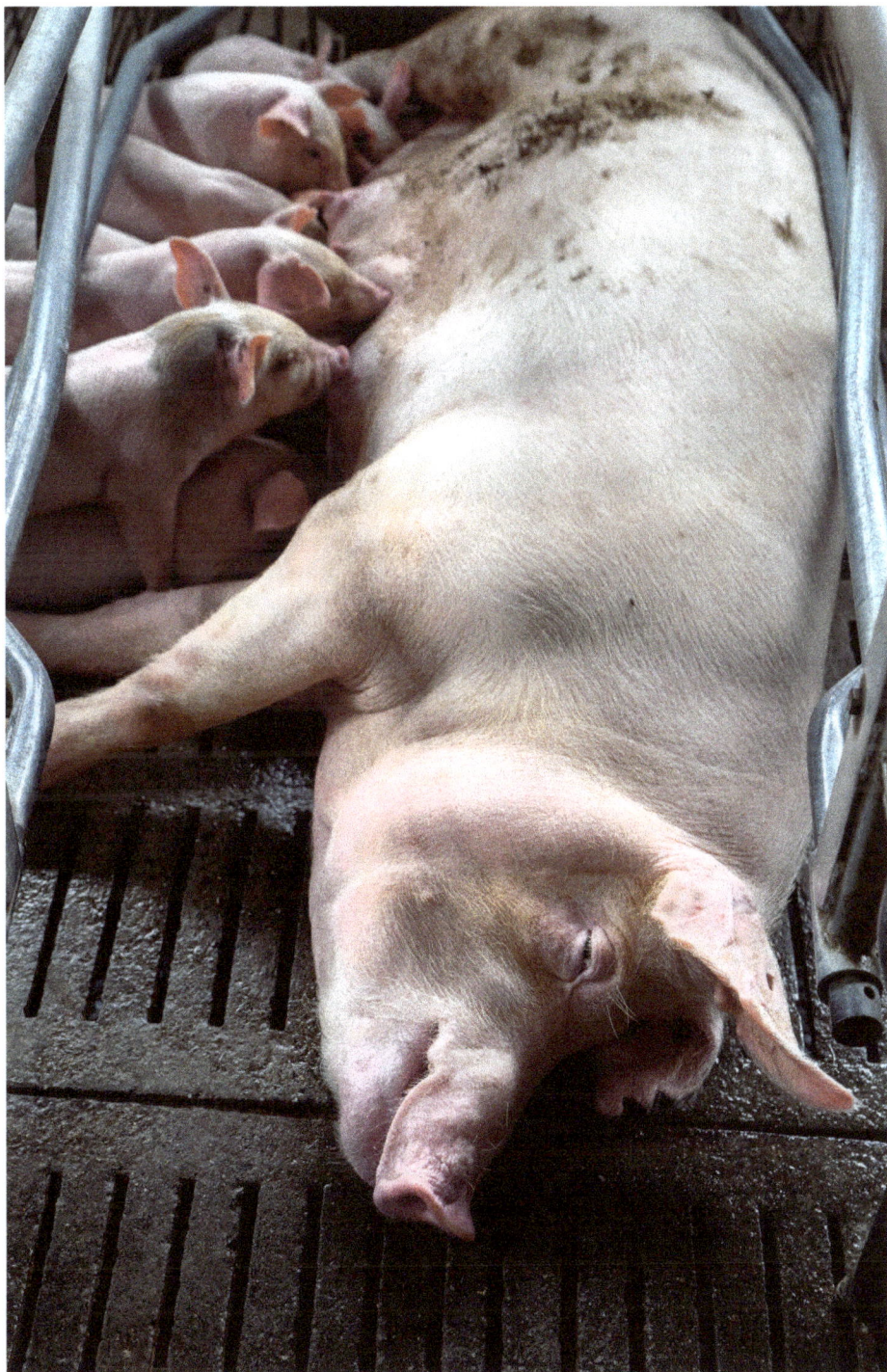

"*Starve your distractions; feed your focus.*"

—Anonymous

CHAPTER 14

BUSINESS SKILLS OF VETERINARY MEDICINE

KNOW THYSELF

The practice of veterinary medicine and small business ownership demands two distinct skill sets. Veterinarians can own and operate a vet practice, but they should understand the myriad duties that come with each role. Buying an existing practice, in whole or in part, effectively commits the veterinarian to the fiduciary responsibilities of business ownership, along with the duties of ethical clinical support and business management.

A veterinary medical practice requires technical and scientific mastery along with compassion and humility. On the other hand, business ownership necessitates a different focus. Owners must tend to property security, location maintenance, contracts, quality control, recordkeeping, and accounting. A healthy dose of assertiveness is needed to be an effective leader/manager-veterinarian/practitioner. One must be able to lead and be willing to make tough decisions, including hiring, training, coaching, and firing staff as needed and accepting the necessary financial risks associated with practice ownership.

BUSINESS KNOWLEDGE AND ACUMEN

The owner of a vet practice needs to understand the principles of sound business relationships as well as the legal requirements ubiquitous to healthcare provisions. The skills in treating a patient are not the same as working with legal entities, property managers, and employees. In addition, employees and contractors do not share business risks. Thus, caution must be exerted in making choices that affect other people.

If bookkeeping or accounting responsibilities are assigned to an employee, the owner must exercise due diligence in ensuring that all functions are completed. In the end, the buck stops with the veterinarian – whether legal, ethical, or fiduciary. Even when delegated, the responsibilities lay with the veterinarian. From big-picture concepts like the state of the economy to the tiniest details of insurance deductibles, vets must understand, analyze, make course corrections, and execute.

Acumen is essential too. Not all veterinarians who want to own a business have the 'sixth sense' to anticipate the unexpected and stay on task with both the practice of veterinary medicine and the management of the practice. Business organization is very different from animal care and treatment.

PERSONALITY TRAITS—ARE YOU AN EXTROVERT?

Extroverts derive energy from the presence of other people. Introverts, on the other hand, need time alone for restoration when fatigued. One can nurture extroversion if nature does not grant this ability naturally. However, a comfort level with people in varied situations is necessary for a practice owner.

DO YOU NEED THE APPROVAL OF YOUR EMPLOYEES?

Vet practice owners must be confident and believe in their capacity for good decision-making. Veterinarians are not always liked and, at times, may have to make life and death recommendations. Because you are human, you will stumble in any number of ways. Perhaps you fail to communicate effectively about a procedure to be done. Maybe you unwittingly put a staff member in the position of managing an unpleasant pet owner.

Whatever the case, your staff may complain, criticize, or even quit. Frankly, even if you miraculously managed not to make mistakes, your administrative decisions could be misinterpreted by your employees. The point is, you must respect your staff members and treat them well without giving them power over your confidence as a practitioner.

When agendas conflict, there can only be one boss. As with effective parenting, veterinarian-managers must forsake the temptation to prioritize popularity over responsibility. Veterinarians must learn to delegate responsibilities efficiently and hold employees accountable for performing the tasks required.

LISTENING TO STAFF MEMBERS

On the other hand, just as the boss must hold a high standard, they must also understand the stressors faced by employees. In the business of your vet practice, it will not be just you whose family depends on the income generated. The practice must succeed in the interest of the employees involved too. Listen to those who work for you so that you can be attentive and flexible.

BEYOND THE OFFICE WALLS

Practice owners must build a relationship with the community to ensure a steady stream of patients. People share information with one another within a society, and referrals are the best way to attract patients. We also live in a digital community. The internet age has changed businesses and business practices.

Websites can provide both positive and undesirable feedback from the public. This internet glow of satisfaction or even the perception of lackluster care cannot be stopped. This wave of commentary means that every patient can write about you, your associates, your staff, and your practice.

All veterinarians—especially business owners—must accept the risk of being negatively portrayed on animal lover review sites. Websites highlight and share information. In general, a veterinary medical practice needs to establish an online presence.

You may assign staff members to manage the details of social media posts and replies. However, again, it is the veterinarian's name and reputation on the line. It is the veterinarian who is praised or criticized. A shy person or someone afraid of public opinion will find it uncomfortable to be a practice owner.

Some veterinarians truly enjoy entrepreneurship. They embrace the challenges of owning a business. Others, though, find that their quality of life could be improved by working for another type of entity—a vet hospital, another veterinarian, a corporate farm, a business, the government, or an animal care service organization.

FARM ANIMAL CARE AND FOOD ANIMALS

Farms filled with animals for personal use, enjoyment, or food production abound across much of the United States. Farm animal owners spend considerable time tending to their nutrition, health, and welfare. Veterinarians who support these farms may not have a physical office in a building, but they also run a business. As a result, business practices can look very different among different veterinarians.

Veterinarians, responsible for the care of animals raised for food production and human consumption, have a duty and commitment to animals and people. While providing medical care, conducting research, and determining diagnoses, much of their obligation and commitment is to:

- protecting animal health through care, nutrition, and support
- preventing disease through testing, vaccinations, etc.
- examining animals in distress
- diagnosing and treating those exhibiting an illness or injury
- considering environmental conditions of livestock
- offering feedback to farm owners regarding their animals
- delivering offspring and managing the reproduction and nutrition
- monitoring exercise and movement of animals
- developing disease management protocols
- discovering information about new diseases, surgical techniques, and medicines
- identifying and controlling disease outbreaks
- overseeing food safety, including regulatory requirements
- mentoring staff and supporting the continued learning of those working on the farm
- ensuring safety, sanitary conditions, and cleanliness
- euthanizing animals
- documenting reasons for animal health conditions
- recordkeeping, accounting, and business management

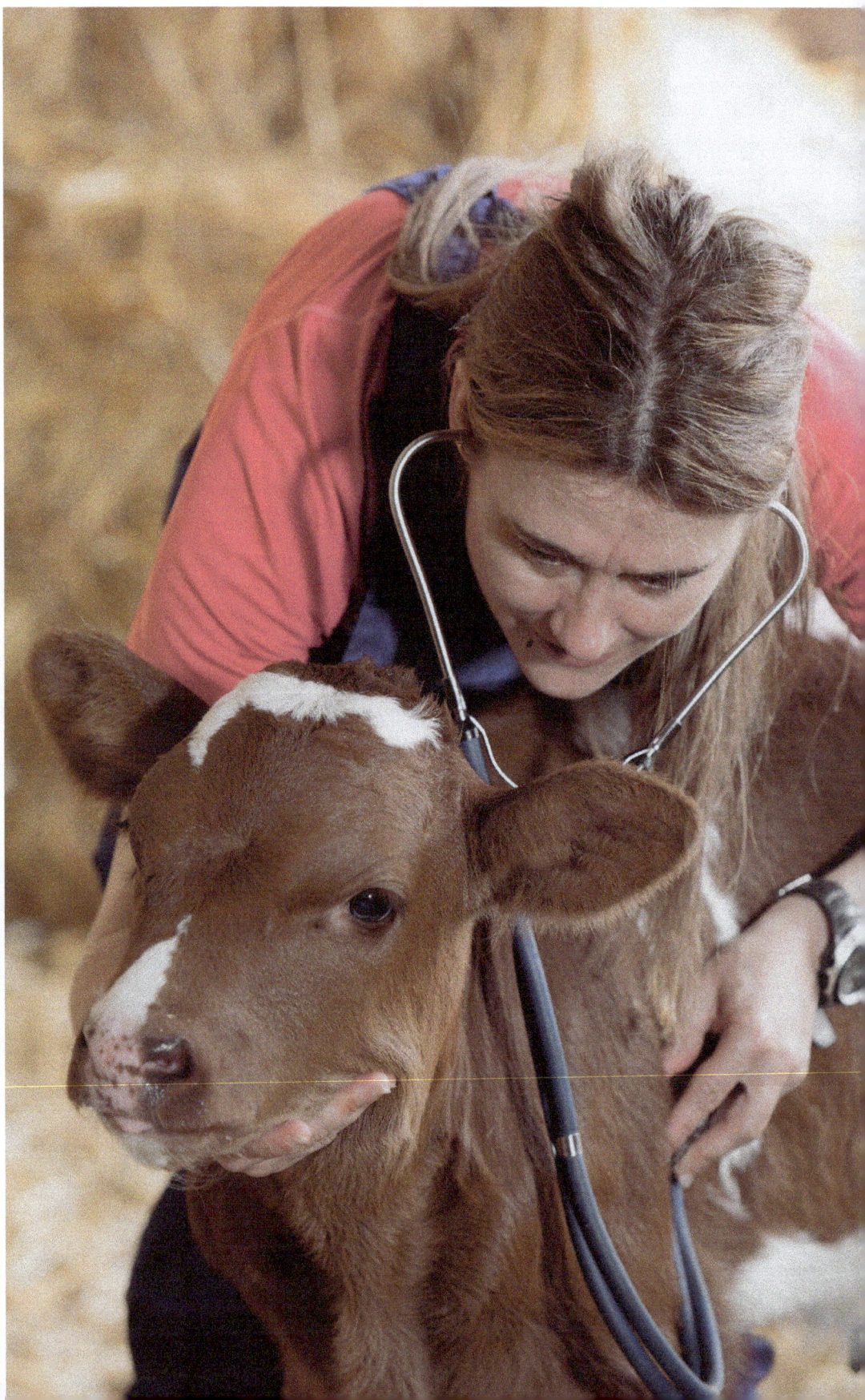

PART 3
PREPARATION

"

"A dog is the only thing on earth that loves you more than you love yourself."

— *Josh Billings*

CHAPTER 15

MAJOR AND ACADEMIC REQUIREMENTS: COURSEWORK, GPA, PREREQUISITES

GPA REQUIREMENT

The University of California Davis admissions site lists the following information as the minimum requirements for their vet med program.[1] However, the actual student profile, given in the chart at the back of this book, shows that the average student from California had a GPA of 3.7 and a science degree. For out-of-state students, the average GPA was 3.96. Other schools have high overall GPAs also, including Texas A&M with a 3.72, Tufts with a 3.72, and Cornell with a 3.73.

Typical applicants have a:

- 2.5 GPA or higher (2.5 is a minimum)
- 180 veterinary experience hours (this varies widely)
- Three professional recommendations with at least one from a veterinarian
- Successful completion of the required prerequisites (courses must have a grade of C and higher; a C- will not be accepted)

1   UC Davis Veterinary Medicine, "Criteria for Admission," *UC Davis Veterinary Medicine*, n.d., https://www.vetmed.ucdavis.edu/admissions/criteria-admission

A bachelor's degree from a regionally accredited university (some do not require a degree)

However, students can get accepted with a wide range of GPAs. First, an average means that some scores are undoubtedly lower than the average though probably not significantly unless there are extenuating circumstances. Vet schools with lower overall average GPAs include Lincoln Memorial with a 3.4, Michigan State with a 3.32, Tuskegee with a 3.4, and Western University with a 3.24.

PREREQUISITES

The prerequisite requirements vary widely from school to school. However, almost all schools require a year of **biology, chemistry, organic chemistry, and physics**.

Most require **biochemistry, cell biology, genetics, and physiology.**

A few require **animal nutrition, zoology, and medical terminology**.

Other requirements across the board. Investigate the specific courses mandated for each school's admissions process for the schools you are considering. Specific prerequisites are listed in the school profiles located at the back of the book. You may also find them on the chart provided here by the University of Massachusetts: https://www.vasci.umass.edu/sites/vasci/files/prereqchart_final-for_website_2.13.20.pdf

BACHELOR'S DEGREE REQUIREMENT

As of June 2021, only two U.S. veterinary medical colleges required a bachelor's degree: UC Davis and Tuskegee University. Since many prerequisites are required, by default, most students earn a bachelor's degree.

AP AND CLEP CREDIT

The counting of AP credit varies by school. Tuskegee University's site says, "Yes. We will accept them as long as it's documented on an undergraduate transcript. However, we may still require you to enroll in some college classes in the science area."[2] Tuskegee University also accepts CLEP credit and classes taken at foreign

---

2   Tuskegee University, "Frequently Asked Questions (FAQ)," *Tuskegee University,* n.d., https://www.tuskegee.edu/Content/Uploads/Tuskegee/images/CVM/Frequently_Asked_Questions.pdf

higher education institutions. Courses placed on a U.S. college transcript with a grade do not undergo a review, while those not on a U.S. transcript must be evaluated to determine acceptability.

The following chart was adapted from a University of North Alabama document.

Vet School	Notes Regarding AP Credit
Auburn University	AP credits appearing on a college transcript are accepted. AP scores are not reviewed.
Colorado State University	CSU's veterinary program accepts AP credits for veterinary prerequisite courses if the course(s) appear on an official transcript at the university in which the student matriculated.
Iowa State University	AP credits are accepted as long as the student's undergraduate institution rewards credit for a specific course that we would accept as meeting our requirement. We will also accept credit if the scores match Iowa State's requirements for fulfilling a particular course.
Kansas State University	AP credits are accepted if the courses are listed by name on a college transcript for credit. Specific AP courses must be delineated.
Massey University	AP credits are not accepted from a high school transcript. However, if a college or university awards AP credit for class(es), then these courses will be considered against the prerequisite requirements.
Mississippi State University	We will accept AP credit provided the courses and credit is listed on the transcript.
North Carolina State University	At NC State, AP courses can be used to fulfill prerequisites. Regardless, the applicant's undergraduate institution must list the AP course by name (Biology, Calculus, English, etc.) on its transcript, indicating the number of credits granted. Note: AP courses are not considered when calculating grade point averages.
Oklahoma State University	We try to honor the requirements and rules of undergrad programs. Oklahoma State honors AP credit for English, for example, though we seldom see AP credit for higher-level courses. Only graded courses go into the GPA calculation.
Oregon State University	Oregon State accepts AP credit awarded, even for prerequisite requirements.
Purdue University	Purdue accepts AP credits if they are listed on an official university transcript. In addition, Purdue accepts credit by exam.

Tufts University	The Cummings School accepts AP credits as long as they are given credit on the applicant's college transcript.
UC Davis	Currently, UC Davis accepts AP credit for lower-division science requirements and English, social studies/humanities, and statistics. However, UC Davis is changing admissions processes which may exclude AP credit in the future. The AP credit must appear on the applicant's transcript and include the subject title and the number of units.
University of Florida	The UFCVM accepts AP credits based on the rules of their undergraduate institution. For example, UF requires a 4 on AP tests to earn undergraduate credit. For example, students applying from UF with a 4 on the AP English exam would meet our requirements.
University of Guelph	AP credits are not considered for prerequisite purposes for DVM applicants. Likewise, we will not consider credit awarded for IB, A Levels, or CAPEs.
University of Illinois	The University of Illinois allows AP credits for some classes but not for prerequisite science courses. These must be earned at the college level.
University of Minnesota	The University of Minnesota accepts AP credit for prerequisite classes if the applicant's primary undergraduate institution awards subject area credit documented on that transcript. For example, if a student receives 3 credits for freshman English based on AP scores, these will count toward English prerequisites.
University of Missouri	AP credit is only awarded if the undergraduate institution specifies the course and credit on the student's college transcript. AP test scores are not evaluated or accepted separately.
University of Tennessee	AP coursework fulfills prerequisite courses (usually English, freshman biology course(s), or foreign language) as long as the AP credit is noted on the official transcript and credit is earned for an appropriate level college course.
Washington State University	AP scores can be used to fulfill prerequisite requirements. However, due to differences in college policies, AP scores are evaluated after WSU receives the AP score sheet and student's earned scores.

VET SCHOOLS REQUIRING CASPER FOR 2022 ADMISSIONS

Kansas State University	Oklahoma State University
Lincoln Memorial University	Purdue University
Long Island University	Ross University (St. Kitts)
Michigan State University	Texas Tech University

UC Davis

University of Florida

Virginia-Maryland College of Veterinary Medicine

VET SCHOOLS REQUIRING GRE FOR 2022 ADMISSIONS

Auburn University

Louisiana State University

Oklahoma State University

Ross University (St. Kitts)

Tuskegee University

UC Davis

University of Georgia

Western University

VET SCHOOLS THAT ACCEPT INTERNATIONAL STUDENTS

Colorado State University

Kansas State University

Lincoln Memorial University

Long Island University

Louisiana State University

Michigan State University

Oklahoma State University

Purdue University

Ross University (St. Kitts)

Texas Tech University

Tuskegee University

UC Davis

University of Georgia

Western University

THE PERKS OF VETERINARY MEDICINE

Becoming a vet doctor comes with plenty of perks. Most applicants who want to become veterinary doctors pursue this career option because of their genuine love of animals, even if the paycheck is not as high as other professions.

Applicants often go the extra mile to gain hundreds of hours of animal care experience. This knowledge not only aids in gaining admission but also lays a solid foundation for subsequent vet school academic and clinical training. To bolster admissions chances, applicants take up roles in vet clinics with titles such as volunteers, interns, groomers, veterinary technicians, or veterinary assistants. Since the process is highly competitive, many applicants also pursue research.

VET SCHOOL TRANSFER

Many vet schools accept few transfer students due to their unique curricula, focus, and methods of learning. Furthermore, small animal classes cannot easily fit into a large animal curriculum. Generally, a student must drop out for a seat to open up. Also, the material does not match, so students will either repeat learning the information ot they will be behind by not knowing what was taught beforehand. To transfer, you must have earned high grades. Schools are not eager to take students who did poorly.

Oregon State University, for example, excepts transfer students who have completed all of the previous curricula. Contact the OSU Admissions Counselor. You will need a transcript for all coursework completed (3.0 or higher is required), an updated personal statement, current resume or CV, letter of recommendation from a faculty member, and application fee.

For some vet schools, mainly where the curricula are different, you must start from scratch. Western University explains, "This is mainly due to the unique structure of our curriculum (Problem-Based Learning). Our concern is that someone who was not involved in the first or second-year curriculum would be at a disadvantage in their last two or three years."[3]

---

3   Western University, "Doctor of Veterinary Medicine (DVM) FAQs," *Western University,* n.d., https://prospective.westernu.edu/veterinary/dvm/faqs/

> "By learning you will teach; by teaching you will learn."

> — Latin Proverb

CHAPTER 16

ACADEMIC ACTIVITIES AND PRE-MED ADVISING

PRE-VET ADVISING

Most research institutions have individual and group pre-vet advisory sessions for prospective vet students. On smaller campuses, that advisor may serve a broader set of students within multiple pre-health disciplines. It is advisable to meet with your pre-vet or pre-health advisor as early as possible to establish a connection.

Ask questions and get advice about proceeding on your academic pathway. Not only will your advisor have college-specific knowledge about your professors, courses, or trajectory, but they might also know about individual vet schools. Navigating the requirements is challenging. However, your advisor may be able to steer you in the right direction, given your unique circumstances.

Ideally, you will build a team of supporters around you while preparing to apply to vet school. No matter how large or small the team, your pre-vet advisor will be an essential player. That individual is also likely to have the most up-to-date information about changes from year to year regarding the admissions process. After all, that is their job.

ACADEMIC CLUBS

Academic clubs are popular and often serve as both a social network and academic community for students with similar interests. Students seeking intellectual stimulation and collegial groups are more likely to suffer from an abundance of choices rather than a dearth of opportunities. As your 'free time' becomes infrequent and you must choose only those activities that make the most sense, each moment also becomes more valuable.

How many activities can you do well without sacrificing other responsibilities? Students planning to apply to vet school must hold priorities in a delicate balance. Taking time away from schoolwork in the interest of staying healthy is necessary without letting too much of that time go to waste in the interest of staying academically competitive.

Ideally, students can engage a few organizations that offer camaraderie while also scaffolding their futures. Pre-Vet Clubs are especially popular because they are the pathway clubs to healthcare professional programs. Not only do these groups bring in speakers, but they also connect students with summer programs, research, internships, clinical experiences, and mentorship opportunities.

Collaborating with other pre-vet students allows you to learn avenues for success as well as pitfalls that sometimes lead students to take a gap year before gaining admission. In addition, you get to network with veterinarians while acquiring the crucial information you need to plan your application process and future career.

Health professions' clubs provide an academic society away from your coursework to collaborate with students traveling along your same journey. You may see these same students in the future. They may be colleagues on the same boards, or you might meet them at veterinary medicine conferences. Through these groups, you may establish a bond that could last for life. However, you will also develop shared academic and personal interests aside from veterinary medicine.

Honorary societies such as Omicron Delta Kappa and Mortar Board are not healthcare-specific. They are accessible to students from a variety of majors and might round out your organizational involvement.

Some schools have living-learning communities (LLCs) where you can participate in activities with students outside of your primary interests. These LLCs often provide social outlets within the context of intellectual curiosity. Take a deep breath, make thoughtful decisions, and have a responsible amount of fun!

Pre-Vet Societies have been established on many college campuses and deserve a look from all people considering careers in veterinary medicine. The National Institute of Food and Agriculture offers 4-H clubs on 100 college campuses. Collegiate 4-H clubs offer opportunities for service, leadership, and professional development. Speaking at schools and discussing opportunities with young people, you can share your knowledge and help people simultaneously. There are often contests, opportunities to serve as a judge or assist with animal service projects.[1]

VETERINARY MEDICINE FRATERNITIES

Another option would be to start a chapter of one of the veterinary medical fraternities below. This option offers you the chance to demonstrate leadership while offering a valuable forum on your college campus.

Alpha Psi (AΨ)

Alpha Psi is a professional fraternity for those interested in veterinary medicine. The fraternity was started in 1906 at The Ohio State University College of Veterinary Medicine. In 1914, a chapter was started in Canada at the University of Guelph Ontario Veterinary College and became the organization's first international chapter. Today, there are eight active chapters, though there were once eighteen. Some early colleges of veterinary medicine closed, as did their chapters. This organization once had a newsletter, bringing the chapters together and sharing information. It looks like a great opportunity for leadership for any student driven to unite these groups.

Omega Tau Sigma (ΩTΣ)

Omega Tau Sigma is a professional fraternity for those interested in veterinary medicine. This fraternity began at the University of Pennsylvania School of Veterinary Medicine in 1906 and spread to other colleges. In 1914, a chapter was started in Canada at the University of Guelph Ontario Veterinary College and became the organization's first international chapter. Today, there are twelve active chapters of Omega Tau Sigma. This fraternity also had a pre-pandemic newsletter and needs a leader to unite the clubs.

---

1   USDA, "Collegiate 4-H Programs," *USDA*, n.d., https://nifa.usda.gov/sites/default/files/resource/Collegiate-4-H-Programs.pdf

> *Desire is the key to motivation, but it's determination and commitment to an unrelenting pursuit of your goal – a commitment to excellence – that will enable you to attain the success you seek."*

– Mario Andretti

CHAPTER 17
RESEARCH AND PUBLICATIONS

S tudents often enter college believing they are a vessel to be filled with knowledge. Yet, knowledge continues to expand. Research pushes the boundaries of what is known to the next level. You will benefit by supporting a science team, serving on a farm/ranch research project, or volunteering on an international animal protection study.

EXPANDING KNOWLEDGE AND BREAKTHROUGH SCIENCE

In February 2021, *Science Daily* shared a scientific development that may reverse previously incurable conditions in dogs. By inducing stem cell generation and transplanting these cells to regenerate damaged tissues, scientists seek to revitalize organs and injured areas in dogs and other animals.[1]

In June 2021, 10,500 veterinary professionals came together to hear presentations on current research at the 38th annual Veterinary Meeting & Expo. One demonstration revealed a portable, iPad-sized ultrasound diagnostic tool that can examine extremely small nerve vessels previously unable to be seen.[2]

---

1   Osaka Prefecture University, "New Stem Cell Therapy in Dogs – A Breakthrough in Veterinary Medicine," *Science Daily,* February 3, 2021, https://www.sciencedaily.com/releases/2021/02/210203090512.htm

2   North American Veterinary Community, "New Technologies and Breakthroughs in Veterinary Medicine Take Center Stage at VMX 2021," *PR Newswire,* June 10, 2021, https://www.prnewswire.com/news-releases/new-technologies-and-breakthroughs-in-veterinary-medicine-take-center-stage-at-vmx-2021-301310089.html

An article published in 2021 presented a development in particle physics that may change the way scientists understand subatomic particles. The research, leading to a possible new "Standard Model", was conducted by the Fermi National Accelerator Laboratory, a joint venture of the University of Chicago and the Universities Research Association (URA).[3]

In May 2021, researchers at Duke University developed fully recyclable, printable electronics using graphene that could be used to develop next-generation technology.[4]

In July 2021, researchers at the University of California, San Francisco, successfully tested an experimental brain implant that allowed a man to "speak" after not being able to talk for a decade. The *New England Journal of Medicine* article describes how people may one day communicate ideas without using vocal cords but just by thinking. This implant translates brain signals into words through a digital transmission on a computer screen.[5]

RESEARCH ADVANCES SCIENCE

Advancements in veterinary medicine continue to improve techniques and save animals' lives. Across all medical fields, research in immunology, cancer biology, and biochemistry makes strides because researchers seek greater understanding. University faculty could not do this without student research support. In college, I researched the regeneration of nerves in the extremities of mice in late stages of diabetes. Years later, scientists are now able to regenerate nerves.

Whatever research projects you choose will take science one step farther toward understanding immunology, pathology, and genetics. Medical advances take the first step toward prevention and treatment. If you are serious about veterinary medicine and the care of animals, you should consider conducting research. By helping to improve the science underlying veterinary medicine, you will gain a firmer foundation in what cutting-edge discoveries mean on a broader basis.

---

3   Dennis Overbye, "A Tiny Particle's Wobble Could Upend the Known Laws of Physics," *The. New York Times,* April 7, 2021, https://www.nytimes.com/2021/04/07/science/particle-physics-muon-fermilab-brookhaven.html

4   Duke University, "Engineers Have Developed the World's First Fully Recyclable Printed Electronics," *SciTech Daily,* April 26, 2021, https://scitechdaily.com/engineers-have-developed-the-worlds-first-fully-recyclable-printed-electronics/

5   Rolfe Winkler, "Brain Implant Lets Man 'Speak' After Being Silent for More Than a Decade," *The Wall Street Journal,* July 14, 2021, https://www.wsj.com/articles/brain-implant-lets-man-speak-after-being-silent-for-more-than-a-decade-11626296422?mod=djemalertNEWS

Research is not required for admission to vet school. However, if you do pursue this avenue, take it seriously and participate actively. Being certified as a vet technician or paramedic is just as valuable and takes about the same amount of time. Choose whatever fits your interests, abilities, and passions. Your knowledge of science and the scientific method in alternative forms is far more important than the name of an important researcher on the laboratory's door.

FIVE CUTTING EDGE RESEARCH AREAS IN VETERINARY MEDICINE

(1) ANIMAL HEALTH CARE

Veterinary medicine's emphasis on animal health is highly valued particularly in the realms of medical and personal care. Research in animal health care focuses more on animal health management driven towards proper reproductive growth. Also, it focuses on examining the health status of animals on the farm.[6]

Researchers carefully observe animals and their behaviors. Any deviation from the norm may imply sickness or disorder. In addition, researchers test pharmacological agents and consider options to treat sick animals and prevent disease outbreaks.

(2) ANIMAL DISEASES

Like humans, animals are susceptible to some diseases which may affect the normal functioning of their internal and external organs. When this happens, it affects animal production. Therefore, disease diagnosis and control are crucial to vet medicine.

Research in these areas examines the nature of animal diseases, causes, prevention, and control. Field research helps to interpret the different types of animal disease and their causes. Sick animals, especially food animals, can cause significant economic loss. Some of these diseases can be transferred to humans.

Veterinary medicine in animal science focuses on preventing and treating domestic, wild, and research animals. However, the basic agricultural concerns impact the prevention, control, and eradication of diseases.[7]

---

6   Marta Hernández-Jover, Lynne Hayes, Robert Woodgate, Luzia Rast, and Jenny-Ann L.M.L. Toribio, "Animal Health Management Practices Among Smallholder Livestock Producers in Australia and Their Contribution to the Surveillance System," *Frontiers in Veterinary Science 6*, (2019): 191, https://www.frontiersin.org/articles/10.3389/fvets.2019.00191/full

7   William Burrows, "Animal Disease – Non-Human," Encyclopaedia Britannica, Updated August 9, 2018, https://www.britannica.com/science/animal-disease

(3) ANIMAL FEEDING

Veterinary research on animal feeding is concerned with providing proper nutrition essential for animal growth, development, and productivity. Animals have specific requirements and cannot feed on just any available food material. It has to be specific or those recommended by vet researchers with experience in animal feeding. Though many livestock owners are forced to manage their expenses by feeding animals alternative food supplements only, it can affect their feeding pattern.

Research in animal feeding also examines animal food supplements and normal animal nutrition with some diet methods in animal management. Researchers examine the quality of specific food nutrients added to animal food designed to complement nutrients in the diet or make up for a deficiency.[8] Animal feeding must be done right as some nutrients are essential for the growth and maintenance of the body to provide sufficient energy.

(4) LIVESTOCK MANAGEMENT

Livestock management research helps raise the quality of animals from birth to the point of sale or productivity.

Livestock management plays a critical role in enhancing food security, nutrition, and the overall welfare of middle-class citizens in developing countries. For this reason, research in livestock management is pivotal to guarantee improved animal productivity in line with health care measures.

(5) ANIMAL PRODUCTIVITY

Research carried out in this field determines the appropriate level of production in animal and livestock management. Results identify factors that aid or affect animal productivity. Researchers in this line of work study domestic animal species and frequently work with livestock to understand the biological and chemical processes by which animals grow to production levels. Animal scientists also study the diverse relationships between animals of different species and how they can be crossbred.

EVERY STEP YOU TAKE IS PROGRESS

Even in a small lab working on a small project, science takes a step forward. Understanding how this process works is valuable and contributes to your ability

---

8   Journal of Animal Research and Nutrition, "Home," *Journal of Animal Research and Nutrition*, n.d., https://animalnutrition.imedpub.com/

to succeed and keep abreast of discoveries. There is much that veterinarians, and scientists in general, do not know. By working in a lab, you take ownership of a larger project. Even if you inject a hundred mice a week, you are still part of a big picture and can better understand connections.

Progress begins with the scientific process and discovery. Often your research qualifies for college credit. Most colleges offer independent study credits whereby you write up a plan, get signatures, and complete the project.

WORKING WITH A PRINCIPAL INVESTIGATOR (PI)

The first step is to find a lab where you can do substantive work and ultimately develop your own research project. At first, though, you will be at the bottom of the totem pole. Start looking for projects during your first or second year so that you can progress. Many labs have funding available. If not, there are usually university research scholarships. Summer research often comes with fellowship funds.

Typically, you begin a project by surveying the literature on topics surrounding the lab's investigation and understanding the research goals. Most of the work you do will be technical or procedural work with cells, solutions, animals, or data entry.

Whatever you do is valuable. You will work at the discretion of your principal investigator (PI), a post-doc, or a graduate student. While you will typically work under their supervision and complete tasks as required, you may be invited to lab meetings or colloquia where you can expand your knowledge.

Part of the training in veterinary medicine is to master the terminology. There are thousands of terms. Through research, meetings, mentorship, data entry, analysis, and writing, you will learn more about the instrumentation, tests, and implications that will also help you in your classes.

Do not be afraid to ask a question. PIs and post-docs have many more years of training and were once in your position. Everyone needs to learn from scratch. You are no different. Do not be afraid if you do not know everything.

WORK IN AREAS OF YOUR INTEREST

You should be interested in the work you do. Often, you will work on this research project for a year or more. You should find it truly fascinating and not just because there is an opening. When you apply to vet school, you are likely to use this experience as one of the experiences on your application. You may discuss it in your interview. If you are enthusiastic, interviewers can tell from your expressions. If you just did it to 'look good', that will be apparent as well. Sincerity is important.

PUBLICATIONS

If you have worked continuously in a lab supporting the research project, you will likely be listed in the publication as a contributor. The first author on a paper is typically the PI. The second might be a post-doc or graduate assistant. You may not be one of the first two. Nevertheless, having your name on a publication means that you were a significant enough part of the process to be named at all. However, being one of the last authors on a paper is fine. Look for chances to conduct an independent research project, publish your findings, and present them in a poster session.

"Success is never accidental."

— Paul Berg

CHAPTER 18

CLUBS, SERVICE, AND SCHOOL INVOLVEMENT

BALANCE AND INVOLVEMENT

Vet school allows students to advance not only intellectually but also personally. Through activities and involvements, students enrich their lives by participating in extracurricular activities that might "round out" their education, such as research, community service, and school activities. For example, students gain basic or clinical research, take part in State Fair activities, collaborate with undergraduate students as part of a mentorship program, volunteer with a variety of organizations, conduct research in wet laboratories, and participate in lunch hour talks.

Activities should be balanced with one's educational obligations. However, even given the demands of the rigorous course load, most students have some time in their schedules to "become involved."

Participating in class activities, community service, or scholarly pursuits outside of class can be beneficial in a variety of ways that enable students to: [1]

MEET CLASSMATES

- create new, long-lasting friendships
- work with faculty members
- add diversity to your résumé

---

1   University of Minnesota, "Extra-Curricular Activities," *University of Minnesota,* n.d., https://open.lib. umn.edu/cvmwellbeing/chapter/getting-the-most-out-of-vet-school-extra-curricular-activities/

- become more competitive for internships
- take a break from lectures
- put lab skills to use
- learn more about a topic
- provide a sense of achievement
- help you gain confidence

SOCIAL AND SCIENTIFIC RESEARCH

Discovery is an art and a science. Innovations and biomedical research change the world, improving health, safety, and life. Understanding how research is conducted is a key to becoming a scientist. As a veterinarian, new developments will be unveiled in journals. Read these, knowing how scientific research works, drawing from your experiences.

Students who participate in research, describe their experiences, and often present a publication, demonstrate to the committee that they are competent in the process of scientific inquiry, experimental design, and, when the advances are published, scientific writing. While completing research and publishing in a journal is not required for admission to most veterinary schools, honing research abilities helps students stand out against the crowd.

As a result, veterinary schools evaluate research and activities regardless of the type of commitment to determine a student's fortitude to complete veterinary school successfully.[2]

CLUBS FOR CURRENT & PROSPECTIVE VET STUDENTS
(just a few examples to create on your campus or join)

ACVIM (American College of Veterinary Internal Medicine)

This non-profit student group is North America's largest veterinary medical student organization. They are always looking for volunteers, provide certifications, and offer awards to students for research and service. The ACVIM is dedicated to improving the lives of animals and increasing awareness. There are currently 32 chapters, and the link provided explains the process of starting a new chapter.[3]

2   Truman State University, "Pre-Vet Studies: Extracurricular Activities," *Truman State University,* n.d., https://www.truman.edu/majors-programs/majors-minors/pre-veterinary-studies/pre-vet-studies-extracurricular-activities/

3   ACVIM, "Student Chapter Information," *ACVIM,* n.d., https://www.acvim.org/resources-for/students/student-chapter-info

At the UC Davis chapter, students learn about ACVIM specializations and residency training in cardiology, cancer, SA internal medicine, and neurology through journal clubs, rounds, wet labs, and lunch talks. In addition, students learn to interpret current research and practice integrating academic knowledge into a clinical context. Educational opportunities extend beyond lectures and labs.[4]

Alpha Psi

This national veterinary medical fraternity was established in 1907 at Ohio State University and spread to vet schools throughout the United States. The goal is to honor students for their academic excellence and build lifelong relationships by creating professional ties with members.

American Association of Equine Practitioners (AAEP)

The AAEP is an international organization that started with 11 charter members focused on equine veterinary medicine. The organization has now grown to 9,300 veterinarians and vet students in 61 countries.

American Association of Feline Practitioners (SCAAFP)

This national organization offers students and professionals education, training, support, scientific investigation, and standards of practice for those who work with felines and are interested in feline medicine. With student chapters throughout the country, the goal is to improve the health and welfare of cats. Learn more at catvets.com. The Ohio State University's chapter website explains, "Our club focuses on enrichment, behavior, handling, and feline-unique diseases." The chapter includes the following Feline Medicine Club. [5]

American Pre-Veterinary Medical Association (APVMA)

The American Pre-Veterinary Medical Association is a national organization of and for pre-vet students. With clubs throughout the country, students considering veterinary medicine come together on their campuses through a symposium to meet and discuss issues related to animal care and veterinary medicine. Communication and idea-sharing are encouraged between clubs and organizations.[6] Leadership opportunities are available on the local, regional, and national levels.

---

4   Aggie Life, "ACVIM Student Chapter," *UC Davis,* n.d., https://aggielife.ucdavis.edu/organization/acvim-student-chapter

5   The Ohio State University, "Feline Medicine Club," *The Ohio State University,* n.d., https://vet.osu.edu/education/feline-medicine-club

6   APVMA, "Home," *APVMA,* n.d., https://www.apvma.org/index.html

Each year, a veterinary school hosts the two-day APVMA Symposium, typically held in March. This event allows club members to travel to the symposium, participate in veterinary lectures and laboratories, and meet current veterinarians. In 2020, for example, students were allowed to visit an open house at the Oklahoma State Veterinary School. In 2021, the event was sponsored by Michigan State and held virtually. Over 500 people attended.

Animal Welfare and Behavior Medicine Club

This organization focuses on behavioral animal care and animal welfare. Members discuss the behavior of animals more thoroughly than in veterinary medicine classes. The clubs' goal is to pique fellow students' curiosity and raise their understanding. By bringing in guest lecturers and wet labs, the club seeks to advance the education of students interested in animal behavior and welfare, ranging from canine cognition and positive reinforcement training in primates to clicker training chickens.[7]

Avian & Exotic Animal Medicine Club

The Avian & Exotic Animal Medicine Club provides opportunities for veterinary students to learn about exotic animal health, medicine, and surgery while also developing technical skills to treat these animals. The club hosts lectures and wet labs for veterinarians, technicians, veterinary students, interested members of the public, and an annual conference.[8]

Caduceus Club

Caduceus is a social club for veterinary students and faculty/staff at the university's school of veterinary medicine. It hosts TGIF get-togethers roughly monthly on a Friday, inviting those affiliated with UC Davis Veterinary Medicine Teaching Hospital (VMTH) to enjoy delicious food, drink some beer or wine, and spend time talking with friends and mixing with faculty. The gatherings encourage students to break from their studies and cultivate relationships with their classmates and professors.[9]

---

7   Aggie Life, "Behavior Medicine and Animal Welfare Club," *UC Davis,* n.d., https://aggielife.ucdavis.edu/organization/behavior-medicine-and-animal-welfare-club

8   Aggie Life, "Avian and Exotic Medicine Club," *UC Davis,* n.d., https://aggielife.ucdavis.edu/organization/avian-and-exotic-medicine-club

9   Aggie Life, "Caduceus Club at UC Davis School of Veterinary Medicine," *UC Davis,* n.d., https://aggielife.ucdavis.edu/organization/caduceus-club-at-uc-davis-svm

Camelid Medicine Club

Camelid Medicine Club offers veterinary students at UCD SVM lectures, hands-on wetlab, and physical exam opportunities with alpaca and llama breeding communities in Northern California.[10]

Canine Medicine Club (CMC)

The Canine Medicine Club (CMC) is a veterinary student-run organization at UC Davis focused on increasing veterinary students' educational and service opportunities in canine medicine-related projects.[11]

Christian Veterinary Fellowship (CVF)

This club at Virginia Tech is a student chapter of the Christian Veterinary Mission (CVM). The organization's goal is to promote and support spiritual growth on campus as well as professional development. Virginia Tech's vet school students have participated in short-term service trips to Honduras, Haiti, Uganda, Malawi, Kenya, and Nicaragua.[12]

Colorado State Equine Clubs

- Polo Club
- Ranch Horse Club
- Rodeo Club
- English Riding Club
- Collegiate Horseman's Association
- Mountain Rider's Club
- Equine Assisted Activities & Therapies Club
- Intercollegiate Horse Show Association Team

Equine Medicine Club (EMC)

The EMC at UC Davis provides exposure to horse medicine, surgery, and reproduction to students in the School of Veterinary Medicine. The goal is to

---

10 Aggie Life, "Camelid Medicine Club at UC Davis," *UC Davis*, n.d., https://aggielife.ucdavis.edu/organization/camelid-medicine-club-at-uc-davis

11 Aggie Life, "Canine Medicine Club at UC Davis School of Veterinary Medicine," *UC Davis*, n.d., https://aggielife.ucdavis.edu/organization/canine-medicine-club

12 Gobbler Connect, "Christian Veterinary Fellowship," *Gobbler Connect,* n.d., https://gobblerconnect.vt.edu/organization/cvf

educate veterinarians to promote the wellbeing of horses and provide educational opportunities for horse owners, breeders, and riders.[13]

FARM Club: Food Animal Reproduction and Medicine Club

The FARM Club assists students interested in reproduction and production medicine to obtain extracurricular learning and networking possibilities. Additionally, the club seeks to provide future clients with reliable scientific data while educating the general public about the food they consume. This commitment begins in elementary school and continues as food animal veterinarians.[14]

Feline Medicine Club

This OSU club, affiliated with the SCAAFP, is dedicated to improving feline medicine through education and training. In addition, the UC Davis club aids local shelters and provides financial support to the sister group, the Orphan Kitten Project, through fundraising events. These clubs also provide vet students coordinated roundtable talks, special lectures, and wetlab experiences.

Food Animal Club

This club, at the University of Florida College of Veterinary Medicine, supports students in earning their certificate in Food Animal Veterinary Medicine (FAVM). The club sponsors events with faculty mentors to offer hands-on animal training along with discussions on food animals. The club also holds weekend and evening wet labs.[15]

Fracture Program Club of Veterinary Medicine

The UC Davis School of Veterinary Medicine's Fracture Program Club works in conjunction with the UC Davis Fracture Program for Rescue Animals that offers free surgical care to shelter dogs and cats with orthopedic fractures. In addition, the club contributes to the overall program by raising money and providing post-surgical care. Students can foster these patients, learning about wound care, medicine administration, and physical therapy while also providing a calm and loving recovery environment.

---

13 Aggie Life, "Equine Medicine Club at UC Davis School of Veterinary Medicine," *UC Davis*, n.d., https://aggielife.ucdavis.edu/organization/equine-medicine-club-at-uc-davis-school-of-vet-med

14 Aggie Life, "FARM Club: Food Animal and Reproduction Medicine Club at UC Davis School of Veterinary Medicine," UC Davis, n.d., https://aggielife.ucdavis.edu/organization/farmclub-at-uc-davis-school-of-veterinary-medicine

15 University of Florida Veterinary Education, "Food Animal Medicine," *University of Florida,* n.d., https://education.vetmed.ufl.edu/dvm-curriculum/certificates/food-animal-medicine/

Global Veterinary Alliance (GVA)

This global veterinary outreach program includes campus clubs and travel experiences for those who want to provide medical assistance, post-op care, and support to animals worldwide. GVA seeks to improve the health and welfare of animals worldwide. By facilitating global volunteerism, GVA offers services, resources, and education to underserved populations. The goal is to increase worldwide access to veterinary care, including a pre-pandemic trip to offer services in Nicaragua.[16]

Integrative Veterinary Medicine Club (IVMC)

The IVMC seeks to raise awareness of non-conventional medical treatments while providing education and training for vet practitioners, the public, and technicians. The goal is to understand usual circumstances and make informed judgments. To that purpose, IVMC leaders invite speakers to discuss state-of-the-art treatments and approaches they employ with their patients, including acupuncture, chiropractic, massage, herbal drugs, homeopathy, and cold laser therapy.[17]

Lab Animal Medicine Club (ASLAP)

The ASLAP club serves students interested in laboratory animal medicine as they advance in their careers by providing opportunities to learn, discuss, and share ideas through wetlabs, seminars, journal clubs, and facility tours.[18]

Student Chapter of the American Veterinary Medical Association (SCAVMA)[19]

The SCAVMA has 37 chapters participating in campuses inside and outside of the United States. Each represents the American Veterinary Medical Association (AVMA), presents information from the AVMA, and supports students on university campuses.

The Cornell SCAVMA sponsors lectures, assists students in learning from a clinician, and organizes social and service events throughout the year. SCAVMA delegates are elected for two-year terms and represent Cornell and national conferences.[20]

---

16 Aggie Life, "Global Veterinary Alliance," *UC Davis,* n.d., https://aggielife.ucdavis.edu/organization/global-veterinary-alliance

17 Aggie Life, "Integrative Veterinary Medicine Club," *UC Davis,* n.d., https://aggielife.ucdavis.edu/organization/integrative-veterinary-medicine-club

18 Aggie Life, "Laboratory Animal Medicine Club, Student Chapter of ASLAP at UC Davis School of Veterinary Medicine," UC Davis, n.d., https://aggielife.ucdavis.edu/organization/laboratory-animal-medicine-club-at-ucd-svm

19 AVMA, "The SAVMA Chapter Program," AVMA, n.d., https://www.avma.org/membership/SAVMA/SAVMA-chapter-program

20 Cornell University College of Veterinary Medicine, "Student Organizations," *Cornell University College of Veterinary Medicine,* n.d., https://www.vet.cornell.edu/education/doctor-veterinary-medicine/student-life/student-organizations

Suture Lab/Job Opportunities

The club at the University of Arkansas offers a suture lab for practice. The club's website lists jobs throughout the community for students to obtain hands-on experience in the veterinary medical business. The suture lab allows students to practice suturing with "skin-like" materials for a more realistic experience. In addition, clinics and shelters from all around the community approach the Pre-Vet Club in search of dedicated students interested in gaining veterinary expertise.[21]

SVECCS (The Student Veterinary Emergency and Critical Care Society)

The Student Veterinary Emergency and Critical Care Society is a national, student-run veterinary emergency and critical care society. Chapters may be started by using this link.[22]

The SVECCA at MSU CVM has grown rapidly, offering a wide range of themes in veterinary medicine. Their purpose is to offer helpful information on typical emergency and critical care scenarios for feline, canine, bovine, equine, and exotic animals. The MSU CVM club provides hands-on experiences in addition to lectures.[23]

Wildlife Exotic Zoo Avian Aquatic Animal Medicine (WEZAAM)

The WEZAAM group at MSU CVM introduces members to various animal species not often discussed in the classroom or on rotations. The club meets to discuss veterinary care for exotic animals. WEZAAM provides a platform for students interested in wildlife and exotic medicine. Club dues cover guest lectures, lunch, wet labs, and field trips.[24]

---

21 University of Arkansas, "Pre-Veterinary Club," *University of Arkansas,* n.d., https://animal-science.uark.edu/students/clubs/prevet-club.php

22 NSVECCS, "Prospective Chapters," *NSVECCS,* n.d., https://www.sveccs.org/prospective-chapters.pml

23 Michigan State University College of Veterinary Medicine, "Student Organizations," *Michigan State University College of Veterinary Medicine,* n.d., https://cvm.msu.edu/students/student-clubs

24 Mississippi State University College of Veterinary Medicine, "Clubs and Organizations," *Mississippi State University College of Veterinary Medicine,* n.d., https://www.vetmed.msstate.edu/student-life/student-organizations

"Never believe that animals suffer less than humans. Pain is the same for them that it is for us. Even worse, because they cannot help themselves."

— Louis J. Camuti

CHAPTER 19

CLINICAL EXPERIENCES AND SHADOWING

EXPERIENCE IN ANIMAL CARE

Those wishing to work with animals in a variety of capacities should gain practical experience with them.[1] Gaining experience with veterinarians is an essential part of the preparation process. Whether you are assisting in a clinic or shadowing a vet on a farm, every moment is a learning opportunity that will add to your familiarity and understanding of veterinary medicine.

Working with livestock and breeding animals, or working in a zoo, aquarium, or pet store offers valuable experiences. Other options provide useful skills as well, like assisting at an animal shelter. Shelters and rescue organizations always need volunteers to help with a range of tasks such as cleaning, feeding, doing kennel chores, providing basic obedience training, and assisting with the puppy or kitten adoption.

To gain business experience, run a pet-sitting service or a pet walking service. This initiative displays your interest in being both an animal lover and an entrepreneur. This type of business is inexpensive to begin and can be run as a small-scale side job.

---

1   Charlotte Kerridge, "How Do I Get Veterinary Work Experience?," *VetRecord Careers*, October 26, 2018, https://www.vetrecordjobs.com/myvetfuture/article/how-do-i-get-veterinary-work-experience-/

Each of these animal experiences presents opportunities for varied engagement with animals outside of those you might own. Pet ownership and academic assignments are not included.

While in college or during the summers, learn as much as possible about animals while also developing skills. Animal science, biology, equine science, and marine biology are examples of majors that can include significant laboratory work and hands-on experience working with animals. In addition, take advantage of learning about anatomy and physiology through dissections and laboratory work.

Volunteer opportunities abound in zoos and animal rehabilitation centers for students and those curious about what goes on behind the scenes. For people interested in working with exotic animals, this could be a terrific opportunity. The selection process for zoo career paths is particularly competitive, with many more candidates than positions available. As a result, prior experience is essential.[2]

Working at a farm or stable can be an excellent opportunity to learn about the behavior of cattle and horses for people interested in large animal or livestock vocations.

VETERINARY EXPERIENCE

Under the guidance of a veterinarian (DVM or VMD), you should engage in veterinary experiences to better understand the field.[3]

Many veterinarian programs require practical animal experience to be accepted. This experience will also provide you with useful references. So, how can you get this necessary experience? Here are a few ways to gain animal-related training:

- Speak to a veterinarian and ask questions
- Shadow a veterinarian to see what they do and how they approach their work
- Work in an animal clinic - job experience is one core asset
- Learn about animal welfare
- Take a summer internship or a paid job as a veterinary assistant
- Earn a certificate as an animal technician
- Develop animal handling abilities

2 Mary Hope Kramer, "How to Get a Job at the Zoo," *The Balance Careers,* Updated December 11, 2019, https://www.thebalancecareers.com/zoo-careers-and-salaries-125932

3 Iowa State University College of Veterinary Medicine, "Veterinary, Animal, and Research Experience," *Iowa State University College of Veterinary Medicine,* Updated April 22, 2021, https://vetmed.iastate.edu/future-dvm-students/apply-to-the-college/pre-veterinary-requirements/veterinary-animal-and-research-experience

- Investigate animal behavior and physiology
- Volunteer at a shelter or a rescue center
- Begin a pet-sitting business
- Choose to major in an animal-related degree program
- Clean and feed animals in a zoo or aquarium
- Serve in a wildlife rehabilitation center
- Assist on a farm or in a stable
- Intern in animal husbandry
- Work in the food production or meatpacking industry
- Travel abroad on international animal protection missions

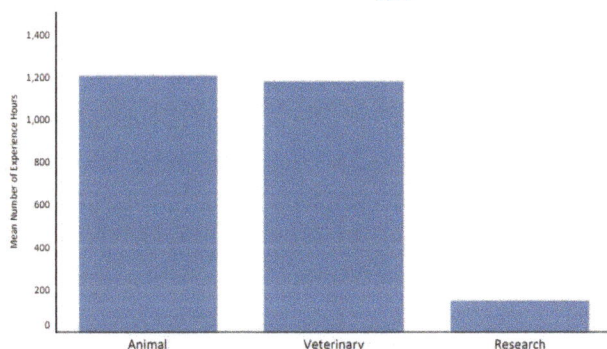

Mean Number of Experiential Hours Applicants Gathered Before the Class of 2023 Vet College Year (2019 AAVMC Annual Data Report)[4]

INTERNSHIPS

One of the best ways to obtain experience dealing with animals is to participate in an internship program. Numerous opportunities are available, including

- beef and cattle industry
- aquaculture and fisheries
- beehive management

---

4   AAVMC, "Annual Data Report 2018-2019," *AAVMC*, 2019, https://www.aavmc.org/assets/Site_18/files/Data/2019%20AAVMC%20Annual%20Data%20Report%20(ID%20100175).pdf

- insecticide/pesticide producers
- wildlife rehabilitation
- primate habitats
- reptile facilities
- animal behavior
- equine, marine animals, zoos, canine, and dairy[5]

Veterinary schools also value non-animal and non-veterinary experiences that ideally take place outside of the classroom. Students should endeavor to get involved in community service activities. These activities demonstrate to veterinary admissions officers the types of values you hold and your commitment to giving back to your community.

Veterinary schools prefer students to hold a leadership position. This type of leadership job can be found in various settings, including a team captain, club board of directors, or liaison to a national board.[6]

EXPERIENCE HOURS REQUIRED OR RECOMMENDED

Schools require varying hours of pre-veterinary experience. Though schools have cut back on the hours, some want hundreds of hours while others do not specify the experience hours needed. Reports suggest that admission teams seek students with experiences gathered under the supervision of a veterinarian or research scientist in a vet practice, public health, or other areas of the profession.

For some universities in the U.S., such as the Cornell University College of Veterinary Medicine, applicants must have engaged in two or more areas of vet experience.[7] Applicants can combine animal and veterinary experiences, including small animals, large animals, research, food animals, production, exotic, aquatic, wildlife, or zoological medicine. However, applicants must have in-depth experience in at least one of the two.

Animal experiences may include volunteer work. Occasionally, applicants

5 Mary Hope Kramer, "Pre-Veterinary Internships for Aspiring Vets," *The Balance Careers*, Updated November 19, 2019, https://www.thebalancecareers.com/animal-behavior-internships-125681

6 Hamilton College, "Gaining Experience," *Hamilton College*, n.d., https://www.hamilton.edu/after/healthprofessions/veterinary/gaining-experience

7 Cornell University College of Veterinary Medicine, "Experience," *Cornell University College of Veterinary Medicine*, n.d., https://www.vet.cornell.edu/education/doctor-veterinary-medicine/prospective-students/experience

gain experience without supervision. However, a few vet schools may not count this as experience. Nevertheless, most admission committees do not distinguish between voluntary or paid work. Associate Dean of the University of Illinois College of Veterinary Medicine, Dr. Jonathan Foreman, explained that the critical goal for admission seekers is an accurate idea of the course of study.[8] However, Dr. Foreman advised that candidates get a solid understanding of their vet school, career, and life trajectory, but to do this, direct veterinary supervision is needed.

Students should want to volunteer or work with animals and should enjoy the work they are doing. Otherwise, they risk spending time doing something they do not enjoy, particularly if they are not accepted. The University of Illinois College of Veterinary Medicine does not publish a required amount of time. Frequently, admission processes are holistic, considering a wide range of experiences, though some schools base candidates' admission predominantly on the number of hours of pre-veterinary experience. Still, in other cases, the numbers do not determine acceptance.

At Tufts University's Cummings School of Veterinary Medicine, admissions selection is different. While Tufts does not release a set number of recommended experience hours, it considers work with animals a crucial part of its selection process. According to Ford Barnet, Assistant Director of Admissions, the number of hours, with and without supervision, are not critical since what counts is the type of vet experience.[9]

Applicants must understand both the challenges and opportunities of working as a veterinary medical doctor. Students must also go beyond shadowing and get hands-on experience in veterinary medicine to remind them why they are veterinary doctors, especially when undergoing challenging moments in vet school and work.[10]

Most veterinary experts and schools agree that hands-on experience is critical for anyone seeking to be a veterinarian.[11] Shadowing veterinarians is invaluable.

---

8   Lisa Wogan, "How Much Pre-Veterinary Experience is Enough?," *VIN News Service*, August 3, 2017, https://news.vin.com/default.aspx?pid=210&Id=8147950&useobjecttypeid=10&fromVINNEWSASPX=1

9   Ibid.

10 Tufts University Cummings School of Veterinary Medicine, "Frequently Asked Questions," *Tufts University Cummings School of Veterinary Medicine*, n.d., https://vetsites.tufts.edu/avm/faqs/

11 Cornell University College of Veterinary Medicine, "Experience," Cornell University College of Veterinary Medicine, n.d., https://www.vet.cornell.edu/education/doctor-veterinary-medicine/prospective-students/experience

Frequently students who lacked experience found it difficult to get accepted into any program, lacking the demonstration of practical knowledge of the profession.[12]

The number of experience hours reportedly demanded by veterinary institutions has dropped. While the Association of American Veterinary Medical Colleges (AAVMC) does not record this, AAMVC Senior Director Lisa Greenhill noted a decline in the number of hours, as in the case of Iowa State, a university that reduced its experience number to 200 hours.[13]

Additional hours increased the competitiveness within the application process. The need for hours primarily impacted students who excelled academically but had little knowledge of the field. Schools did not accept as many applicants without experience, though these students may have demonstrated soft skills, including interpersonal skills.[14]

Yet, students still feel that they learn much from their work with animals that will help them in vet schools and that these experiences make them more competitive and desirable. Moreover, most applicants far surpass the hours required. Some students take a gap year after earning their degree to increase the number of hours of experience between themselves and other applicants, putting more pressure on applying to vet school.[15]

Dr. Jim Weissman, Clinical Associate Professor and Director of Student Services at Purdue University College of Veterinary Medicine, explained that applications at Purdue are reviewed holistically.[16] Experience in animal health and welfare gained by applicants is unlikely to give the student's application an additional boost since other activities are also considered.

Virginia-Maryland College of Veterinary Medicine decreased the required hours from 300 to 100, with applicants exceeding 100 hours receiving no additional consideration.[17]

---

12 W. T. Clark, L. Kane, P.K. Arnold, I.D. Robertson, "Clinical Knowledge and Skills used by Vet Students During their First Year in Animal Practice," *Aust Vet J.* 80, no. 1-2 (2002): 37-40, https://pubmed.ncbi.nlm.nih.gov/12180876/

13 Lisa Wogan, "How Much Pre-Veterinary Experience is Enough?," Vin News, August 3, 2017, https://news.vin.com/default.aspx?pid=210&ld=8147950&useobjecttypeid=10&fromVINNEWSASPX=1

14 The Ohio State University College of Veterinary Medicine, "presenting a Competitive Application," *The Ohio State University College of Veterinary Medicine,* n.d., https://vet.osu.edu/education/presenting-competitive-application

15 Mary Hope Kramer, "Things You Should Know About Vet School," *The Balance Careers,* Updated October 30, 2019, https://www.thebalancecareers.com/things-you-should-know-about-vet-school-4020896

16 Lisa Wogan, "How Much Pre-Veterinary Experience is Enough?," Vin News, August 3, 2017, https://news.vin.com/default.aspx?pid=210&ld=8147950&useobjecttypeid=10&fromVINNEWSASPX=1

17 Ibid.

HOW MUCH PRE-VETERINARY EXPERIENCE IS ENOUGH?

There is no fixed number of hours that is globally accepted. The actual requirement varies by college and is impacted by the pool of similar applicants. However, multiple admissions directors have advised that gaining 200+ hours of real-life animal care experience in the field is essential for most veterinary school applications.

VIN News Service conducted a recent study of 30 veterinary schools in the United States to determine their policies regarding experience.[18] Out of the 30 schools in the survey, 25 gave feedback. Results indicated that the policies regarding experience varied, with nine requiring a minimum of 40 to 500 hours, nine not specifying the number of hours, though suggesting at least 200 to 500 hours, and seven not specifying a specific number.[19]

Reports recently showed that aspiring students surpassed these recommendations, including in colleges that never specified, recommended, or suggested hours of experience. For example, despite offering no suggestions nor recommendations about the number of hours needed on applications, Dr. Gretchen Delcambre, Director of Admissions at the College of Veterinary Medicine and Biomedical Sciences at Colorado State University, said the average applicant recorded 1000 hours.[20] Elsewhere, the reports were similar.

The University of California, Davis, School of Veterinary Medicine, suggested 180 hours of quality veterinary experience.[21] However, applicants logged in 1600 hours. At the University of Missouri College of Veterinary Medicine, applicants averaged between 350 and 500 hours, despite the minimum 40 hours required by the school.[22] In other schools such as Michigan State University, accepted applicants averaged 1,850 hours of pre-veterinary experience despite the 150 recommended.[23] Meanwhile, at the University of Tennessee, many applicants surpassed 2000 hours.

18 Lisa Wogan, "How Much Pre-Veterinary Experience is Enough?," *Vin News,* August 3, 2017, https://news.vin.com/default.aspx?pid=210&ld=8147950&useobjecttypeid=10&fromVINNEWSASPX=1

19 Ibid.

20 Ibid.

21 UC Davis Veterinary Medicine, "Criteria For Admission," UC Davis Veterinary Medicine, n.d., https://www.vetmed.ucdavis.edu/admissions/criteria-admission

22 University of Missouri College of Veterinary Medicine, "2021-2022 Admission Guide," *University of Missouri College of Veterinary Medicine,* February 2021, https://cvm.missouri.edu/wp-content/uploads/2020/05/2020-2021-CVM-Admissions-Guide.pdf

23 Michigan State University, College of Veterinary Medicine, "Become an MSU Vet," Michigan State *University, College of Veterinary Medicine,* n.d., https://cvm.msu.edu/future-students/dvm

"
"*Dogs are not our whole life, but they make our lives whole.*"

– Roger Caras

CHAPTER 20

TRAINING AND CERTIFICATIONS

BONDING THROUGH ASSOCIATION

A saying goes, "Two heads are better than one." While that may not be the case in every situation, there is great value in collaborating with those interested in similar personal or career paths. In this case, those committed to veterinary medicine can find strength in numbers, primarily because research, techniques, innovations, and business practices evolve. Sharing ideas is an excellent way to stay on top of current trends, regulations, and demands of government entities and animal owners.

The job of a vet can feel isolating. However, depending on one's type of vet practice, involvement in and commitment to veterinary associations can provide a hub, friend group, or colleagues who have the same kinds of questions and seek to resolve challenges by sharing information. Organizational involvement is invaluable to a veterinarian's growth.

Associations are often distinguished by animal and practice type. Furthermore, associations offer networking opportunities, collaboration on cases, and online facilitated forums. In veterinary medicine, there are new discoveries around every corner, and often new adventures to explore.

CONTINUING EDUCATION

A concept you will encounter many times in your professional career is the idea of being a lifelong learner. All veterinarians are required to complete a certain amount of continuing education to maintain their licenses. Some vets embrace professional development far beyond what is mandated, often building reputations as experts in their distinct areas of interest.

Associations provide coursework, certifications, and continuing education units (CEUs) for veterinarians to stay on top of the profession. Many organizations also hold national and/or regional conferences with presentations given by the leaders in the field. To further stay on top of the latest research, veterinarians contribute to and read professional journals that disseminate information about the latest discoveries in the area.

There is solace in knowing that there are groups that serve similar clientele and animal owners. Numerous veterinary organizations provide up-to-date information along with opportunities to cultivate relationships. Veterinary medicine is an evolving profession that demands ongoing engagement.

Technological change has introduced novel approaches such as 3D printing, wireless devices, wearable technologies, and digitized equipment. Additionally, the speed with which all information multiplies ensures dynamic organizational opportunities for the veterinarian and vet school student. Some veterinary organizations are listed below.

Continuing education is essential to those seeking to stay at the top of their careers.[1] State requirements dictate that veterinarians complete continuing education programming to maintain professional licensure. However, continuing education is also valuable to

- remain current in the field
- develop specialize techniques
- update skills with emerging trends
- train for additional skills
- earn advanced certifications
- gain promotions to leadership in veterinary medicine
- prepare to teach at a vet school

---

1   AVMA, "Continuing Education (CE)," *AVMA*, n.d., https://www.avma.org/education/continuing-education-ce

NATIONAL AND INTERNATIONAL ORGANIZATIONS

American Veterinary Medical Association (AVMA)

This nonprofit association brings together veterinarians from around the world devoted to the practice. With 91,000 members representing a range of jobs and industry sectors, the AVMA provides current information to members, holds conferences, and lobbies congress regarding issues related to animals and animal health. Additionally, the AVMA is designated as the accrediting body for U.S. schools of veterinary medicine, maintaining educational standards and ensuring the qualifications and competency of graduating veterinarians.

Student American Veterinary Medical Association (SAVMA)

This association brings together student members from North America, including clubs in the U.S., Canada, and the Caribbean. This group provides a voice for vet students through AVMA student chapters, activities, speakers, and newsletters. In addition, SAVMA promotes the exchange of information and promotes issues in legislative areas that benefit student veterinarians. Schools in foreign countries may join as associate members. SAVMA has approximately 17,000 members in 37 chapters and 1 associate chapter.[2]

Association of American Veterinary Medical Colleges (AAVMC)

The AAVMC is a nonprofit organization that serves and supports veterinary medical colleges by protecting and improving health and welfare worldwide while advancing veterinary medicine. The AAVMC has 74 members, including 33 U.S. veterinary colleges, 5 Canadian schools, and 16 international schools along with affiliate members.

Veterinary Medical College Application Service (VMCAS)

Sponsored by the AAVMC, the VMCAS offers veterinary medical colleges a platform where students may apply to vet school.

American Association of Veterinary State Boards (AAVSB)

The AAVSB brings together veterinary medicine regulatory boards with members in 62 jurisdictions throughout the U.S, Puerto Rico, the U.S. Virgin Islands, and nine Canadian provinces: Alberta, British Columbia, Manitoba, New Brunswick, Newfoundland and Labrador, Nova Scotia, Ontario, Prince Edward

---

2   AVMA, "What is SAVMA?," *AVMA*, n.d., https://www.avma.org/membership/SAVMA/what-is-SAVMA

Island, and Saskatchewan.[3] The goal is to certify veterinarians and protect the public. The AAVSB is the only organization that reports national exam results to the jurisdiction(s) in which a veterinarian wishes to be licensed. It also acts as a public resource for veterinary medical regulation information.

VETERINARY MEDICAL ORGANIZATIONS AND ASSOCIATIONS

1. Academy of Veterinary Allergy and Clinical Immunology (AVACI)

The AVACI is a group of veterinarians who specialize in clinical allergy and immunology in small and big animals. The Academy's mission is to support animal allergy research and share information about it.

2. Academy of Veterinary Consultants (AVC)[4]

The AVC is a group of veterinarians supporting and promoting the interests of the beef cattle industry. The AVC seeks to increase awareness of beef herd importance while encouraging high standards and information exchange. In addition to working with agricultural organizations and regulatory agencies, it offers scholarships and grants to students.

3. American Animal Hospital Association (AAHA)[5]

The AAHA is a nonprofit organization dedicated to the advancement of veterinary medicine. It is a global organization of over 29,000 veterinarians who treat pets. The AAHA is well-known among veterinarians and pet owners for its hospital and pet healthcare standards.[6]

4. American Association of Bovine Practitioners (AABP)[7]

The AABP is an association of veterinarians who are passionate about bovine medicine. It began as a "not-for-profit" organization in 1965 and has since grown to include about 5000 veterinarians. The majority of the members are from the United States along with about 500 Canadian and 200 international members.

---

3   AAVSB, "Licensing Boards for Veterinary Medicine," *AAVSB*, n.d., http://aavsb.org/dlr

4   Academy of Veterinary Consultants, "2021 AVC Summer Conference," *Academy of Veterinary Consultants*, 2021, http://www.avc-beef.org/

5   AAHA, "Ask AAHA: Answers From the Experts," *AAHA*, n.d., http://www.healthypet.com/

6   Michigan State University, "Veterinary Associations and Organizations," *Michigan State University,* July 15, 2021, https://libguides.lib.msu.edu/pethealth/orgs

7   American Association of Bovine Practitioners, "Home," *American Association of Bovine Practitioners,* n.d., http://www.aabp.org/

5. American Association of Equine Practitioners (AAEP)[8]

The AAEP is the world's largest equine veterinarians' professional organization. The association's objective is to enhance the health and welfare of horses.[9]

6. American College of Veterinary Anesthesiologists (ACVA)[10]

The ACVA is a professional organization of veterinarians who specialize in anesthesia. Veterinary anesthesiology has grown in importance due to advancements in anesthesiology, human medicine, and the growth of other veterinary specialties.

7. AASP - American Association of Swine Practitioners[11]

The mission of the AASP is to improve swine veterinarians' knowledge by promoting the development and availability of resources that increase the effectiveness of swine-related professional activities, creating opportunities for personal and professional growth, and advocating science-based approaches.

8. Association of Avian Veterinarians[12] (AAV), Association of Avian Veterinarians, Australasian Committee (AAVAC)[13]

The Association of Avian Veterinarians, headquartered in New Jersey and the Australasian Committee of the Association of Avian Veterinarians (Australia and New Zealand) promote the health and welfare of birds through their respective nonprofit organizations. Members include a wide range of researchers, government entities, zoos, universities, corporations, and students of veterinary medicine.

9. American Association of Veterinary Parasitologists (AAVP)[14]

The AAVP, a nonprofit scientific and educational association with over 450 members, is a division of the AVMA. Members of the AAVP include researchers,

---

8   American Association of Equine Practitioners, "Home," *American Association of Equine Practitioners,* n.d., http://www.aaep.org/

9   Illinois State Veterinary Medical Association, "Veterinary Organizations," *Illinois State Veterinary Medical Association,* n.d., https://www.isvma.org/organizations/

10   ACVA, "Home," *ACVA,* n.d., https://acvaa.org/

11   American Association of Swine Veterinarians, "Home," *American Association of Swine Veterinarians,* n.d., http://www.aasp.org/

12   Association of Avian Veterinarians, "Home," *Association of Avian Veterinarians,* n.d., https://www.aav.org/

13   Association of Avian Veterinarians Australasian Committee, "Home," *Association of Avian Veterinarians Australasian Committee,* n.d., https://www.aavac.com.au/

14   University of Florida College of Veterinary Medicine, "Home," *University of Florida College of Veterinary Medicine,* n.d., http://www.vetmed.ufl.edu/aavp/

148

scientists, veterinarians, vet students, and anyone interested in parasites. The focus of this association is parasites found in companion, food-producing, including domesticated animals and wildlife, which may be transmittable to humans.

10. American Board of Veterinary Toxicology (ABVT)[15]

The ABVT is comprised of veterinarians who aim to educate the general public, private practice veterinarians, and veterinary medical students about toxicologic threats to pets, livestock, and wildlife.

11. American Association of Feline Practitioners (AAFP)[16]

The AAFP specializes in feline medicine, dedicated to giving cats the finest care and treatment available. The AAFP works to boost the standards of feline medicine and surgery through knowledge-sharing. Avenues include disseminating advancements in research, promoting continuing education, supporting ABVP certification in Feline Practice, and encouraging veterinary student interest in feline medicine.

12. American Association for Laboratory Animal Science (AALAS)[17]

The AALAS was established as a professional organization to provide information and support for laboratory animal professionals, including researchers, veterinarians, veterinary technicians, and animal care personnel.

13. American Association of Public Health Veterinarians (AAPH)[18]

The mission of the AAPH is to advance the science and art of public health, epidemiology, and primary care. The association provides an expert forum to discuss and develop professional recommendations and public health resolutions on public health issues that affect the veterinary profession.

14. American College of Veterinary Internal Medicine (ACVIM)[19]

The American College of Veterinary Internal Medicine (ACVIM) is a worldwide

15 American Board of Veterinary Toxicology, "Home," *American Board of Veterinary Toxicology*, n.d., http://www.abvt.org/

16 American Association of Feline Practitioners, "Home," *American Association of Feline Practitioners,* n.d., http://www.aafponline.org/

17 University of Minnesota, "Research Animal Resources," *University of Minnesota*, n.d., http://www.ahc.umn.edu/rar/MNAALAS/

18 AAFSPHV, "Home," *AAFSPHV*, n.d., https://aafsphv.org/

19 ACVIM, "Home," *ACVIM*, n.d., http://acvim.org/

certifying organization for veterinary internal medicine experts in large and small animals, cardiology, neurology, and cancer. The ACVIM is paving the way in veterinary medicine and research to improve animal illnesses and disease diagnosis and treatment.

15. American College of Veterinary Microbiologists (ACVM)[20]

American College of Veterinary Microbiologists is a specialty organization recognized by the American Veterinary Medical Association for certifying veterinarians with a particular interest in microbiology.

16. American Pre-Veterinary Medical Association (APVMA)[21]

The American Pre-Veterinary Medical Association (APVMA) is a college-level national chapter organization dedicated to promoting and stimulating interest in the discipline of veterinary medicine. The organization supports and provides information to its member clubs.

17. American College of Veterinary Nutrition (ACVN)[22]

The ACVN is the AVMA certifying organization to become a Board Certified Veterinary Nutritionist. The ACVN advances veterinary nutrition to improve animal health through nutrition, while providing veterinarians with information and promotion of competencies. The College encourages professional education and the promotion of research in animal nutrition.

18. American College of Veterinary Pathologists (ACVP)[23]

With a peer-reviewed journal, annual meetings, and a rigorous certifying exam, the ACVP promotes excellence in veterinary pathology on the cutting edge of science through information sharing, student chapters, and the commitment to improve animal, human, and environmental health.

19. Association of Reptilian and Amphibian Veterinarians (ARAV)[24]

The ARAV is a nonprofit international association of reptile and amphibian

20 American College of Veterinary Microbiologists, "Home," *American College of Veterinary Microbiologists,* n.d., https://www.acvm.us/

21 APVMA, "Home," *APVMA,* n.d., https://www.apvma.org/index.html

22 American College of Veterinary Nutrition, "Home," *American College of Veterinary Nutrition,* n.d., https://acvn.org/

23 ACVP, "Home," *ACVP,* n.d., https://www.acvp.org/

24 ARAV, "Home," *ARAV,* n.d., http://www.arav.org/

veterinarians and herpetologists who inform and unite members through teaching, idea exchanges, and research. The goal of the ARAV is to improve reptile and amphibian veterinarian care and management by promoting conservation and humane treatment of reptile and amphibian species through education, breeding, and reptilian and amphibian habitat preservation.

20. American Society of Veterinary Ophthalmic (ASVO)[25]

The ASVO offers opportunities for veterinarians to pursue advanced studies by disseminating information regarding animal ophthalmology and encouraging ophthalmologic training in veterinary institutions.

21. American Zoo and Aquarium Association (AZA)[26]

The AZA is a nonprofit organization dedicated to the ecology, education, science, and entertainment of zoos and aquariums. Founded in 1924, the AZA explores the ways where animals and the environment are valued, respected, and protected.

22. American Association for Laboratory Accreditation (A2LA)[27]

The American Association for Laboratory Accreditation is an organization that certifies laboratories. A2LA was established in 1978 as a nonprofit membership organization dedicated to the formal certification of knowledgeable testing and calibration laboratories, inspection bodies, and organizations.

23. Christian Veterinary Fellowship (CVF)

This organization brings together those who support the Christian spiritual belief in service. With 28 CVF chapters, students unite for professional development while being empowered, supported, and encouraged in their faith.

24. Christian Veterinary Mission (CVM)[28]

This nonprofit international organization, based in Seattle, includes more than 5,000 veterinarians and vet students. CVM serves to educate and support veterinarians through service, prayer, and relationships. CVM promotes an international ministry and healing opportunities overseas in dozens of countries.

---

25   ASVO, "Home," *ASVO*, n.d., http://www.asvo.org/

26   Association of Zoos & Aquariums, "Home," *Association of Zoos & Aquariums*, n.d., http://www.aza.org/

27   A2LA, "About Us," *A2LA*, n.d., https://www.a2la.org/about

28   Christian Veterinary Mission, "home," *Christian Veterinary Mission*, n.d., https://cvm.org/

25. International Veterinary Students Association (IVSA)[29]

With 194 member organizations in 73 countries, IVSA supports more than 38,000 members as the largest nonprofit international association for veterinary students. By exchanging ideas, knowledge, and culture, IVSA seeks to "benefit the animals and people of the world by harnessing the potential and dedication of veterinary students to promote the international application of veterinary skills, education and knowledge." Through international events, exchanges are facilitated, including educational opportunities and collaborations.

26. Society for Theriogenology (SFT)[30]

The SFT's mission is to provide information regarding reproductive animal medicine and surgery, including animal reproduction, obstetrics, and neonatology. SFT promotes standards of excellence and provides outreach and education to animal health professionals to foster continual improvements in theriogenology.

27. Veterinarians for Global Solutions (VGS)

VGS is a student organization committed to advancing veterinarians' role to improve vet health care access and support global ecosystems.

LICENSING

Engaging in a series of training is not enough to become a certified veterinarian. As a result, a formal license is required to practice as a Doctor of Veterinary Medicine (DVM). A certified veterinarian will need a state license and sometimes additional licenses to establish their competency in the field. The process of issuing licenses to certified veterinarians is known as "licensing". Licenses are obtained after fulfilling basic requirements in veterinary medicine. While certificates on the side are good to have, state licensing is essential.[31] These state licenses are approved after applicants pass a state board examination. Once obtained, they must be renewed, requiring continuing education.

Some areas of specialization in veterinary medicine require additional licenses, such as livestock, pets, research, and development. The requirements for licensing vary depending on the state and department. In addition, DVM's must complete

29 IVSA, "Home," *IVSA*, n.d., https://www.ivsa.org/

30 Society for Theriogenology, "Home," *Society for Theriogenology*, n.d., https://www.therio.org/

31 Study.com, "Veterinarian Certification and License Information," *Study.com*, June 15, 2021, https://study.com/veterinarian_certification.html

both national and state applications and examinations before they receive them.[32]

NORTH AMERICAN LICENSING EXAMINATION (NAVLE)

- Fourth-year exam
- National Board Examination (NBE) with a locally derived, scaled minimum score of 75% (425 minimum raw score), **AND** the Clinical Competency Test (CCT) with a locally derived, scaled minimum score of 75% (425 minimum raw score); **OR**
- You have passed the NAVLE with the same minimum score criteria.

TRAINING AND CERTIFICATION

Aspiring veterinarians undergo intense formal and informal training to acquire knowledge in animal science, diseases to be certified on the doctoral level. Afterward, students must be licensed through the successful completion of national and state examinations.

Licensing laws protect the public, respecting the belief that:[33]

1. Specialized knowledge and skills are required to practice veterinary medicine
2. The public needs protection from incompetent or unethical practitioners
3. Veterinarians must graduate from an AVMA-accredited program
4. Education and training must continue throughout the veterinarians' careers

The Qualifying Examination tests a veterinarian's knowledge of anatomy and physiology, microbiology, and pharmacology.[34] Once completed, vet students take a 360-question licensing exam, the North American *Veterinary Licensing Examination* (NAVLE).

There are two testing windows each year: spring and fall.[35] Vet students are qualified to take the exams when they reach the final eight months of their program. To become both certified and licensed, vets must submit two

---

32 University of Tennessee Institute of Agriculture College of Veterinary Medicine, "Licensing Requirements and USDA Accreditation," *University of Tennessee Institute of Agriculture College of Veterinary Medicine,* n.d., https://vetmed.tennessee.edu/admissions/dvm/licensing-requirements-and-usda-accreditation

33 AAVSB, "Licensing Boards for Veterinary Medicine," *AAVSB,* n.d., http://aavsb.org/dlr

34 Health Care Pathway, "Veterinarian Certificate and Licensing," *Health Care Pathway,* n.d., https://www.healthcarepathway.com/certification/veterinarian-licensure/

35 Texas A&M University Veterinary Medicine & Biomedical Sciences, "Licensing Requirements," *Texas A&M University Veterinary Medicine & Biomedical Sciences,* n.d., https://vetmed.tamu.edu/dvm/resources/licensing/

applications: one for the National Board of Veterinary Medical Examiners and the other for state licensure.[36]

Certificates guarantee the competency of a veterinarian wherever and however they plan to practice. Basically, these highly prioritized certifications exist to ensure excellence in the national and international community of animals and animal-related products by measuring the skills and knowledge veterinarians must exhibit to support, promote, and mitigate animal health.

Certifications allow practitioners to specialize by demonstrating competency in levels of training and sub-disciplines.[37] Some disciplines include animal growth biology, physiology, nutrition, production systems, and diseases. Sub-disciplines require expert certificates.

Is there specialized training that might set you apart from other applicants when you apply to vet school or afterward as a veterinarian? More importantly, what skills can you learn to help you be a confident and competent vet student and, eventually, a great practitioner? The answers to those questions are the same. Training and certification in the medical field, especially in veterinary medicine, will prepare you for vet school.

To clarify, in this context, "training and certification" refers to the successful completion of a formalized curriculum rather than casual mentorship or job oversight. Therefore, while beneficial and required of most vet school candidates, shadowing is not considered training or certification.

CERTIFICATIONS

Bright students working intently toward a DVM seven to eight years down the road may overlook their eligibility to seek immediate certifications. In other words, your academic and professional efforts toward establishing a veterinary medical career do not disqualify you from experiencing a supportive or auxiliary role in the meantime.

As a busy young adult with a rigorous academic schedule, no doubt, you also have leadership and family responsibilities. Depending on the amount of time you are willing and able to sacrifice in the interest of real-world credentialing, consider

36 Mass.gov, "Apply for a Vet Medicine License," *Mass.gov*, n.d., https://www.mass.gov/how-to/apply-for-a-veterinary-medicine-license

37 University of Reading, "Animal Science," *University of Reading*, n.d., http://www.reading.ac.uk/ready-to-study/study/Subject-area/animal-science-ug

these options.

The most obvious and quickest training is a CPR certification course. Lifeguard certification and Red Cross are other options. What about going a little deeper, though? You might be surprised to know that high school graduates can be certified as EMTs (emergency medical technicians) in a matter of weeks, depending on a given state's requirements. Phlebotomy training is an excellent skill as well, and certification can take as little as four weeks.

VETERINARY LABORATORY CERTIFICATE

Those with a veterinary laboratory certificate are those who study animal laboratory science and have acquired adequate and practical knowledge in research techniques and equipment. They are trained on various animals and are knowledgeable about blood, corpses, and organs. Veterinary laboratory experts study the properties, composition, structure, chemicals, and biological processes in animals.

Upon certification, they have the skills to conduct diagnostic research and investigate meat, milk, and other animal products.[38] They also perform bacteriological, biological, serological, toxicological, pathological-anatomical, and histological investigations. The certificate acquired in this field is similar to the veterinary technician certificate,[39] allowing personnel to work as laboratory technicians.

VETERINARY ASSISTANT CERTIFICATE

This certificate allows personnel to work as assistant veterinarians, providing medical health care for animals. Personnel with this certificate take blood samples and administer medications to animals. They also assist veterinarians during animal examinations and other health procedures.

Candidates who wish to acquire this certificate must undergo formal training for a specific amount of time and complete a program in the field. Although states are not required to give credentials to veterinary assistants, those interested can test for optional certification, such as the Approved Veterinary Assistant credential

---

38 The Free Dictionary, "Veterinary Laboratory," *The Free Dictionary*, n.d., https://encyclopedia2.thefreedictionary. com/Veterinary+Laboratory

39 Keystone Healthcare Studies, "Veterinary Technician," *Keystone Healthcare Studies,* n.d., https://www. healthcarestudies.com/Veterinary-Technician/USA/Vet-Tech-Institute

offered by the National Association of Veterinary Technicians in America.

VETERINARY RECEPTIONIST CERTIFICATE

The veterinary receptionist certificate demonstrates skill in the customer service sector of veterinary medicine, including specialist training in record-keeping systems to support clinical services. Attending to customers is one of the major functions of a veterinary office. The veterinary receptionist answers phone calls, responds to questions, and screens clients while scheduling appointments.[40]

Additionally, vet receptionists process credit card payments and prepare bank deposits. A veterinary receptionist certificate has a short training period with a minimum level of required education.

BUT IS A CERTIFICATION NECESSARY?

No. The subject of certification is raised for two reasons:

1. You will encounter people in vet school who started DVM training with certifications. Many individuals earn these credentials irrespective of their eventual goal. Some veterinary technicians pursue a DVM. For instance, you may meet someone who has worked as a licensed laboratory technician but only recently realized a desire to be a small animal vet.

2. Students who want exposure to a particular body of knowledge for the structure of the program, clear objectives, and a sense of accomplishment which comes through certification.

Formal training is not required of a vet school applicant, though. So, what kind of experience or training is most likely to strengthen your candidacy? It would help if you were the decision-maker when it comes to any unique training or credentialing. Students probably tire of advice like this, but it stands: you must determine your own best course. If there were a formula, everyone would follow it and lack uniqueness and individuality.

---

40 Mary Hope Kramer, "What Does a Veterinary Receptionist Do?," *The Balance Careers,* Updated July 16, 2019, https://www.thebalancecareers.com/veterinary-receptionist-125839

PART 4

PRE-APPLICATION: TESTING AND RECS

"The average dog is a nicer person than the average person."

– Andy Rooney

CHAPTER 21

CHECKLISTS

☐ GRE

☐ Letters of Recommendation

☐ Personal Statement

☐ Shadowing/Volunteer Activities

☐ Application

☐ Essays

☐ CASPer

☐ Interviews

☐ Updates

☐ Admission

When You Start

☐ Choose a task management calendar system (online or notebook)

☐ Write down requirements and responsibilities

- Coursework, assignments, discussions, tutoring/advising, mentoring, research, community service, athletics, music/art, exercise/meditation, family, friends, social activities, cleaning/organizing, trips, and breaks

- Animal Care Activities – work and/or shadow activities in a vet clinic, farm, stable, shelter, or other location

- Application requirements like dates applications open/close, testing, letters of recommendation, etc. (see timeline)

☐ Create file folders to organize information from schools

Summer/Fall (Before Applying)

☐ Pre-health advisor meeting

☐ Pre-health committee letter

☐ Pre-requisite classes

☐ Connect with AVMA, AMA, AAVMC, VMSAR, VMCAS, TMDSAS

☐ Research vet schools

☐ Purchase GRE preparation book

☐ GRE tutoring, test prep class, or independent study

☐ Register for GRE

☐ Prepare for GRE

☐ Download previous year's AAVMC, VMCAS, and TMDSAS applications to review

Winter/Spring (a year and a half before you plan to begin vet school)

☐ VMCAS Opens January 21st

☐ Take GRE

☐ Outline your personal statement

☐ Ask a minimum of three people if they will write your letters of recommendation (LOR) – one should be a veterinarian

☐ Input names of those submitting your electronic letters of recommendation (eLOR)

☐ Follow up with committee letter of recommendation (if required by the undergraduate institution)

☐ Follow up with individual recommenders

☐ Write your personal statement (one-page essay not exceeding 3,000 characters)

☐ Write supplementary essays

☐ Request transcripts.

☐ Send transcripts to application services

May/June

☐ May 1st - Complete TMDSAS (if applying for Texas vet schools)

☐ May 12th – First date to submit VMCAS (however, since vet school admissions are not rolling, wait until you can include your summer activities, experiences, classes, etc.)

☐ Input personal statement and school-specific questions

☐ Fill in courses and grades section (have all transcripts on hand)

☐ Select colleges

☐ Take/retake GRE if necessary (last test date accepted is typically August 31st)

☐ Take/submit TOEFL test to VMCAS as soon as possible, last date September 15th (only for international students)

☐ Register and take CASPer (most schools accept scores by the September 15th VMCAS deadline)

Summer/Fall

☐ Check formatting and spelling

☐ Certify, pay, and submit

☐ Review/error check on VMCAS and TMDSAS

☐ August 15th recommended deadline to submit AAVMC VMCAS application at some schools

☐ The earlier you submit, the sooner your application can be verified by VMCAS

☐ AAVMC VMCAS and TMDSAS applications close on September 15th

☐ Check application status (monitor for LORs, transcripts, fee payments, verification)

☐ Interview offers (schedule dates as soon as you receive requests for interviews)

☐ Prep for Interviews

☐ Interviews begin as early as October

☐ Follow up with schools

☐ Complete and submit FAFSA to receive financial aid

☐ Admissions decisions (December – March)

Winter/Spring

☐ Interviews continue through February

☐ Admissions continue until March

☐ April 15th (the day after if the date falls on a weekend) – National Deadline (admitted students must accept or decline admissions offers)

☐ Update waitlist schools on new accomplishments

☐ Show expressed interest in waitlist schools

☐ Applicants who are not accepted should consider requesting a counseling appointment in April/May from vet schools where they applied. Students must reapply through VMCAS to be reconsidered

☐ May – July Orientation

☐ New Student Orientation Week

VET SCHOOL APPLICATION TIMELINE

Veterinary school in the U.S. is a four-year degree program that follows undergraduate degree coursework - 3 to 5 years undergraduate plus four years of veterinary school.

Many new graduates take an additional year of general or specialty clinical training after graduating from veterinary school. Some complete a 2- to 5-year residency program, leading to board certification. This additional training allows them to practice in medical and surgical specialties, including neurology, cardiology, dermatology, orthopedic surgery, equine medicine, and zoo medicine.[1]

Classroom education, laboratory work, and clinical practice make up most of your first three years of vet school, including animal anatomy, physiology, behavior, immunology, and pathology. You will also learn preventative animal care, as well as diagnosis and treatment of fractures, injuries, and diseases.

During your fourth year, you will complete clinical rotations in a veterinary clinic or animal hospital, where you will observe procedures and receive hands-on experience under the supervision of a certified veterinarian.[2]

---

1   VIN Foundation, "Blog | How Long Do I Have to Go to Veterinary School?," *VIN Foundation,* n.d., https://iwanttobeaveterinarian.org/how-long-do-i-have-to-go-to-veterinary-school/

2   Mary Dowd, "How Many Years of School Does it Take to Be a Vet?," *Chron,* Updated July 1, 2018, https://work.chron.com/many-years-school-vet-9669.html

When applying to veterinary school, it is critical to develop a plan. Nevertheless, your timeline should be flexible. Course schedules, extracurricular activities, and deadline modifications, particularly during the pandemic, contribute to the need to make adjustments to your schedule.

Check VMCAS, VMSAR, and TMDSAS for recommended due dates, though the standard due date is September 15th. Submitting by the recommended August 15th date for some schools, like the University of Florida, where admissions staff will help you avoid delays, expedite processing, and increase your chances that no glitch will prevent the omission of a test or recommendation.[3]

THE APPLICATION CYCLE RECAP

April to August

- Take the GRE
- Confirm vet school requirements
- In January, you can get started on the VMCAS. In May, you can dive more fully into VMCAS and submit if you like.
- Begin the application process by filling in the blanks
- If your question is not answered in the VMCAS instruction manual, please contact VMCAS associates directly
- VMCAS is open for four months, from May to September 15th. Applications are submitted online. The VMCAS website includes school-specific recommended deadlines.
- Keep volunteering, participating in clinical opportunities, and working with a veterinarian

June to September

- Send letters of recommendation to VMCAS - particular institutions may have different requirements. Letters must be received before the September deadline.
- Early to mid-August is the best time to apply. Applying early enables students to mitigate any application delays or problems that need to be addressed before the September deadline.
- Each year, the VMCAS deadline is September 15th. There are no exceptions.
- Schools that require additional application materials will inform applicants on how to obtain these and the procedure for submission

---

3   University of Florida College of Veterinary Medicine, "Admissions Important Dates," *University of Florida College of Veterinary Medicine,* 2021, https://education.vetmed.ufl.edu/admissions/application/application-timeline/

- Ensure that official transcripts are provided to VMCAS
- Submit the GRE

November to April
- Interviews are held between December and March; some do not have interviews for all next-round considered applicants.
- Admission offers are typically sent out by e-mail. Dates on websites may change. Check each school's calendar for specific dates.

TEXAS MEDICAL & DENTAL SCHOOL ADMISSIONS (TMDSAS)

- **TMDSAS Opens: May 3rd**
- **TMDSAS Application:** September 15th, 5:00pm
- **Secondary Application Deadline:** September 15, 5:00pm
- **CASPer Test:** Due date for Texas A&M is September 9th, while the due date for Texas Tech is October 14th, 2021, 6:00 pm (7:00 pm EST). Check the college websites to confirm dates.

"Study hard, no matter if it seems impossible, no matter if it takes time, no matter if you have to stay up all night; just remember that the feeling of success is the best thing in the entire world."

– Unknown

CHAPTER 22

TESTING PLAN AND PREPARATION

You are prepared.

You have a checklist.

N ow you must manage your dates and deadlines. It is hard to overstate the importance of task management. While planner pads, online task management programs, or a system of phone reminders are helpful, the tasks included in applying to vet school are only a few you must complete. Planning a year in advance is not too early. Prevent deadlines from sneaking up on you!

THINK AHEAD

Remember that an early application does not significantly improve your chances of getting accepted as it does for medical or dental school. Vet school acceptance is not on a first-come, first-served basis.

Mindful planning pays dividends. Your life probably already consists of some combination of the following: coursework, assignments, discussions, tutoring/advising, mentoring, research, service, shadowing, athletics, music/art, exercise/meditation, family, friends, social activities, cleaning/organizing, trips, and taking a break. The veterinary school admissions process adds complexity to an already-packed schedule. However, careful organization will help you take things one day at a time.

ACADEMIC DOCUMENTATION

Students with credits earned from multiple sources, such as Advanced Placement or different institutions, should maintain a spreadsheet of their coursework and grades. Having your academic information in one place will come in handy when checking and double-checking your progress. Also, you will have all the necessary information at your fingertips when it is time to complete the application itself. Official transcripts will also need to be requested when you submit your application.

EXTRACURRICULAR DOCUMENTATION

Every meeting, game, and social gathering of your undergraduate experience does not need to be recorded, but you should document the following:

- Anything that informed your desire to study veterinary medicine
- Document undergraduate research (and graduate, if applicable) relevant to the study of veterinary science and animal care
- Any activity in which you officially represented your institution

Examples of such activities include, but are not limited to: musical groups, art training, solar car competitions, robotics competition, athletics, speech and debate, mock trial, Model United Nations, chess tournaments, college-sponsored service trips, science contests, and 4-H clubs.

- Any activity in which you held a leadership position

Leadership skills are valuable in veterinary medicine. Leadership in social clubs, athletic teams, science teams, or competition groups are practical experiences that may lend themselves to running a practice or leading a team at a hospital. Document your role, along with the goals you set and the objectives you accomplished.

TESTING PLAN AND PREPARATION

At one time, not too long ago, colleges required the Veterinary College Admissions Test (VCAT). Some also accepted the Medical College Admissions Test (MCAT) in place of the VCAT. These are no longer required. However, this only makes the focus even more intense on the number of your upper-division science classes. VCAT and MCAT tests allowed colleges to determine vet school acceptance through

BCPM (Biology, Chemistry, Physics, and Mathematics) aptitude.

During the pandemic, curricula, normally taught, were not delivered. With inconsistent preparation, provisions to skip material, and pass/fail options, admissions committees know less about the student's capabilities. Thus, there is likely to be a greater emphasis on science courses.

However, many of the schools are still requiring the GRE and CASPer.

The GRE is required for Auburn, Louisiana State, Oklahoma State, Ross University (St. Kitts), Tuskegee, UC Davis, University of Georgia, and Western University.

The CASPer is required at Kansas State, Lincoln Memorial, Long Island University, Michigan State, Oklahoma State, Purdue, Ross University, Texas Tech, UC Davis, University of Florida, and Virginia-Maryland.

Veterinarians must also pass a standardized license exam after graduation, and some graduates may be required to complete state standardized tests.

GRADUATE RECORD EXAMINATION (GRE)

The GRE assesses students in three areas: analytical writing, verbal reasoning, and quantitative reasoning.

Students must demonstrate their ability to communicate effectively and clearly. Test takers must also be able to evaluate and analyze written passages and solve problems in geometry, arithmetic, algebra, and data analysis.[1]

- Analytical Writing – Assesses critical thinking and analytical writing ability, particularly expressing difficult concepts clearly and effectively
- Verbal Reasoning – The Verbal Reasoning test assesses the ability to analyze and evaluate textual content, as well as verbal and analytical reasoning skills
- Quantitative Reasoning – Assesses fundamental mathematical problem-solving skills

Official GRE scores are sent directly from ETS to VMCAS via a unique VMCAS GRE code for each program. Upon your request, VMCAS can obtain official GRE scores from ETS at any time during the application cycle, including after your application has been e-submitted.

---

1   ETS, "GRE," ETS, n.d., http://www.ets.org/gre/

Licensing Exam

To qualify for licensure, students must pass the North American Veterinary Licensing Examination. This 8-hour standardized test of practical and written questions is required to practice as a veterinarian in North America (NAVLE). This exam is offered in a four-week window in November and December and a two-week period in April across North America and specific international locations. This veterinary school exam has a countrywide pass rate of 95%.

State Exam

Some states also require veterinarians to take standardized exams specific to their state. These exams assess a candidate's knowledge of state laws and regulations as well as veterinary skills. Each state has its standards for maintaining a valid veterinarian license. The AAVSB created the Registry of Approved Continuing Education (RACE) to assist veterinarians in determining which courses are available for licensure renewal in their state.

WHAT TO EXPECT AFTER SUBMITTING YOUR APPLICATION

After you complete, sign, pay, and submit your initial application, the documents and school choices are not automatically sent to the schools you chose.

Your application must undergo a verification process. First, AAVMC, VMCAS, and TMDSAS must receive all transcripts and required information. You can submit your application before the letters of recommendation arrive, though they are still required afterward. You can also submit the application without the GRE or CASPer.

Do not wait until you take the GRE or CASPer. While VMCAS will not send your application to schools until they received your GRE scores, delaying submission puts you farther behind in the verification process. Your application will go into a queue for review. There may be hundreds ahead of you, so submitting your application before the September 15th deadline will allow you to ensure everything is processed. All applications must be verified before they are sent on to the schools.

AAVMC VMCAS and TMDSAS match each college, course, and grade input with the transcripts submitted. If you make a mistake, the application may be sent back to you for you to fix. Additional verification will take place. Make sure you send in the correct information and double-check for errors.

While you are waiting, you may think the process is taking a long time.

However, it is in the best interest of the processing service to complete the verification in a timely manner. While it can take a few weeks to process and send your applications to schools, your application will move through faster if you submit early and are at the front of the queue. Vet school acceptance does not require early submission. However, you can better monitor your application and ensure that everything is completed by the hard and fast September 15th deadline.

INTERVIEW DATES AND PLANNING

Only a few schools announce their interview dates well ahead of time. Even so, you will not know if you will get an interview. Nevertheless, you may need to travel to the school, though many schools offered virtual interviews during the pandemic. An interview signifies that you are at the top of the pack, arriving at the next round of cuts.

You should be excited. However, this puts a burden on your schedule. Plan your coursework and responsibilities around your interview. Make sure you squeeze time into your schedule to prepare for your interviews.

Know enough about that particular vet school to know what is important to them. In speaking with an admissions director from a vet school, she mentioned that she found it disheartening that an interviewee knew little about the school and had no interest in the culture or community of that city or state. Thus, it is essential to read through the website, sift through blogs, contact people at the school, and learn about the vet school's culture - more thoroughly than when you selected the school initially and later wrote your secondaries.

DIGITAL OR PAPER FILING SYSTEM

Research schools, request information, collect notes from vet school college fairs (virtual or in-person), and get letters and materials in the mail. Create a system that works for you to file this information away. Organization is extremely important so that you have a system to track:

- Transcripts
- Letters of Recommendation Requests
- Essays and Supplementals
- Resume Versions
- Separate Folders for Each School on Your List
- Application Copy
- Interviews and Thank You Notes

- Communications with Admissions
- Passwords, Access Numbers, IDs

FLEXIBILITY

Since some of your school assignments, requirements, and responsibilities are known, and some are unknown, you need to be flexible. Map out on a calendar everything you know you need to accomplish. Block out your course, job, and volunteer schedule. Then, predict and plan times to set aside for those upcoming requirements that you do not know. Leave two chunks of time each week for application requirements.

BE PREPARED!

Preparation for the vet school application process is much easier through disciplined recordkeeping and organization. If a hundred college students described their method(s) for documenting and tracking information, you would receive one hundred replies. Everyone is wired a little differently and has been exposed to various tools, technological and old-school alike.

FINAL NOTES

It will be handy to include in your records the names of possible recommenders and contact information of anyone you have spoken to in vet school admission, as well as contacts you have made in veterinary medicine. Make a note of these people when you record the relevant activity.

Only very disciplined students recognize and protect personal time for journaling and reflection. If you do keep a journal, consider incorporating it alongside the other application materials you compile. The notes may be invaluable once you begin the writing tasks of your vet school applications.

The best advice?

Find what works for you and stick with it.

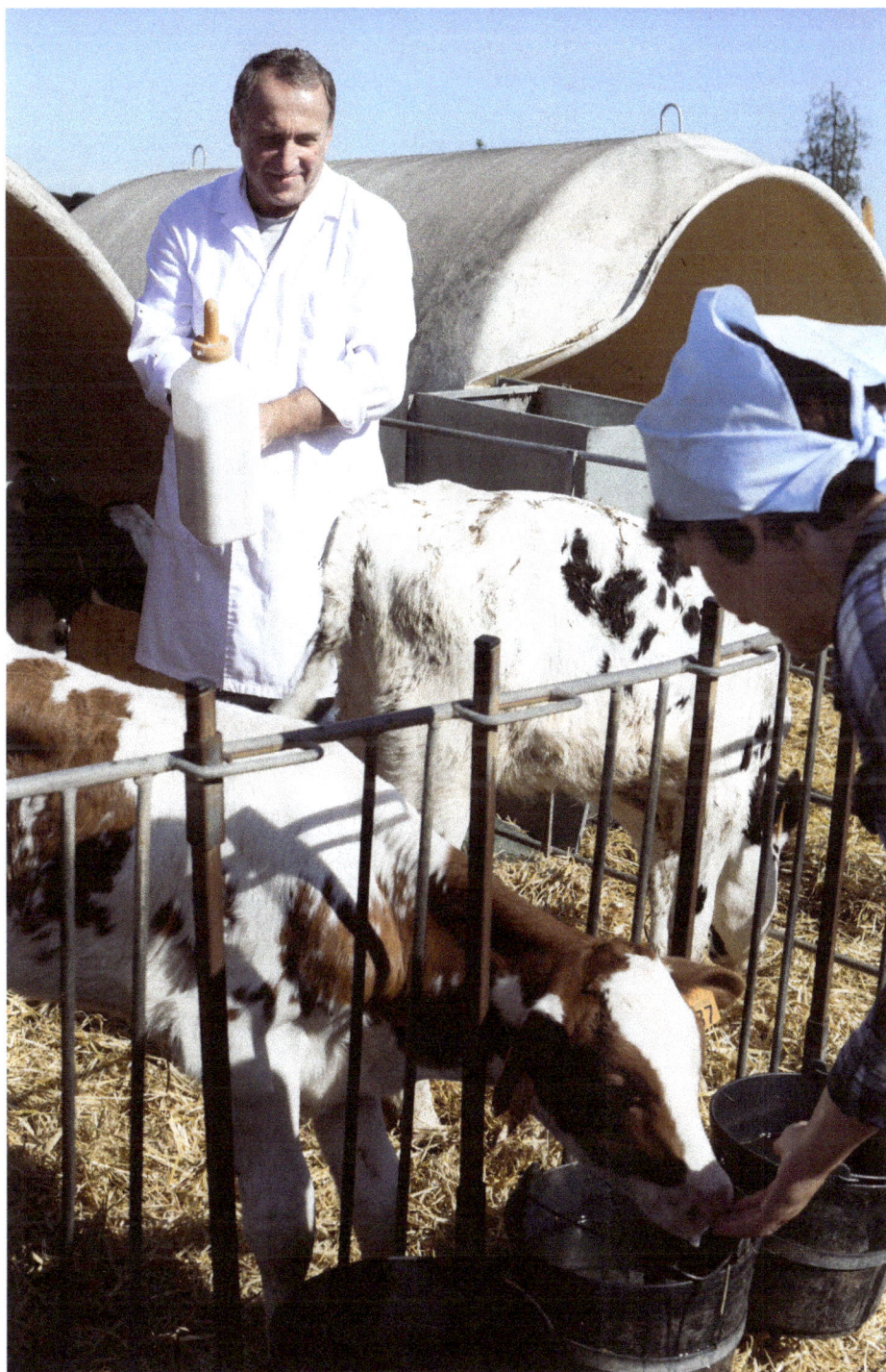

"*Success is not a miracle. Nor is it a matter of luck. Everything happens for a reason, good or bad.*"

— *Brian Tracy*

CHAPTER 23

TOEFL AND INTERNATIONAL TESTS

International students can apply for admission to nearly all U.S. vet schools.

International Student: A native of a foreign country who is in the process of completing or has completed their undergraduate education in the U.S. or from any other country who wishes to attend vet school in the United States on a student visa.

TOEFL, IELTS, CAEL

The first step for all non-native English-speaking students is to demonstrate English proficiency. To do this, non-native speakers of English need to take the Test of English as a Foreign Language (TOEFL) or the International English Language Testing System (IELTS).

Occasionally, the Canadian Academic English Language (CAEL) test is allowed. Minimum scores must be met on the listening band, writing band, and speaking band in one sitting, as is the case with Michigan State. However, please check the websites for current information.

Some schools waive this test requirement if higher education degrees are earned where the language of instruction was English.

The TOEFL/IELTS requirements for four DVM programs are listed below:

- **Colorado State** – minimum TOEFL score of 80 (iBT) or IELTS of 6.5.

- **Tufts** – TOEFL is not required if the college language of educational instruction was English

- **UC Davis** – minimum TOEFL score of 105, taken by August 31 and sent to the school code 4834.

- **UPenn** – scores in the 90th percentile, or, if applicants earned an undergraduate or graduate degree in the English language, TOEFL may be waived.

- **Iowa State** - minimum TOEFL score of 600 (PBT), 100 (IBT), or IELTS 7.0[1] - Applicants who do not receive the minimum requirements will not be considered. At the College of Veterinary Medicine's discretion, the English examination requirement for students who have graduated from a U.S. college may be waived.

Applicants from Puerto Rico are U.S. citizens and typically do not need to submit these scores. However, it is important to note that generally, those students who must take the test need to have a recent score, typically within the last two years.

TESTS FOR INTERNATIONAL APPLICANTS TO U.S. VET SCHOOLS

Note: The 150 – 300 hours of veterinary professional experience or veterinary research required by most vet schools for entering students may be waived for students entering in 2021 and 2022, depending upon the school. Check the school's website.

Test of English as a Foreign Language - TOEFL iBT (Internet Based Test): Applicants who desire to take the TOEFL iBT must complete each subsection in its entirety within a single administration. Typically, vet schools require that the tests be taken within the past two years.

The TOEFL iBT is a four-hour test that covers the following areas:[2]

- Answer questions based upon a reading passage

- Listen to a passage once and answer questions regarding the interaction

- Read texts and vocally respond to questions which is digitally recorded and evaluated

---

1   Iowa State University College of Veterinary Medicine, "Home," *Iowa State University College of Veterinary Medicine,* n.d., https://vetmed.iastate.edu/

2   International Student, "TOEFL," *International Student,* n.d., https://www.internationalstudent.com/test-prep/toefl/

- Write a passage based upon a given prompt

International English Language Testing System - IELTS: Applicants who choose to take the IELTS must complete the academic version in a single examination administration. Typically, vet schools require that the tests be taken within the past two years.

The IELTS consists of:

- 40 questions based on four recordings of monologues and dialogues
- 30 minutes of audio content including a variety of accents
- 40 questions based on three reading passages that may feature graphics from sources including books, journals, and newspapers (60 minutes)
- 2 writing assignments: a short formal essay and a description or explanation of a table, chart, or other figures (60 minutes)
- 11 – 14 minutes of a face-to-face interview, responding to broad inquiries about themselves and familiar topics provided on a card and participate in an organized discussion. This segment may be done up to seven days before or after the other three sections (completed in one sitting)

Canadian Academic English Language – CAEL:[3] All sections of the CAEL must be completed together - listening band, writing band, and speaking band. Applicants must acquire the minimum needed marks for all required areas of the CAEL Assessment.

Graduate Record Examination - GRE: All sections are required (verbal, quantitative, and analytical writing). The test takes approximately 3 hours and 45 minutes (six sections with a 10-minute break after the third).

GRE scores are used to evaluate applicants' potential for graduate-level study in a variety of fields. Although GRE Subject Tests are required for some graduate programs, they are not required for veterinary medical schools. The Subject Tests evaluate knowledge in a specific topic, whereas the General Test evaluates verbal thinking, quantitative reasoning, and analytical writing skills.

There are three sections to the GRE:

- **Verbal Reasoning:** This section assesses applicants' abilities to analyze and evaluate written content, synthesize knowledge, understand linkages between sentence components, and recognize relationships between words and concepts. Each set of 20 questions lasts 30 minutes

3   Canadian Academic English Language (CAEL), "Home," *CAEL*, n.d., https://www.cael.ca/

- **Quantitative Reasoning:** Most questions are multiple-choice, although a few require applicants to enter a number or make a quantitative comparison. This section tests quantitative reasoning skills and an understanding of basic arithmetic, algebra, geometry, and data analysis.
- **Two Analytical Writing Essays:** 60 minutes
  1. present a point of view on a specific topic
  2. argument analysis - This section assesses candidate's ability to express themselves, present evidence, and correctly use the English language

TRANSCRIPTS

All students to DVM programs must submit transcripts. However, for those students applying to vet schools from other countries, the courses and programs must be evaluated by a standardized method. One of those is the World Education Services (WES), where the courses are translated. This requirement is not necessary if the degree program was taught in English.

INTERNATIONAL STUDENT APPLICANT TO VET SCHOOL

To apply, complete all parts of the VMCAS application in English, inputting undergraduate schools, coursework, and grades in the same way as other applicants. There are no differences in the required essays and supplemental applications. You will need to check the websites to determine if the schools you have chosen accept international students. Almost all do.

FINANCIAL AID AND SCHOLARSHIPS

International students will have to look harder for financial aid and scholarships since most of the available assistance is through the U.S. federal government for citizens and permanent residents. Scholarships have varied requirements. However, some of these are strictly merit-based. You may qualify for one of these options. Check to see if any apply.

All students need to show the ability to pay using a form supplied by the financial aid office online or in person. The form is not complicated. However, signatures are required, often including a parent and a bank official from the financial institution where your school funds are located. The bank must confirm that funds are available. The U.S. government requires international student applicants to certify that they can provide adequate funding to cover the cost of a U.S. education.

Admission cannot be finalized, and an I-20 issued until the Office of Admissions verifies the applicant's complete Graduate Student Certification of Available Finances form. Check with the vet school financial aid office to see what they suggest. Some financial aid offices are excellent with helpful staff who truly want to help you find the money you need. These staff members believe that if their admissions offices accepted you, they picked you from a long list of excellent candidates and truly want you to attend. They will help.

However, there are a few financial aid offices where the staff cannot be bothered and brush you off by sending you down a rabbit hole with no cheese on the other side. Do not get discouraged or think the whole school is like that. Particularly during the pandemic, some staff members responded once a week and only vaguely answered questions, while others went over and above the call of duty even if they were in isolation. Customer service was hit or miss.

LOANS

Private loans are available through banking institutions as well. If you have a U.S. co-signer, you can often get a loan for the full cost of attendance, depending on the co-signer's creditworthiness. If you choose the loan option, just make sure you have read through the requirements, as there will be provisions regarding interest, repayment, and postponement. Focus on the interest rate and repayment because you might want to try a second or third bank.

Don't settle for the first option until you do your research. There is a huge difference between Full Deferral, Interest Only, and Immediate Repayment. The interest, terms, and conditions could make a difference of $100,000.

Also, remember, you may choose a residency program and thus remain in school for much longer. Residencies are not required. However, you may choose to complete a three-year residency after vet school. Thus, to pay for school and possibly your extended education afterward, many vet schools suggest that you consider using the private company, eduPASS, for assistance.

Tufts DVM website says, "First-year international students are not eligible for institutional financial aid. There are several private student loans for which international students may apply. The student must have a loan co-signer who is a United States citizen or permanent resident. Additional information may be found on the eduPASS website."

INTERNATIONAL STUDENT VISA PROCESS

International students who do not have U.S. citizenship or permanent residence must obtain a student visa to lawfully attend school in the United States. This international visa allows students to stay in the United States for a set amount of time to attend an approved school, language program, or academic exchange program. Upon completion, the student visa expires. Students must then leave the United States, although students may return as a tourist or on another visa, such as a work visa.

Applying for a student visa in the United States requires planning. Be sure to apply for the visa at least three to five months before your program begins. The process for applying for a U.S. student visa differs at some U.S. embassies or consulates. Thus, it is critical to check the guidelines on the embassy or consulate's website before applying.

Prospective students must undergo the following stages:

Apply and Be Accepted to a U.S. Student and Exchange Visitor Program (SEVP)-approved school

International students must apply to a veterinary medical school and be accepted. Accreditation is crucial because it ensures that the anticipated degree will be recognized by other institutions, professional organizations, businesses, and government departments around the world. Only SEVP-approved institutions may enroll students in the Student and Exchange Visitor Information System (SEVIS) and supply students with the necessary documentation needed to apply for a U.S. student visa.

All U.S. vet schools on VMCAS are accredited. For other schools, students can find authorized institutions by visiting the U.S. government's "Study in the States" webpage.[4] You will be requested to show proof of sufficient financial resources.

There are three categories of student visas available in the United States:[5]

F-1 visa:[6] This visa is meant for high school or college/university study in the United States, and it is available to both undergraduate and graduate students.

---

4   Department of Homeland Security, "School Search," *Department of Homeland Security,* n.d., https://studyinthestates.dhs.gov/school-search

5   U.S. Department of State, "Study & Exchange," *U.S. Department of State,* n.d., https://travel.state.gov/content/travel/en/us-visas/study.html

6   U.S. Department of State, "Student Visa," *U.S. Department of State,* n.d., https://travel.state.gov/content/travel/en/us-visas/study/student-visa.html

This is the one offered by veterinary medical schools.

M-1 visa: This visa is for non-academic or vocational study in the United States. These programs are usually short-term and focused on a particular career, for example, culinary school or a medical training program.

J-1 visa: This visa is for study abroad students, scholars, interns, and au pairs.[7] If you qualify for a J visa, you will be sent a SEVIS-generated document called Form DS-2019.

If you are accepted to vet school, you are eligible for an F-1 visa and will be provided a SEVIS-generated document, Form I-20.

Note: International students on F and M visas are managed by the SEVP, whereas Exchange Visitor Programs and international students on J visas are managed by the Department of State (DoS).

Pay SEVIS Fee

The SEVIS charge must be paid three days before submitting the U.S. visa application. To pay, complete either an online or paper form found on the SEVP website of the U.S. Immigration and Customs Enforcement (ICE).[8] Provide the requested information precisely as it appears on your I-20 form. The page describes how to pay using various debit or credit cards, checks, foreign money orders, and Western Union Quick Pay. Check the website to ensure your payment has gone through or to check on the progress. You may have a third party (such as a sponsor) pay the charge on your behalf.

Once completed, print a payment confirmation for proof to be used at your U.S. student visa interview. In addition, if you modify your non-immigrant status or seek any other U.S. immigration benefits, you may be required to show the confirmation to the customs officer at the U.S. Port of Entry of your choice.[9]

Complete Student Visa Application

Schedule an appointment with a U.S. consulate or embassy in your country to apply for a U.S. student visa once you have received your SEVIS form and paid the SEVIS fee. In addition, you will need to attach recent photos. Since visa processing

7   Hannah Muniz, "10 Steps to Get a US Student Visa: Full Application Guide," *PrepScholar,* January 3, 2021, https://blog.prepscholar.com/how-to-get-a-us-student-visa

8   U.S. Immigration and Customs Enforcement, "Pay Your Fee," *U.S. Immigration and Customs Enforcement,* n.d., https://www.ice.gov/sevis/i901/

9   International Student, "How to Apply for an F1 Visa," *International Student,* n.d., https://www.internationalstudent.com/immigration/f1-student-visa/how-to-apply-f1-visa/

periods vary, apply as soon as possible, regardless of when your program is set to begin. Your visa can be approved up to 120 days before your scheduled arrival in the United States. Most countries maintain a website that explains their specific requirements.

Pay Visa Application Fee

The visa application fee, also known as the Machine Readable Visa Fee (MRV) is required. Check the fee payment instructions on your embassy or consulate's website since payment methods differ. However, there are three general options for paying the non-refundable, non-transferable visa application fee:

1. In-person at an approved bank
2. By phone (you will receive a fee confirmation number)
3. Online (you must print your receipt)

Set Up Visa Interview Appointment

The final step is to schedule and attend a visa interview. You can do so by contacting the U.S. embassy or consulate in your area, either online or over the phone. Pay the MRV fee ahead of time since you may be asked for your MRV fee number.

Your visa application is incomplete until you interview with a consular officer. If you need to schedule your interview in a different U.S. embassy or consulate than the one where you originally applied, your information can be retrieved using the barcode from your DS-160 at any U.S. embassy or consulate.[10]

Bring the following documents:[11]

1. Transcripts and degrees from prior colleges and universities attended
2. Scores on standardized tests such as the TOEFL, LSAT, GRE, GMAT, or other tests
3. Financial proof that you or your sponsor (i.e., your parents or a government sponsor) has enough money to cover your tuition, travel, and living expenses while in the U.S.
4. A written list of prior employers and schools

---

10 U.S. Department of State, "Visa Appointment Wait Times," *U.S. Department of State,* n.d., https://travel.state. gov/content/travel/en/us-visas/visa-information-resources/wait-times.html

11 Laura Bridgestock, "Graduate Admissions Tests at a Glance: GMAT, GRE, LSAT, TOEFL, & IELTS," *Top Universities,* Updated April 17, 2021, https://www.topuniversities.com/student-info/admissions-advice/graduate-admissions-tests-glance-gmat-gre-lsat-toefl-ielts

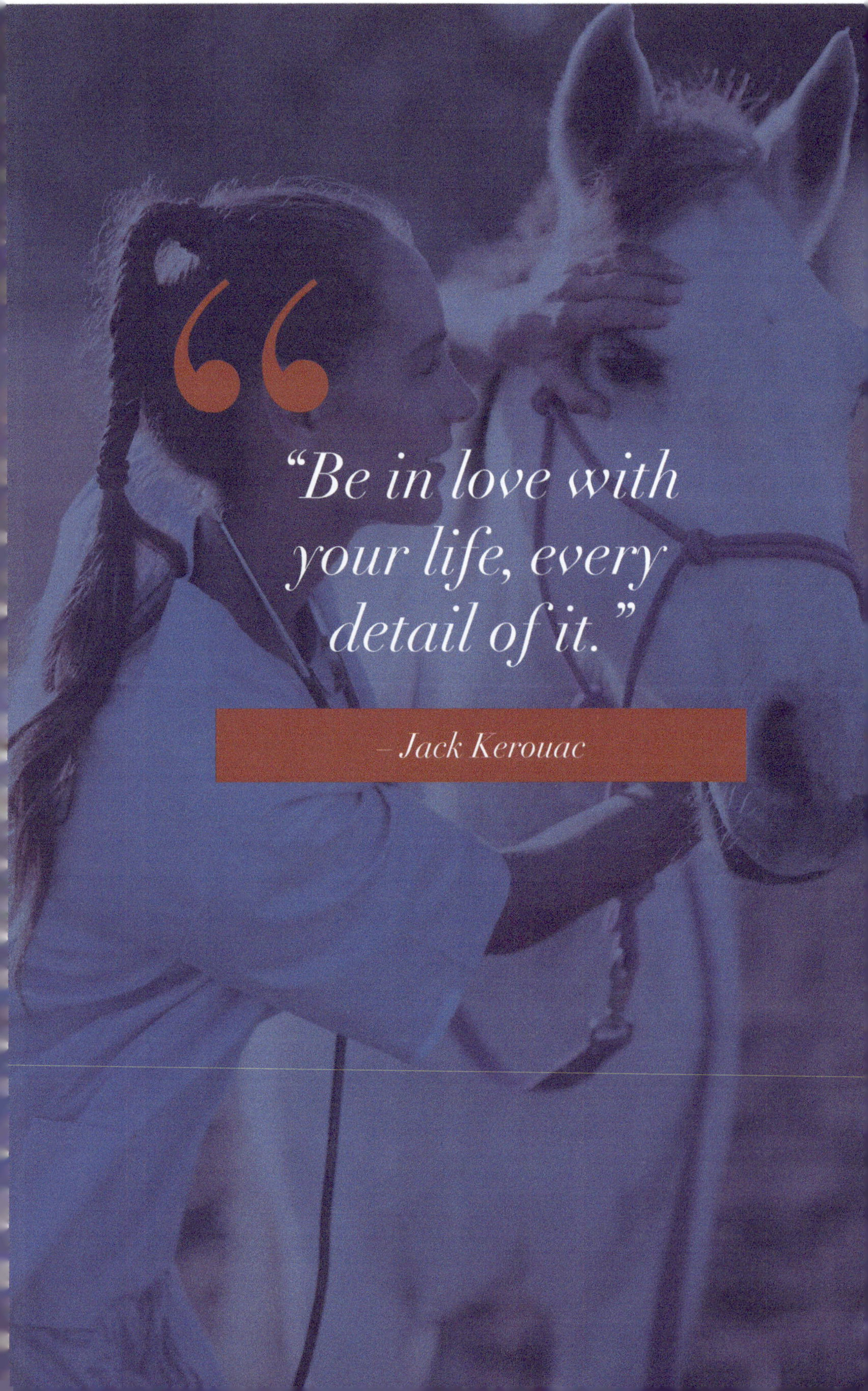
"Be in love with your life, every detail of it."
– Jack Kerouac

CHAPTER 24

RECOMMENDATIONS & COMMITTEE LETTERS

CASPer is the Computer-Based Assessment for Sampling Personal Characteristics administered by Altus Assessments to determine the non-academic qualities that may determine if you would make a good veterinarian. CASPer is a situational judgment test that is designed to assess decision-making in specific scenarios.

Test takers are asked to judge a situation. Using their on-the-spot judgment, they respond to an ethical, personal, or other situational dilemma in a medical setting. After reviewing the choices provided, they respond with the appropriate alternative they believe best fits the vignette.

The questions vary from capabilities to thinking skills to give vet schools a clearer picture of the applicant's decision-making, problem-solving, and situational management abilities. Both in vet school and in the practice of veterinary medicine, individuals must be able to manage and resolve difficult problems quickly and appropriately.

While these behavioral skills were once not considered, increasingly vet schools have sought to gain a deeper insight into applicants' actions and reactions when put under pressure. Relationship-building and communication are valued skills that vet schools consider essential to becoming a good practitioner.

The Purdue DVM program website states that the test is mandatory, but they believe the test is essential in helping the admissions team make better decisions about candidacy. Specifically, the Purdue site notes, "In implementing Casper, we are trying to further enhance fairness and objectivity in our selection process. All applications are reviewed holistically, and the information Casper provides will be of additional benefit to the Purdue University College of Veterinary Medicine Admissions Committee."

THE CASPER TEST ASSESSES:

- Collaboration
- Communication
- Empathy
- Equity
- Ethics
- Motivation
- Problem Solving
- Professionalism
- Resilience
- Self-Awareness

THE TEST

75 – 90 Minute Test Questions: Progress to the next section is automatic. There is an optional 10-15-minute break halfway through.

12 Scenarios (8 Video-Based & 4 Word-Based): Each is followed by 3 open-ended questions (5 minutes).

Not Computer Scored: Each test is individually scored by more than one specially-trained evaluator.

The CASPer test includes 12 sections: 8 video-based and 4 word-based scenarios. After each vignette, you will be required to answer three probing questions in five minutes or less. Halfway through the test, you will be offered an optional 10-15-minute break. The test typically takes between 75-90 minutes to complete.

Your test will be anonymously scored by multiple graders. Thus, your final score will not be judged differently and will give a strong and reliable representation of your personal and professional decision-making skills. Studying is not required.

TEST SCORES FORWARDED AUTOMATICALLY

After scoring is completed, tests are forwarded to the designated schools you listed on your application.

NOTE: Spelling Mistakes Do Not Impact Your Score

Since you can take the test from your choice of appropriate locations, you can create an environment that works for you. It is helpful for you to eliminate distractions from your environment ahead of time since this will help you think more clearly. If you believe headphones will help you, most test centers will let you use them.

Read the prompt thoroughly. Reflect and think through what you want to write in response to the three open-ended questions. You only have five minutes, and you want to be broad but clear. Since you have five minutes to complete each response, use your time wisely.

Focus on what you are trying to relay rather than the spelling or format. Since a different reader will rate the next section, they will not be prejudiced on what you might have done wrong in a previous section. Also, there are 12 sections, so you may do better on another if you make a mistake on one.

You also have a short break to relax, collect your thoughts, and get some refreshing water. Draw upon your life experiences as you respond and explain how you would act based on your life situations. Research shows that test takers who use the full amount of time score higher. So, do not rush or feel stressed during the test. Take your time.

Cheating can be detected by the trained eye and violates the agreement test takers sign. If cheating is determined, scores are withheld, and information is sent to each of the programs. Furthermore, cheating takes time and sophistication. Since the consequences are high, it is not worth the time or risk. You cannot really prepare to have good judgment except to relax and think through what you would do. You've got this!

Preparing for the test is enough. Relax and be yourself.

TEST FOR VETERINARY MEDICAL SCHOOL - CSP-10101 – U.S. PROFESSIONAL HEALTH SCIENCES

Dates & Fees (CASPer: $25, plus $12/school)

Specific information about dates and fees is typically released in April before the application cycle and varies by program and country. Fees are nonrefundable, so make sure you have the test date and location you desire ahead of time. The fees are only valid for the original/current admissions cycle. Add all vet school programs to which you are applying. When you complete the test, your scores will be sent to those schools. CASPer fees vary by type and country. Check the CASPer site

Ten considerations before taking the test:

1. Check your account to confirm your test date and time
2. Disable VPNs, Firewalls, and Plug-ins
3. Ensure that your webcam is working and that you have up-to-date Chrome or Firefox browsers
4. Complete the System Requirements Check
5. Familiarize yourself with the test question types and format
6. Practice with the sample scenarios at *https://takecasper.com/test-prep/*
7. Prepare with additional situational scenarios
8. Find a quiet place where you will not be disturbed and remove noises and other distractions
9. Take the full time to respond and review your choices
10. Relax and be yourself Note: Applicants are not permitted to take the CASPer test more than once per admissions cycle

These vet schools require the CASPer (subject to change):

- Kansas State University College of Veterinary Medicine
- Lincoln Memorial University College of Veterinary Medicine
- Long Island University Veterinary Medicine
- Michigan State University College of Veterinary Medicine
- Oklahoma State University College of Veterinary Medicine
- Purdue University College of Veterinary Medicine
- Ross University School of Veterinary Medicine
- Texas Tech University College of Veterinary Medicine
- UC Davis School of Veterinary Medicine
- University of Florida College of Veterinary Medicine
- Virginia-Maryland College of Veterinary Medicine

ACCOMMODATIONS

If you require testing accommodations for CASPer, you will need to submit the Accommodations Request Form.[1] This form must be completed at least three weeks before your desired test date and must be signed by you and a licensed professional. You may ask additional questions at *support@takecasper.com* or use the chat feature on the lower part of your screen.

---

1   Take Casper, "CASPer Test Accommodations Request Form," *Take Casper,* Updated October 2019, https://takecasper.com/wp-content/uploads/2019/10/CASPer-Test-Accommodations-Request-Form-English.pdf

"The aim of Positive Psychology is to catalyze a change in psychology from a preoccupation only with repairing the worst things in life to also building the best qualities in life."

– Martin Seligman

CHAPTER 25
CASPER TEST

etters of recommendation, letters of evaluation, and/or committee letters are required for the application process. Your submissions to AAVMC, VMCAS, and TMDSAS are incomplete without letters of evaluation, although they do not need to be submitted by the time you send your application. However, VMCAS requires recommendations to be completed and submitted to VMCAS and TMDSAS by September 15th, when the application closes at 11:59 pm Eastern Standard Time.

To ensure that VMCAS and TMDSAS will get these on time, request your transcripts early. Recommenders need time to formulate what to write. Since recommenders find it useful to have information available to them about your interests, progress, and goals, providing them with your current resume and personal statement assists them in formulating their thoughts.

HOW MANY AND WHAT ARE THE REQUIREMENTS

The VMCAS site states that you may submit a minimum of three electronic letters of recommendation and a maximum of six. When a college has a preference of the types of letters, they will describe their requirements on the site. Letters of recommendation on paper are no longer accepted. Your letters (eLORs) must be sent digitally.

Typically, vet schools want one to be from a veterinarian. Other assumptions are that one letter will be from a bio, chem, or physics teacher and another from a professional reference from a research advisor, animal care leader, veterinarian, animal science professor, or employer. Another faculty member will strengthen your application.

While you do not need to provide all six, you must provide at least three letters. Science teachers are the best because they can assess your ability in classes closest to the field of veterinary science. You might also choose the leader of your research team, volunteer effort, farm owner, or someone who knows your academic and professional performance.

Your application can be verified as complete, even if the recommendations arrive after your application is submitted. The letters you submit will provide a fuller picture of who you are as an applicant and how you will perform professionally. The individual might offer insights into your commitment to veterinary medicine and your ability to perform under pressure. These individuals have observed your work and are the eyes and ears of the admissions committee.

Since many schools consider a student holistically, they rely on those who can attest to your abilities, personality traits, and work ethic. Individual vet schools may have additional requirements. In the supplemental applications, a vet school might request a letter of recommendation from a source that offers them the further information they need.

COMPOSITE OR COMMITTEE LETTER

Your undergraduate institution may offer the opportunity to request a committee letter. Committee letters are not as common for vet school admissions as they are for medical or dental school. Some vet schools DO NOT look at the committee or composite letter, and some will NOT even accept the committee letter as one of the six letters they will consider in the process. Check each school's website to be sure.

Note that the "Health Professions Committee Letter" process is often laborious. Students loathe the labyrinth of rules, regulations, and procedures just to initiate the process. Furthermore, each school has a unique process, including essays, statements, resumes, interviews, and forms completed along a strict timeline. Thus, unless your school requires you to submit a committee letter, this effort might be better spent gaining clinical or research hours. If they do, contact your pre-health advisor early to determine what you should do.

INDIVIDUAL LETTERS OF EVALUATION

Start early! You will need to build relationships with a few people who will become your recommenders. These letters will come from your professors, advisors, lab supervisors, volunteer supervisors, veterinarians, clinical practitioners, or others who have worked with you in a professional capacity. Planning ahead of time is helpful. Faculty may not know individual students well enough at some schools, where science class sizes are large.

They may not be able to objectively evaluate the student's academic performance or professionalism in group clinical settings, particularly during the pandemic. All they may know about a given student is that they earned an A in the class, which does not say much about the student as a future vet student or practitioner and amounts to a very weak recommendation. This situation makes asking a professor awkward and may lead the professor to say, "No." Furthermore, professors may not be willing to write the recommendation because they feel uncomfortable doing so. Thus, you should find a recommender who will write a good letter. This situation necessitates that you get to know your professors well enough so that they can provide a solid, impactful assessment of your personal qualifications as well as your academic ability.

Often principal investigators (PIs) on a research project also do not know their assistants well since they spend most of their time mentoring their master's and doctoral candidates. Typically, if you are on one of these teams, the only person you will communicate with is the doctoral student.

Students often ask if they can use the doctoral student as their recommender. The answer is yes. Why? They are, in effect, your supervisor and the one with whom you work on a day-to-day basis in the lab. They know you best and have a good sense of how to assess your abilities.

Getting good letters of evaluation is a function of getting to know your recommenders and determining their ability to write a good recommendation. They can do this best if you communicate well in advance, get to know them and provide them with the information they need to write the best evaluation.

MONITORING THE RECOMMENDATION PROGRESS

You can track the progress of your application through the portal. There, you will discover who opened, started, and submitted your letters so that you can follow up. The process is safe, secure, straightforward, and quick. You should not worry about this process. The only thing you need to do is monitor, track, and determine where you stand with your recommendations. If any individuals have not submitted, contact them with a nice note. You may need to resend the request if the first time you sent the eLOR e-mail is lost in their inbox.

PART 5

WHERE AND HOW TO APPLY

"*If you are not willing to learn, no one can help you. If you are determined to learn, no one can stop you.*"

– Zig Ziglar

CHAPTER 26

WHAT TO LOOK FOR IN A VET SCHOOL?

There are many factors to consider in applying to vet school. However, each person is different. What might be most important to one student, like cost, location, or residency opportunities, may not be as important to another who is more concerned with research faculty, cutting-edge facilities, and high academic achievement of incoming students.

Aspiring vets often choose veterinary medicine because they love animals. Though this is okay, it is not good enough. Veterinary medicine is a highly-skilled, science-focused profession and requires a strong work ethic. For most vet colleges, a strong work ethic together with solid experience is a top priority. Therefore, candidates who possess these qualities have a better chance of securing an interview.

- Is the veterinary medicine training especially rigorous, competitive, collaborative, problem-based?
- If the out-of-pocket cost is significantly more at one school than another school, is the outcome worth the investment?
- Is location important, like near your farm or where your family lives?
- Is the vet school known for research, clinical, urban/rural experiences?
- Are clinical rotations near the campus, alternative site, small clinics, or large urban hospital?
- What are the costs, drawbacks, or opportunities of foreign vet schools?

- Is studying veterinary medicine outside the U.S. worth the risk?

The next page lists considerations when thinking about the vet schools to which you plan to apply.

CONSIDERATIONS

Cost	Types of Clinical Experiences
Debt Burden of Graduates	Job Prospects
Income After 10 Years	Prestige
Equipment	Animal Patient Interaction
Technology/Internet	Scholarship Possibilities
Simulation Labs	Demographic Makeup
Virtual Reality	Collegiality/Competitiveness
Production	GPA Range
Farm Animals	GRE Range
Food Animals	CASPer Required
Reproductive Medicine	Weather
Small/Large Animals	State Where There is Growth
Research/Clinical Focus	Political Viewpoint
Supportive Environment	International Students
Alumni Support	Average Age of Admits
Location	% of Nontraditional Admits
Endowment	Prerequisites
Acceptance Rate	Rankings
Dropout Rate	Difficulty of Classes
Pass Rate on Board Exams	Student Feedback
In-State/Out-of-State Apps	Difficulty to Apply
Length of the Program/Summers	Friend/Family of Alumnus
Religious Foundation	Student-Faculty Ratio
Clinical or Research Focus	Specialty Subjects
Number Who Get Residencies	Student Life

OPPORTUNITY, COST, AND STRESS

With the high cost of a veterinary medical degree and low starting salaries, think carefully about how much you are willing to spend. Colorado State explicitly asks students to respond to the prompt, "Academically, financially, and personally challenging. What drives you to pursue a DVM degree and face those challenges?"

Thus, with the rigor of classes and the cost of a veterinary medical education as high as a home mortgage, it is critical to figure out the value of a particular school's education and how you will pay. Unlike medical school, your income is not correlated to the cost or prestige of the school. Finally, emotional wellbeing is essential to the practice of veterinary medicine due to the stresses of the job.

A study conducted at the University of California, Davis revealed that 38.9% of first-year vet students experienced symptoms of depression and a feeling of uncertainty about growing debt in subsequent years.[1] Stress impacts veterinarians' lives with injured patients who cannot speak, and both veterinarians and pet owners needing to make life and death decisions. It is interesting to note, in comparison, that depression was found in a quarter of medical students who study humans though the rigor and training are similar.

A Veterinary Wellbeing Study conducted in 2020 by Merck Animal Health and the AVMA, determined that veterinarians are 2.7 times more likely to die by suicide than those in the general public.[2] Also, while female veterinarians think about suicide more, male veterinarians have a higher rate of attempts. This comprehensive study examined areas such as job satisfaction, compensation, burnout, substance use disorder, cyberbullying, and suicide.

AGE & GENDER OF INCOMING STUDENTS

It may not surprise you that many vet schools have more than five times as many women as men. However, you might be surprised to know that, at some schools, you will have classmates as old as your parents. For the University of Florida class of 2025, there are students as old as 45 and an applicant range up to 63. At Michigan State, 90% of the incoming class are female with an age range

1   Munashe Chigerwe, Karen A. Boudreaux, and Jan E. Ilkiw, "Assessment of Depression and Health-Related Quality of Life in Veterinary Medical Students: Use of the 2-Item Primary Care Evaluation of Mental Disorders Questionnaire (PRIME-MD PHQ) and the 8-Item Short Form-8 Survey (SF-8)," *Journal of Veterinary Medical Education* 45, no. 3 (2018): 358-366, https://jvme.utpjournals.press/doi/10.3138/jvme.0217-022r

2   Merck Animal Health, "Merck Animal Health Veterinary Wellbeing Study II," *Merck Animal Health*, n.d., https://www.merck-animal-health-usa.com/about-us/veterinary-wellbeing-study

of 20-33. For the class of 2025, UPenn's average age is 23.4; the average age at UC Davis is 23. Tufts class of 2024 had students up to 51 years old. Thus, students of all ages apply, and one is never too old to do so.

RANGE OF EXPERIENCES

More than ten percent of the University of Florida's entering class had graduate degrees. In addition, approximately ten percent double majored in college. More than 75% of the admitted class majored in biological or animal sciences. Six students in Michigan State's incoming class had a graduate degree; three were accepted without a bachelor's degree. Ten students in UC Davis' class of 2025 had a master's degree with an average of 1698 hours of veterinary experience; twelve students accepted to the incoming class had previously applied. One student applied three times and was accepted on their third try.

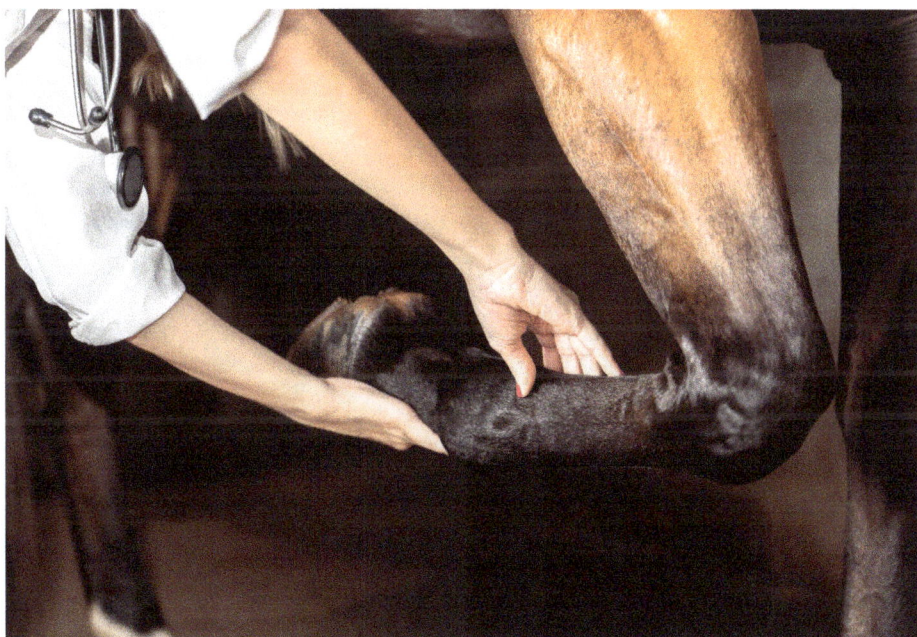

"The ones who are crazy enough to think that they can change the world are the ones who do."

— Steve Jobs

CHAPTER 27

THE PERILS OF RANKINGS

t is fairly safe to assume that the top ten colleges ranked on the national or international level are very good for one aspect of a veterinary education or another. However, since needs, experiences, and goals differ, rankings have only marginal utility. Nevertheless, students and their families are eager to find a quantifiable way to assess the quality and value of a given vet school and discover which schools offer a better quality of education. Unfortunately, there are few ways to thoroughly assess veterinary medical programs without a significant time investment. Thus, many base their choices upon ranking systems.

Here are a few other considerations:

- Residency Matches – Note that most schools say they match nearly everyone, but students may not be matched to their choice of specialty, and the statistic may eliminate a subset of students.

- Accreditation – Vet schools may be put on probation due to changes in delivery or other criteria. Check this out.

- Theory, Research, or Clinical Focus – The way you want to learn and the style of teaching varies from school to school. One student commented that at his vet school (name left out in case this data point was an aberration), students had to learn everything on their own since the teachers did not teach.

- Facilities – Many schools have simulations, and all schools have clinical experience, but some of those opportunities are not on campus or near where you live.

- Certifications – A few schools offer specialized certifications in food animals, food production, and small animals. You might want to demonstrate your proficiency in a specific area. For example, the University of Florida College of Veterinary Medicine has certificate programs in (1) Aquatic Animal Health, (2) Food Animal, (3) Shelter Medicine, and (4) Veterinary Business Management.

The American Veterinary Medical Colleges (AVMA) Council on Education (COE) does not rank, recommend, or compare schools.[1] The goal is for every veterinary medical school to have high standards met by accreditation and continual improvement. Published systems or publications that rank vet schools are considered questionable, viewing these with caution.

Even so, while veterinary medical schools often downplay rankings, when they appear on one of the lists, they often share that ranking on their website. For example, Colorado State University's College of Veterinary Medicine website boasts that *U.S. News and World Report* ranked CSU CVM #3 in the U.S.[2] And, in another example, UC Davis is "ranked #1 in the nation by *U.S. News & World Report* and #1 globally by QS World University".[3]

VET SCHOOL RANKINGS

Comparing one vet school to another is complicated. The factors that are most important to some – cost, location, job prospects, and income potential – may be very different than the factors for another – prestige, state-of-the-art technology, and the likelihood of a top-notch residency.

People are different. Their needs and preferences are different as well. Wanting to pick the "best" school, people rely on rankings. However, how do you factor in debt burden, scholarship opportunities, weather, collegiality, religious foundation, and patient interaction when some cannot be quantified. Would you get more, better, or diverse experiences in a rural area, big city, or specialty clinic? Thus, your ranking based on your needs could be very different than another applicant's ranking.

Thus, the "best" vet schools depend on your criteria. However, rankings still

1 AVMA, "What is the Best Veterinary School?," *AVMA*, n.d., https://www.avma.org/education/accreditation/colleges/what-best-veterinary-school

2 Colorado State University, "College of Veterinary Medicine and Biomedical Sciences," *Colorado State University*, n.d., https://vetmedbiosci.colostate.edu/dvm/

3 UC Davis, "School of Veterinary Medicine – Achievements," *UC Davis*, n.d., https://www.vetmed.ucdavis.edu/index.php/achievements

exist. Here are a few.

U.S. News & World Report Top Ten Vet Schools

1. UC Davis
2. Cornell University
3. Colorado State University
4. North Carolina State
5. Ohio State University
6. Texas A&M University
7. University of Pennsylvania
8. University of Wisconsin
9. University of Florida
10. University of Georgia

Using the American Association of Veterinary Medical Colleges Cost Comparison Tool, the ten most expensive vet schools (out-of-state or private) in the U.S. are:[4]

1. Long Island University
2. Midwestern University
3. Ohio State University
4. University of Arizona
5. University of Pennsylvania
6. University of Minnesota
7. Tufts University
8. Colorado State University
9. Western University
10. Michigan State University

The ten least expensive vet schools (in-state tuition) in the U.S. are[5]

1. Purdue University
2. North Carolina State University
3. University of Georgia

---

4   AAVMC, "Cost Comparison Tool," *AAVMC*, n.d., https://www.aavmc.org/becoming-a-veterinarian/funding-your-degree/cost-comparison-tool/

5   Ibid.

4. Kansas State University

5. Texas Tech University

6. Iowa State University

7. University of Illinois Urbana

8. Washington State University

9. TexasA&M University

10. Virginia-Maryland Regional College

The 2020 Shanghai Rankings, are as follows:[6]

1. Ghent University, Belgium

2. Nanjing Agricultural University, China

3. University of Veterinary Medicine Hanover, Germany

4. University of Copenhagen, Denmark

5. The Royal Veterinary College, the UK

6. University of Edinburgh, the UK

7. Autonomous University of Barcelona, Spain

8. University of Veterinary Medicine Vienna, Austria

9. University of California, Davis, the US

10. University of Bern, Switzerland

Quacquarelli Symonds (QS) is also a worldwide ranking. The top vet schools on this list for 2021 are:[7]

1. The Royal Veterinary College, UK

2. University of California, Davis, US

3. Utrecht University, the Netherlands

4. University of Edinburgh, UK

5. Cornell University, US

6. University of Guelph, Canada

7. The Ohio State University, US

8. University of Cambridge, UK

9. University of Copenhagen, Denmark

---

6   Shanghai Ranking, "2021 Global Ranking of Academic Subjects," *Shanghai Ranking*, 2021, https://www.shanghairanking.com/rankings/gras/2021/RS0304

7   QS Top Universities, "Veterinary Science," *QS Top Universities*, n.d., https://www.topuniversities.com/university-rankings/university-subject-rankings/2021/veterinary-science

10. Vetsuisse Faculty Bern and Zurich, Switzerland

These rankings certainly do not mean that other vet schools are not good or do not have excellent faculty.

Take these rankings as somewhat subjective. Ultimately, you should base your decision on the factors that are most important to you.

PRIORITIES AND LIMITATIONS

The decision about where to apply is a function of your priorities. Some of these criteria are presented in this book. You may not have the grades and scores to get accepted into a university like the University of Pennsylvania. However, if you are close but out of range, you may have a good shot for many other schools. This limitation should inform your decision.

You can still apply if you are not in the middle 50th percentile, but your chances are decreased. Your best bet is to create a chart of schools and list the most important factors to you. Each individual's chart would be unique based on your own set of priorities and circumstances.

With the cost of some vet schools skyrocketing at well over $400,000 for four years, many students include costs and access to scholarships toward the highest of their considerations. As a result, the debt burden of vet school graduates is extraordinary.

HOW MANY APPLICATIONS?

The next question to ask yourself is, how many vet schools will you put on your final list? More sounds better to have choices until you must complete the secondary applications and discover that there are essays required for each and more research. You might be better off applying to fewer schools and doing them well. A good target is to research 20 schools and narrow the list down to between 14-16 schools. This number is still a lot of work, but it is more reasonable than 30.

Furthermore, there are costs associated with these applications. The VMCAS fees for 2022 are $220 for the first school and $120 for each additional school. This means that if you apply to 16 schools, the cost just for applying is $2,020. This consideration is important, though there is a process you can undergo to get a few of the fees waived if money is a concern.

TOP VET COLLEGES IN THE WORLD

Getting into a vet school can be a tough hurdle for applicants. However, a 2021 report showed that the acceptance rate in Vet Colleges in the U.S., UK, and Europe ranged from 3.9% to 73%, which was impressive compared to the 3% to 16% registered by medical schools.[8]

When applying for vet schools in the U.S., vet schools require 45 to 90 hours of undergraduate science credit.[9] Pre-veterinary courses are similar to those for medical and dental school. Aspiring vets must have an academic background in general biology, cell biology, biochemistry, physics, organic or inorganic chemistry, genetics, and knowledge in basic human sciences and calculus.[10]

Applicants must consider things such as university requirements, location, rankings, and tuition fees. With this in mind, there are plenty of veterinary medical colleges students can choose from in the U.S. and Europe.

University of California, Davis

Currently ranked the second-best veterinary school in the world, according to the 2021 QS ranking, UC Davis is a public research institution with an impeccable history of academic excellence and groundbreaking research. UC Davis offers the Doctor of Veterinary Medicine, Master of Preventive Veterinary Medicine program, and related graduate academic M.S. and Ph.D. programs. The acceptance rate at UC Davis is 38%.[11]

Cornell University

Founded in 1865, Cornell University is a private university in New York and is a member of the Ivy League. Cornell University is widely recognized as a leader in veterinary medical education, animal medicine, and biochemical research. They offer continuing education and top-notch DVM training. Cornell's acceptance rate is low — 10 percent.[12] Although Cornell is a private school, tuition is lower for New York residents.

8   Med Edits, "Medical School Acceptance Rates, Admissions Statistics + Average MCAT and GPA for Every Medical School (2021)," *Med Edits,* 2021, https://mededits.com/medical-school-admissions/statistics/

9   Veterinary & Animal Sciences, "So You Think You Want to Go to Vet School – Frequently Asked Questions," *Veterinary & Animal Sciences,* n.d., https://www.vasci.umass.edu/sites/vasci/files/so_you_think_you_want_to_go_vet_school.pdf

10 University of South Alabama, "Pre-Veterinary," *University of South Alabama,* n.d., https://www.southalabama.edu/departments/academicadvising/pre-health/pre-veterinary.html

11 World Scholarship Forum, "17 Best Vet Schools in the World 2021 | Updated," *World Scholarship Forum,* 2021, https://worldscholarshipforum.com/best-vet-schools/

12 Cornell University, "Facts about Cornell," *Cornell University,* n.d., https://admissions.cornell.edu/facts-about-cornell

Royal Veterinary College, London

The RVC is a federal university founded in 1791 in London. Royal Veterinary College is the best in the UK and one of the best in the world. The tuition for successful applicants is estimated at £9,250.[13]

University of Cambridge

Founded in 1209 and the second oldest university in the UK, the Veterinary department is a front-runner in veterinary science and medicine. The university is widely recognized for its excellent teaching and research. The University of Cambridge is ranked 4th in the world for Veterinary Medicine, according to QS rankings. Tuition, however, is very costly for international students — £55,272.[14] For UK and EU students, the tuition is set at around £9,250.

Utrecht University

Located in the Netherlands, Utrecht University is one of the best universities globally, ranking high in the world. The faculty of veterinary medicine is one of the best globally, with a primary focus in areas such as patient care. In addition, the university has a central animal research facility and offers several academic programs in veterinary medicine.

13 Royal Veterinary College University of London, "Tuition Fees for UK, EU, International and Channel Islands Students – 2021/22," *Royal Veterinary College University of London,* 2021, https://www.rvc.ac.uk/study/fees-and-funding/fees#panel-tuition-fees-for-undergraduate-students

14 World Scholarship Forum, "17 Best Vet Schools in the World 2021 | Updated," *World Scholarship Forum,* 2021, https://worldscholarshipforum.com/best-vet-schools/

" "In America, with education and hard work, it really does not matter where you came from; it matters only where you are going."

– Condoleezza Rice

CHAPTER 28

REFINING YOUR LIST

You want to apply to enough schools so that you have choices, but, keep in mind, the cost of applying can be alarming.

APPLICATION FEES

For the 2021-2022 application season, applicants will pay a $200 flat fee for the TMDSAS and, for the VMCAS, an application to one vet school costs $220 with $120 for each additional school. Thus, 10 schools would be $1,300, and 16 schools would be $2,020.

NOTE: some schools have a supplemental application fee that is paid directly to the school. Fortunately, not all schools have a supplemental application fee. Even so, with this kind of expense just to submit applications, you want to look carefully at what you want in a vet school and how many schools you will consider.

FEE WAIVER

TMDSAS does not offer a fee waiver program. However, VMCAS will waive the initial application fee for one school on a first-come, first-served basis for students with exceptional needs. All additional applications will need to be paid for by the applicant. All fee waiver requests must be submitted by

August 13th.[1]

PREREQUISITES AND DEGREE REQUIREMENTS

Each college has a prescribed set of prerequisite courses. Additional courses are listed as recommended. These prerequisites often include a combination of courses in math, science, social science, and humanities. Every college has its own set of rules and limits regarding AP/IB credits, community college courses, pass/fail, and/or online courses that can be used to meet prerequisites and requirements. You may request a waiver of one or more requirements from most schools if there are extenuating circumstances.

To ensure that you have the latest information, you should conduct thorough research using the Veterinary Medical School Admissions Requirements (VMSAR).[2] This site offers a centralized platform to research and consider vet school requirements. Additionally, individual school websites and admissions offices are also good places to investigate vet school options and gain more in-depth, school-specific information.

A bachelor's degree is not required to apply and enroll in most DVM programs. If you satisfy the prerequisite requirements, you may be eligible to apply after only two years of undergraduate schooling. This scenario is infrequent since the process is competitive, but it is not impossible with enough AP credit and upper-division coursework.

Veterinary medicine schools in the United States and Canada are almost all four years in length. Typically, the process includes three years of nonclinical or didactic instruction and one year of clinical training. A few colleges provide a two-and-a-half-year preclinical program followed by a one-and-a-half-year clinical program.

Note: Some students have specific questions about prerequisites. For example, the university may want an upper-division biochemistry class, but their college only offers one that appears as a lower-division class. Another student's college may not offer a class with the same name but with the same content. Thus, students should contact the school directly. This request for clarification may take

---

1   Liaison International, "VMCAS Application Fees and Fee Waivers," *Liaison International,* n.d., https://help. liaisonedu.com/VMCAS_Applicant_Help_Center/Starting_Your_VMCAS_Application/Getting_Started_with_ Your_VMCAS_Application/3_VMCAS_Application_Fees

2   AAVMC, "Veterinary Medical School Admission Requirements (VMSAR)," *AAVMC,* 2021, https://applytovetschool. org/

multiple tries, but be persistent. Eventually, you will get a response.

1. **Review Prerequisite Requirements**

Minimum Prerequisites:

All submitted applications must meet the following basic standards in order to be considered for admission to the School of Veterinary Medicine:

- GPA of 2.5 or better
- Differing hours of veterinary experience (check the website)
- Three expert references, including one from a veterinarian.
- It is necessary to have met all of the conditions (course grades must be a C or better; a grade of C- will not be acceptable.)
- A regionally approved bachelor's degree is not always required.

Keep in mind that these are the basic minimums; competitive submissions will have significantly higher GPAs and experience. International applicants must meet additional criteria.

- A 2.50 grade point average is necessary for admission (on a 4-point scale, A=4). To determine an application's initial ranking, two GPAs are used:
- BCPM (Biology, Chemistry, Physics, and Math) GPA. This BCPM GPA includes all science courses as deemed by VMCAS.
- Through the last 45 semester/68 quarter units, GPA should include any graded courses taken but not limited to undergraduate, graduate, or prerequisite courses.

UNDERGRADUATE PREPARATION

- Most veterinary colleges in the United States do not require a bachelor's degree.
- It is critical to maintain high grades in veterinary school prerequisites. However, maintaining a 4.0 throughout your undergraduate years is not required.
- Finish the prerequisites at a pace that allows you to maximize your learning and GPA while engaging in non-academic pursuits such as extracurricular activities, employment, volunteer work, clubs, research, and animal/veterinary experiences.
- There are no standard prerequisites for veterinary colleges. The AAVMC Veterinary Medical School Admission Requirements (VMSAR) website (applytovetschool.org) or the veterinary school website are the best sites to look up prerequisite requirements. As a guide for applicants, AAVMC maintains a requirements chart, which is available online.

- Advanced degree – Applicants frequently obtain an advanced degree to increase their scientific knowledge, develop research skills, or raise their GPA.
- The holistic review process places a premium on recent academic courses.

ADMISSIONS STATISTICS

Once you picked out vet schools that have the type of learning meeting your criteria, focus on small/large animal, coursework, costs, and other factors, dig into the probability of your application.

How are admissions applications assessed?

Supplementary applications are examined after they are filed to ensure that they are complete and eligible. Any applications that are missing application materials or do not match the eligibility requirements (i.e., a minimum GPA, veterinary experience hours, and one eLOR from a veterinarian) will be rejected.

Step 1: Two GPAs (the most recent 45 semester/68 quarter hours and all scientific courses), the quantitative GRE score, and the total composite scores from the three eLORs are used to rank all complete and qualifying applications.

Step 2: Interviews are held for the top applicants

Step 3: The school's admissions committee will assess candidates' actual experience, including veterinary and other animal experiences, research opportunities, VMCAS essay questions, the personal statement, letters of recommendation, leadership and community service, education, life experiences, and motivation for a veterinary career. These criteria will all be put into consideration during the application review.

Step 4: Students will then be interviewed. Their interview results will be ranked. For example, if the MMI is used, results will be given a score at the end of the MMI interview process. The admissions committee will get together to talk about the MMI results. The dean will discuss an initial ranked list of the best candidates based on expected class size (those offered admission) after which candidates further down the list, but still on the list, will be waitlisted.

SCHOOL SELECTION CRITERIA

To refine your list, you must determine the criteria that are most important to you. These may include clinical opportunities, research, faculty, tuition, location, size of the student body, difficulty of classes, and many other factors. Make a chart of the factors that are most important to you and investigate these on VMSAR and each school's website.

FOLLOW UP

- Check the status of your application materials in the applicant portal.
- Check your email communication for important updates or requests.
- Follow up with any application issues prior to the application deadline.
- Indicate a minimum of three recommenders.
- Follow up with each recommender to ensure that they submit the recommendation by the deadline.
- Submit transcripts for all coursework directly to VMCAS.
- Send GRE scores to VMCAS using the appropriate GRE code.
- Communicate per the ideals and principles of the veterinary profession.
- Applicants to vet schools are expected to conduct themselves in a manner that demonstrates responsibility.
- Exhibit a high level of professionalism, integrity, good judgment, and potential.
- Take ownership of all aspects of the application and admissions processes.
- Review the admissions requirements and application procedures for both VMCAS and each designated vet school.
- Communicate with both VMCAS and admissions officers in a professional and timely manner.
- Provide all required information on the VMCAS application.
- Complete the VMCAS accurately and by the application deadline.
- Provide all required information on the supplemental applications accurately and by the school-specific deadlines.
- Log into the VMCAS application to check for important messages.
- Notify each admissions office if you do not plan to attend a scheduled admissions interview.
- Respond to admissions offers by the April 15th Common Reply Date.
- Contact vet schools that you have decided not to attend.

"

"There are two ways
of spreading light: to
be the candle or the
mirror that reflects
it."

– Edith Wharton

CHAPTER 29

INTERNATIONAL MEDICAL EDUCATION

P rospective veterinarians should know that several universities outside of the U.S. offer options worth considering. If you are fluent in a language other than English, you have even more choices. However, many of the accredited foreign universities are English-speaking as in the U.K., Australia, New Zealand, St. Kitts, Granada, and all but one in Canada.

North American vet schools outside the U.S. offer potential options for training. While countries worldwide train veterinarians, not all are accredited by the American Veterinary Medical Association (AVMA) Council on Education (COE). Check the accreditation status to determine whether the level of education can be translated to U.S. education.

Nevertheless, many vet schools abroad are accredited by the American Veterinary Medical Association (AVMA). The hurdles that must be overcome translating education for medical school are not the same for vet school. Veterinarians trained in an AVMA-accredited university may practice in the U.S.

However, those studying at non-accredited foreign universities have the additional hassles of testing, certification, and fulfilling equivalency requirements before being eligible. Transferability of credentials requires the Program for the Assessment of Veterinary Education Equivalence (PAVE) and the Educational Commission for Foreign Veterinary Graduates (ECFVG) certification program.

U.S. ACCREDITED FOREIGN UNIVERSITIES

West Indies

Ross University (St. Kitts) St. George's University (Grenada)

Mexico

Universidad Nacional Autonoma de México (Federal District)

Canada

University of Calgary (Alberta) University of Saskatchewan

University of Guelph (Ontario) Université of Montréal (Quebec)

University of Prince Edward Island

The United Kingdom

University College Dublin (Ireland) University of Glasgow (Scotland)

University of Edinburgh (Scotland) University of London (England)

Oceania

Murdoch University (Australia) University of Sydney (Australia)

University of Melbourne (Australia) Massey University (New Zealand)

University of Queensland (Australia)

Europe

State University of Utrecht (The Netherlands) VetAgro Sup (France)

APPLYING TO CANADIAN VET SCHOOLS

Only one out of every six applicants to Canadian vet schools are accepted. The probability decreases for students from the U.S. Part of the reason is that there are only five vet schools in the entire country. While they do accept international student applicants, it is highly competitive. Furthermore, at the University of Montreal, you must be fluent in French.

The following universities accept applications on VMCAS for U.S. students but require that Canadian applicants apply to the school directly and do not accept the VMCAS.

- University of Guelph-Ontario Veterinary College (Canada)
- University of Prince Edward Island - Atlantic Veterinary College (Canada)

- University of Saskatchewan – Western College of Veterinary Medicine (Canada)

As with other vet schools, detailed information may be found either on the institutional websites or within the Veterinary Medical School Admissions Requirements (VMSAR) utility.

Like their American counterparts, Canadian vet schools often require interviews before extending an offer of admissions. There is little difference, if any, between the two countries when it comes to their interview objectives and processes. Anyone from the U.S. considering a Canadian vet school should know that they are statistically more likely to be admitted to a U.S. institution. Canadian vet schools give preference to Canadian residents. Also, do not overlook the obvious challenges inherent in attending a program in another country.

Keep in mind that the adventures gained through international study come with their own unique set of challenges. The crossing of international borders is regulated. Differences in policies, teaching styles, and methodologies can be fraught with hassles. Also, world affairs can cause disruptions depending on the geopolitical context and, as evidenced by the COVID-19 pandemic, the state of public health.

A U.S. passport does not constitute sufficient documentation for a U.S. resident to attend vet school in Canada. A study permit must be acquired once you accept an offer. Background checks are often required as well.

For students who are not proficient speakers and readers of French, living in parts of Canada may stretch the comfort zone, particularly at the University of Montreal, where the language of instruction is French. The extent to which French is employed, both in the public square and the classroom, will depend on the school's province.

When the time comes for you to look ahead to your veterinary medical employment, licensure and its requisite testing will become common threads of conversation. As implied earlier in this passage, a U.S. student at a Canadian vet school should have no trouble acquiring a license to practice in either country. Still, the student should understand that the path to licensure might vary from that of other classmates.

Finally, Canada's top-ranked veterinary medical university and one of the top ten vet schools in the world is the University of Guelph's Ontario Veterinary College (OVC) based on the Quacquarelli Symonds (Q.S.) university rankings.

CANADA'S VETERINARY MEDICAL COLLEGES

Quebec

Université de Montréal

Saint Hyacinthe, Quebec, Canada J2S 7C6

http://www.medvet.umontreal.ca

Alberta

University of Calgary

Calgary, Alberta, Canada T2N 4N1

http://www.vet.ucalgary.ca

Ontario

University of Guelph

Guelph, Ontario, Canada N1G 2W1

http://www.ovc.uoguelph.ca

Prince Edward Island

University of Prince Edward Island

Charlottetown, Prince Edward Island, Canada C1A 4P3

http://www.upei.ca/avc

Saskatchewan

University of Saskatchewan

Saskatoon, Saskatchewan, Canada S7N 5B4

http://www.usask.ca/wcvm

VET SCHOOLS IN THE UNITED KINGDOM

In many cases, the admission process for U.S. vet schools is different than it is abroad. Additionally, there are variations in how universities operate, tuition, fees, living, lectures, relationships with professors, etc. There are U.S. accredited vet schools in the United Kingdom. While their curricula must conform to U.S. standards, aspects of their methodology are dissimilar.

Admission requirements for veterinary medical colleges in the U.K. are comparable to the U.S. They seek candidates with a wealth of experiences, strong academics, and well-rounded interpersonal and leadership skills. However, there is a major difference in vet school admissions prerequisites and the length of time to earn a degree.

First, veterinary medicine in the U.S. is a graduate-level course. This means that applicants have most often completed an undergraduate degree emphasizing the sciences, though admissions requirements differ for each university.

However, this is not the case in the U.K. Unlike in the U.S., U.K. residents can apply to vet colleges after high school graduation, starting from the age of 17.[1] When they do, they must complete only five years of vet school as opposed to eight (BS and DVM) that is typically done in the U.S. As a result, U.K. vet training can be appealing.

---

1   Uni Admissions, "Minimum Age Requirements to Study Medicine UK," *Uni Admissions,* n.d., https://www. uniadmissions.co.uk/application-guides/minimum-age-requirements-to-study-medicine-uk/

While this is a plus for those eager to study vet medicine in the U.K., there are rules. For most U.K. vet schools, foreign applicants must earn the top scores in AP and IB exams. Cambridge University requires that students score five on five AP tests in relevant subjects.

In the U.K., applicants with significant experience working with a veterinarian stand a higher chance of getting accepted due to the importance placed on work experience. Some schools in the U.K. also offer foundational classes for students who do not meet the admissions requirements. Sadly, this option is only available to U.K. residents.

A four-year accelerated option is available to students with a bachelor's degree. Universities such as the Dick School of Veterinary Studies and the RVC offer this option.

Another important difference between vet schools in the U.K. and the U.S. is the cost. Generally, the tuition for vet medicine is shockingly high. Americans attending vet school in the U.K., scaled down from the 7-8 years demanded by U.S. vet schools to 5 in the U.K., saves the graduated DVM thousands of dollars.

Further, when four-year courses in universities and colleges in the U.K. were compared with those in the U.S., results showed that their tuition fees were cheaper in the U.K. with a significant price difference.[2] However, students studying vet medicine in the U.K. face cultural differences.[3] Though living in an entirely different environment has its perks, such as meeting new people, trying new things, diversity, etc., it can take quite a lot to settle down in a new environment with unspoken rules.

NON-U.K. EUROPEAN VET SCHOOLS

Studying internationally, outside of the U.K., could be even more challenging for U.S. students. Unlike the U.K., most European countries do not have native English speakers. As a result, applicants seeking admission to vet schools in Europe outside the U.K. will find it more difficult. Language is bound to come up as students may have a hard time trying to communicate. This could happen in the supermarket, asking directions, or simply finding the right room or class. Other

2   Jane Playdon, "How Much Does it Cost to Study in the UK?," *Top Universities,* Updated April 21, 2021, https://www.topuniversities.com/student-info/student-finance/how-much-does-it-cost-study-uk

3   Felix von Wendorff, "Top 5 Challenges of Studying Abroad," *Top Universities,* Updated May 25, 2021, https://www.topuniversities.com/blog/top-5-challenges-studying-abroad

challenges include not knowing what books to buy or where to go and even feeling homesick. As a result, this can discourage some native English students even though tuition in Europe is more affordable.[4]

As a way of helping international students who are native English speakers, most vet schools in Europe have included a crash course in the local language to help international students quickly acclimate.[5] For students who feel lost during lectures, asking for help or discussing challenges with the lecturers is a good step to ease uncertainty.[6]

Studying veterinary medicine outside the U.S. comes with the benefit of having a wealth of international experience, which is why the costs are often worth the risks despite the many challenges involved. Today, employers look for well-rounded students and those who can bring diversity to the workplace.

Vet students studying outside of the U.S. gain experience from another perspective. They become more independent and confident. Another advantage of school in Europe, especially in a part of the European Union (EU), is that the student gets rewarded with an internationally-recognized diploma offering opportunities to work in any country.[7]

AUSTRALIA & NEW ZEALAND

Two countries that should not be overlooked for vet school are Australia and New Zealand. First, there are lots of animals in those countries. Second, there is a significant cattle industry. Third, there are more exotic animals that students are unlikely to treat if they study in the U.S. Thus, Australia and New Zealand are excellent options for locations to study veterinary medicine.

Most vet schools in Australia and New Zealand operate like those in the U.K., where students begin at the undergraduate level, though there are a few graduate entry programs. These programs tend to be less theoretical and more hands-on with clinical activities from the start of your training. Most programs do not focus

4   Study.eu Team, "Study in Europe for Free (or Low Tuition Fees)," *Study.eu,* Updated April 1, 2020, https://www.study.eu/article/study-in-europe-for-free-or-low-tuition-fees

5   Think Poland, "One Year Polish Language Course in Poland, Warsaw," *Think Poland,* n.d., https://www.thinkpoland.org/en/one-year-polish-language-course.html

6   Inter HECS, "Study Veterinary Medicine in Europe," *Inter HECS,* 2017, https://www.interhecs.com/news/study-veterinary-medicine-europe

7   Study.eu, "7 Reasons Why You Should Study in Europe," *Study.eu,* February 26, 2017, https://www.study.eu/article/7-reasons-why-you-should-study-in-europe

on small or large animals but cover the breadth of animal life. With top-notch facilities and faculty, most of the programs are AVMA accredited.

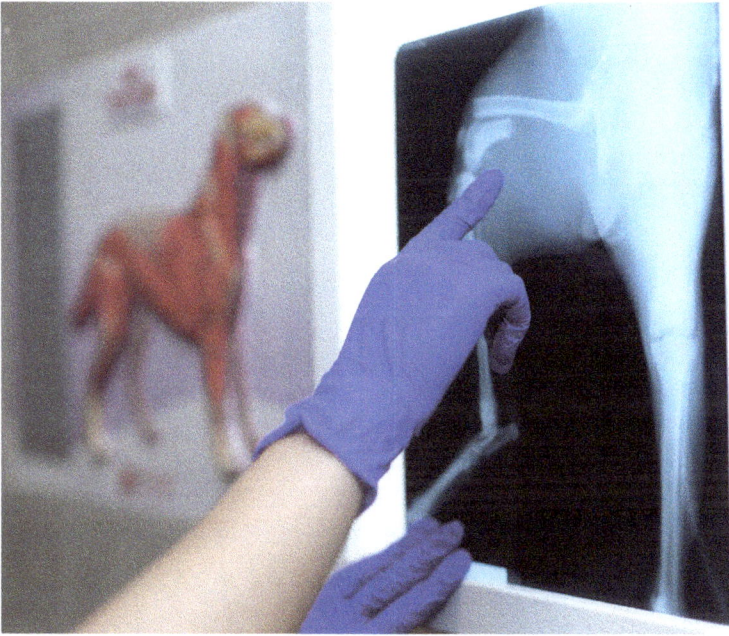

" *"If you pick up a starving dog and make him prosperous, he will not bite you. This is the principal difference between a dog and man."*

– Mark Twain

CHAPTER 30

VMCAS AND TMDSAS APPLICATIONS

APPLICATION SERVICES – VMCAS & TMDSAS

A key step on your path to becoming a veterinarian is to prepare your application to vet school.

The U.S. has thirty-three accredited veterinary medical colleges. There are five in Canada (the Ontario and Atlantic Veterinary Colleges; the Western College of Veterinary Medicine; and the faculties of veterinary medicine at the Université de Montréal and the University of Calgary).

The American Association of Veterinary Medical Colleges (AAVMC) also represents four departments of veterinary science, three departments of comparative medicine, one animal medical center, and fifteen international colleges of veterinary medicine. The AAVMC promotes teaching, research, and service activities on the national and international level.

The AAVMC sponsors the Veterinary Medical College Application Service (VMCAS), which serves thirty-one U.S. veterinary medical colleges, three Canadian veterinary medical colleges, and eleven international veterinary medical institutions.[1] The Texas Medical and Dental Schools Application Service (TMDSAS) is used for the two Texas vet schools, Texas A&M and Texas Tech.

---

1   AAVMC, "Home," *AAVMC*, n.d., https://www.aavmc.org/

TMDSAS DEMOGRAPHIC DATA

For the 2020 entering class, the TMDSAS demographic data show that there were 739 applicants with 161 accepted. Regarding gender, 81% of the applicants were female; the same percentage of females admitted for fall 2020. As for residency, 80% of the applicants were from in-state, though 88% of the accepted students were in-state residents. The average age of the accepted students was 22-years-old and 7% were non-traditional admits. The overall GPA of applicants was 3.51 and the overall GPA of admitted students was 3.74. The BCPM (Biology, Chemistry, Physics, and Math) GPA was 3.41 for applicants and 3.70 for those admitted.[2]

TMDSAS FEE

TMDSAS charges a $200 flat fee payable by credit card. TMDSAS does not offer students the chance for a fee waiver.

VMCAS AND TMDSAS DATES AND SUBMISSION

The Veterinary Medical College Application Service (VMCAS) and the Texas Medical and Dental Schools Application Service (TMDSAS) are user-friendly methods for applying to veterinary medical schools. These applications have numerous parts. While the applications may seem daunting, they are far less so than completing an entire application and submitting each one separately as was once required.

VMCAS – Application for U.S. vet schools
Application opens January 21st
First day to select programs - May 12th
Application due September 15th

TMDSAS – Application for Texas residents applying to Texas vet schools
Application opens May 3rd
First Submit May 17th

The Veterinary Medical College Application Service (VMCAS) serves as your centralized application processing service to apply for veterinary medical colleges. In this location, you will complete one application, fill out your personal

---

2   TMDSAS, "Veterinary School Applicants 2020 Entering Year Final Statistics," *TMDSAS*, 2021, https://www.tmdsas.com/docs/stats/Final-Statistics-Report-Veterinary-EY20.pdf

information, input your coursework, complete your essays, and send your required materials to multiple schools. VMCAS will process your application, verify your information, and send the information to the schools you designate.

VMCAS will not make recommendations. All decisions regarding your admission will be done by the individual schools. However, there are tools for you to use, like Veterinary Medical School Admission Requirements (VMSAR), to help you make good decisions regarding prerequisites, admissibility, and past student results.

You should also go to each veterinary medical college website to become familiar with each school's admissions requirements and processes.

EXPERIENCE

On the application, you will provide your veterinary medical experiences as well as your other extracurricular activities. Begin by preparing an exhaustive list of organizations you have joined, accomplishments you have made, and service projects you have performed. Document these on a chart or Excel spreadsheet with the dates, hours, experiences, accomplishments, and what you learned from the experience. Note the names of individuals who might write reference letters.

- Which of these were most meaningful to you?
- What moments impacted your appreciation for these activities?
- Did you provide leadership in the overall group or any subset, like a speaker event, social, or newsletter?
- What did you learn about yourself during the research process?

Work experience in the veterinary field under the supervision of a veterinarian is an essential demonstration of your commitment to veterinary medicine. You will discover your fortitude and dedication to veterinary medicine while participating in the career you plan to enter. Furthermore, you will demonstrate work ethic, dedication, commitment, responsibility, communication skills, and leadership potential. Shadow veterinarians in different areas of veterinary medicine: large and small animals, large and small clinics, emergency animal medicine, farm animals, etc.

Other avenues for hands-on experience with animals include volunteering at shelters, 4-H clubs, zoos, therapeutic riding facilities, wildlife centers, animal rescue facilities, and farms.

Collaborating on research with a faculty member offers you the chance to understand scientific discovery from a different viewpoint. No doubt, you will read journals or articles on cutting-edge research throughout your career. Knowing the procedures, processes, and can be invaluable to your future while at the same time demonstrating that you can work with people from different backgrounds. You may ask your research advisor to provide one of your recommendations.

APPLICATION PROCESS

When you apply through VMCAS or TMDSAS, you submit a personal essay responding to your professional aspirations and personal characteristics. There are typically word or character limits for the personal statement, activity descriptions, and supplemental essays. Note each of these.

Though this process may seem overwhelming, take your time, and step back to consider your reasons for your commitment to animal medicine. What brought you to a career in veterinary medicine?

The following are the step-by-step process for admission into veterinary schools:

GRADUATE RECORD EXAM (GRE)

It is strongly recommended you take the GRE. While exam requirements differ per institution, many will require the test and recommend a minimum score.

What exactly is the GRE?

It is an exam that assesses your verbal, quantitative, and analytical reasoning skills. It is part of your application portfolio used to assess your abilities. You should prepare for the test. The GRE includes verbal, quantitative, and analytical writing components examined as part of the holistic review process, even though only the quantitative score is typically reflected in an application's initial ranking. If you retake the GRE, the highest score will be used. It must be completed within five years after applying to veterinary school.

- **Recommendation Letters (eLOR)**

As part of VMCAS application, applicants must submit at least three eLORs (refer to VMCAS instructions for more information). Make sure you understand the requirements for each school to which you intend to apply. Select evaluators who can illustrate your critical thinking skills, commitment to the profession, and positive attributes. Letters from veterinarians and science professors are preferred by most schools.

Maintain a positive relationship with the veterinarian(s) and professor(s) with whom you interact. At least one eLOR must be from a veterinarian. Veterinarians, professors, researchers, and others may also be used to attest to a deeper understanding of veterinary medicine and/or academic ability.

In your veterinary school application, there are a lot of moving components. If possible, download or log into the application ahead of time so you are ready to tackle each section. Pay special attention to the portions that ask you to upload documents.

- **Language Proficiency**

Unless they have a bachelor's degree from an English-speaking university in the United States, non-native English speakers must take the TOEFL test. Shoot for a score of 105.

- **Your Competitiveness**

Initially, each application is assessed in three areas:

1. GPAs from the most recent 45 semester/68 quarter hours and all science courses
2. GRE score (quantitative)
3. Three e-recommendation letters (eLORs) minimum

Compare admissions statistics, particularly the GPAs and GRE scores. Out-of-state residents' average scores are higher since there are fewer slots available.

- **Application for the VMCAS**

Applicants must use the VMCAS central application system to apply. There are no paper applications available. The VMCAS system must be used to submit all application materials, including GRE scores, academic transcripts, and letters of recommendation.

- **VMCAS Score Reports and Transcripts**

Request authentic transcripts from all of your previous colleges and have them forwarded immediately to VMCAS.

- **Transcripts and Score Reports for the VMCAS.**

VMCAS must verify all submitted applications. This process might take up to four weeks. If you submit your transcripts before the deadline, you will have a much better chance of having your application verified early and making any necessary corrections.

Note: If other materials such as eLORs or test scores are missing, applications that have reached the "verified" status may still be incomplete. Even if you submitted a supplemental application, if your verified application is missing any application materials after the deadline is reached, it will not be considered for admission.

- **VMCAS Application Fee**

VMCAS APPLICATION COST 2022	
# of Programs	2022 Fee
1	$220
2	$340
3	$460
4	$580
5	$700
6	$820
7	$940
8	$1,060
9	$1,180
10	$1,300
11	$1,420
12	$1,540
13	$1,660
14	$1,780
15	$1,900
16	$2,020

Note that VMCAS does not provide refunds under any circumstances. There are no refunds, even if you accidentally choose the wrong school, miss the deadline, or if materials are not received in time. As soon as the payment is submitted, VMCAS is authorized to process materials whether or not they are complete.

August 13th Deadline – If you chose to participate in and pay for the Professional Transcript Entry (PTE) service, ALL required transcripts must be delivered to VMCAS by this date.

Also, note that once the application is submitted, changes to the VMCAS application cannot be made. If there are changes in contact information, these must be sent directly to the designated school(s) with the correct VMCAS ID.

Finally, electronic recommendations must be submitted by the application deadline.

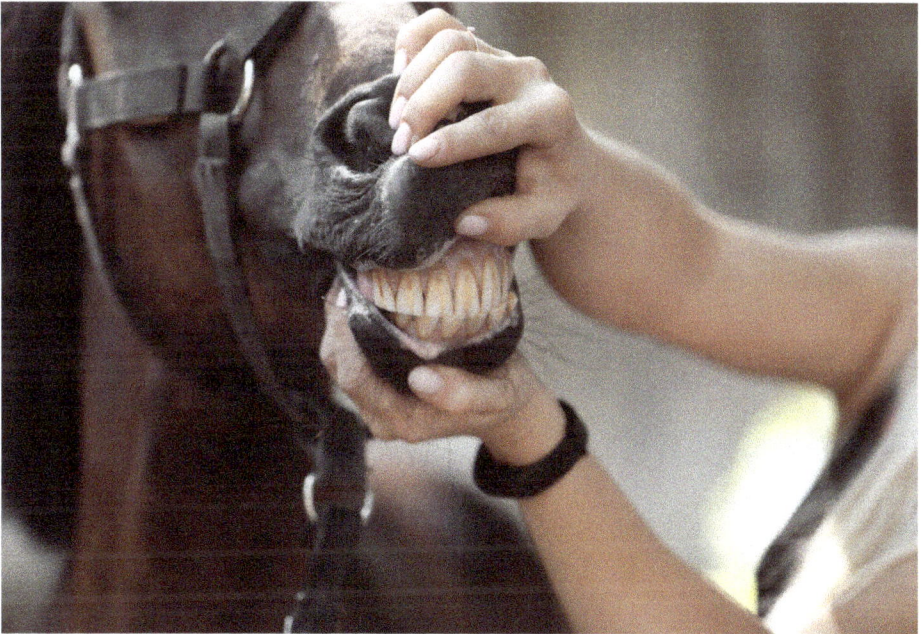

PART 6

THE APPLICATION

"
"If people are doubting how far you can go, go so far that you can't hear them anymore."

— Michelle Ruiz

CHAPTER 31

TELLING YOUR STORY: THE PERSONAL STATEMENT

S tudents pursuing veterinary medicine often spend much of their life around animals. These experiences might have been a dog or cat at home, chickens in a coop, horseback riding, exotic animals at a frequently visited zoo, or their family farm. Your vividly crafted essay is the hallmark of your application which explains your reasons for pursuing this course of study, experiences that led you to this juncture, and your passion for animal science.

PERSONAL STATEMENT

The vet school personal statement clarifies why a student is intent on choosing a career in animal medicine. Applicants writing their personal statement are expected to highlight their values, character, and personality while offering a progression of motivations, interests, and experiences.

1. Common Errors

Applicants are expected to be accurate, concise, and straightforward in their writing. They must avoid wordy sentences and spelling mistakes. Vikki Cannon, the head of admissions and recruitment at the Royal Veterinary College, explains that quality writing is important in vet essays. Though

Cannon argued that bad spelling would not ruin an applicant's admission chances, care should be taken in writing the personal statement since the quality of their essay matters.[1]

Most colleges emphasize that personal essays must be clearly written. Additionally, there are word limits— usually around 5,000 characters (including spaces).

2. Avoid Irrelevant Information

Applicants must ensure that their essays are concise and contain only relevant information. Irrelevant information may affect an applicant's admission chances. Reflect on why you have chosen this career path in vet medicine.

3. Limit the Cliches

Statements like, "I love animals" or "I have always wanted to be a vet since I was…." Admissions representatives know that almost all applicants wanted to be a vet for a long time. This is not new. They are more concerned with what applicants have done.

THE IDEAL PERSONAL STATEMENT

Although there are no formal rules that dictate the contents of a personal statement, nonetheless, admissions representatives are attracted to those statements that stand out. The personal statement is an opportunity to demonstrate your unique traits or qualities and why the university should accept you over other candidates.

Useful Tips

Include why you want to become a veterinarian, the contributions you offer, and specific aspects they appreciate most about animal medicine and healthcare. Below are useful tips and guides that make a definitive personal statement.

1. What led you to consider a career in vet medicine?

Studies were conducted regarding the ideal personal statement. The studies revealed that examiners paid extra attention to why students want to pursue a

---

1   Libby Page, "How to Write a Personal Statement for Veterinary Science," *The Guardian*, January 7, 2014, https://www.theguardian.com/education/2014/jan/07/how-to-write-personal-statement-veterinary-science

career in vet medicine. As a result, applicants must clearly explain their reasons while relaying impactful experiences.

2. What contribution will you make to veterinary medicine?

Admission committees seek intelligent, creative, and passionate students.

3. What are your stand-out achievements?

Describe what you have done that is exemplary, including risks, contests, leadership, and research.

4. What are the other areas of interest?

A typical good personal statement contains hobbies and other areas of interest. Examiners use this to evaluate applicant's capabilities. According to Claire Philips, director of admissions at Edinburgh University's Royal (Dick) School of Veterinary Studies, vet schools look for versatile students who have well-rounded capabilities. In addition to outstanding academic abilities, students should have interests outside work and academics.

5. What veterinary experiences led you to vet school?

Admissions committees look for related, supervised experience. These experiences can be acquired in animal clinics, shelters, veterinarian's offices, or vet hospitals.

AVOIDING PARALYSIS BY ANALYSIS

When the time comes to apply to DVM programs, much of your candidacy profile has already been determined. Your coursework choices have been made, and your grades are a matter of record.

The essay, though--that is the part of the application over which you still have 100% control. Instead of relishing the opportunity to take advantage of that, many hopeful vet students are intimidated by the task. And therein lies the same paradox you probably faced as a college applicant: the ability to write anything makes the task more intimidating than inspiring.

Consider the blank space on your laptop. Do you find yourself threatened or overwhelmed by writing your personal statement? If so, you are not alone. Obviously, there are the 5000 characters you need to generate (approximately 600-800 words, or a couple of double-spaced pages).

However, the source of anxiety around personal statements usually lies in decisions to make about your topic. It can turn into paralysis by analysis, but this is not necessary. Ultimately, you will submit an outstanding personal statement, but the best way to fight off writer's block is to set a more humble intention. Invoking a sports metaphor, start with a solid base hit rather than attempting a home run.

Just think of the essay as a job to be done.

Give yourself a time frame in which you will write a first draft and stick to it. Even if that first attempt is lousy, you will benefit from having written something. You now have a narrative to edit and revise. That assurance can give you the confidence necessary for later effective choices about style, metaphor, and anecdotes.

Your Task:

No matter which application platform you used to apply to your undergraduate school, you probably wrote a personal statement. Your essay was written to meet the same three objectives you have before you now:

1. Articulate your rationale for attending vet school.
2. Demonstrate that you can write clearly
3. Provide evidence of personal qualities which are sought by the vet admisson's committee.

The Rational:

You absolutely, positively must write an essay that convinces the reader that you know what you are getting into, you are certain you want to be a veterinarian, and that you are willing and able to stay the course and succeed. Applicants are understandably most concerned about their admissibility.

It is the burden of the application reader, though, to look beyond the matter of "getting in," focusing instead on the likelihood of graduating from their institution if they do admit you. The same personal statement will be read by admissions personnel at each school to which you apply. Therefore, you should not write anything in your essay which refers to a specific school, e.g., "I have been captivated by the research conducted by Dr. Smith at Big State U."

Your job is more general. You need to make the case that your logical next step is the pursuit of a DVM.

The Most Important Part

Describe the natural consequence of who you are and the experiences which led you to this juncture. The personal statement can be a place to elaborate on information found elsewhere in your application. You tell your story while demonstrating your personality and character.

There is no formula or outline for communicating your "why."

Effective Communication

You must write a clear, grammatically correct, concise, and focused essay. Period.

Getting Help

If you lack confidence in your writing ability, by all means seek assistance throughout the writing process. If you are in college, there are plenty of places where you might find help. Officially, the college's writing center is a traditional go-to, but you can also check with your pre-vet advisor or even seek out a fellow student.

If you are not currently in college and need help writing, go online to find help. Tutoring services abound. If you wish to engage an online writing tutor, be judicious as you browse and make sure the company is reputable. I offer this advice from long years of experience in assisting students in fleshing out ideas and in editing.

Unfortunately, the internet is home to lots of writers-for-hire--that is, people willing to write your personal statement for a fee. If you find yourself on one of those sites, move along. Frankly, authenticity is one of the primary objectives of your writing. Having someone do it for you is a very bad idea. Your essay will suffer for it, to say the least. More importantly, it's the wrong thing to do.

Awesomeness

How do you accomplish the task of selling yourself as a great person? The awkward task of addressing your virtues is difficult for most. "Everyone says I am the nicest person they have ever met." Ick. Instead, adopt the "show, don't tell" approach. How "you do you" can take many forms. It may be conveyed through anecdotes.

You can also influence the reader to pull for you simply by writing from an authentic perspective and sharing your vision or your unique personality traits.

All About Animals:

How does this vet school personal statement differ from your previous college application essays? Despite accomplishing the same objectives as a college admissions essay, your personal statement for vet school will differ in the following ways:

1. Your personal statement must be vet, vet, and more vet. To be sure, your personality should shine through your statement, but not at the loss of focus. Your undergraduate college application essay did not have to be "about" any specific topic. For vet school applicants, though, the personal statement provides your best opportunity for making your case, for articulating the reasons you will be a successful vet student and positive member of their community.

2. Needless to say, your personal statement should reflect the maturity of someone your age and be written with the technical expertise one expects of a college graduate.

3. Explanations of any aberrations, suspensions, or details which might weaken your candidacy should be included in the personal statement.

Two Final Tips:

First, I beg you, please limit the number of people from whom you seek feedback on your writing. Experience has proven to us that, if you show your personal statement to 100 people, 97 will suggest a substantive edit. Adjustments must be considered carefully. If someone suggests, for example, that you include a story for which there simply is no space, you may begin to doubt your own content.

Whatever the case, I suggest that you share you writing with a maximum of three people. Even with just a small number of readers, if you are happy with your statement as it is, let it go. If you got help, Instead of, "Would you please read this and tell me how to improve it?" say, "Finally! I feel great about my personal statement!

Would you mind proofreading it for me? Let me know if you have any significant concerns about the content, but I think I just need a grammar and spelling check." Or, "I have the word count right and included the important points, but if you see an error, I would appreciate it if you pointed that out."

Second, save every draft you write, making a copy of it before opening and renaming another copy for edits or revisions. Just do it. You will appreciate accessing the various drafts when you think your revision may not have been an improvement.

And now, write on!

TEN BRAINSTORMING IDEAS

1. Do you consider yourself compassionate? If so, which experiences have developed that quality in you?
2. If you had to identify one moment when you knew you wanted to be a veterinarian, what would it be?
3. Would your fifteen-year-old self be surprised that you are applying to vet school? Why or why not?
4. What was the most valuable day of your shadowing or vet practice experiences?
5. Which two or three people outside of your family do you consider your vet role models?
6. Has anything unique in your background led you to study veterinary medicine?
7. When was holding your pet, riding your horse, or taking care of the animals on your farm worth a thousand words?
8. If you witnessed an animal in pain, what difference did the veterinarian make?
9. What difference did an animal hospital make to your pet?
10. What would life be like if you did not have a pet?

Share the knowledge you have gained from veterinarians you have met or worked with and how they inspired your pursuit to become a veterinarian.

In conclusion, well-written, relevant, and thoughtful personal statements are important. Allow yours to express yourself and show admission committees why you deserve a chance to be a veterinarian.

"We can judge the heart of a man by his treatment of animals."

— Immanuel Kant

CHAPTER 32

ACTIVITY STATEMENTS, "MOST MEANINGFUL", & COVID-19 ESSAYS

With volunteer experience, research positions, and animal support jobs, most vet school applicants have created a resume or curriculum vitae. During the application process, you will want to revisit that resume and tweak it either for the application or to bring to your interview.

Thus, it is time to draw on that skill set once again. Whether or not a vet school application requires the submission of a resume, you should compile one from scratch or update one that you have.

HIGHLIGHTING YOUR EXPERIENCES

1. You will find it handy to have an updated resume. You will need to write statements on your activities. Thus, a current, up-to-date list of what you have done and accomplished will prove invaluable as you begin.

   The hardest part of resume creation is jogging your memory to recall important jobs, research, activities, etc. Almost no one can, in one sitting, create a resume that fairly and thoroughly represents key accomplishments and personal attributes.

2. Tweak your resume to demonstrate reasons why you are an

excellent vet school candidate. "Sleep on it" to recall important pieces of information initially omitted. And once the vet school application is online and ready for your entries, the clock will be ticking. Prepare your resume well in advance.

3. Unless instructed otherwise, have your resume with you during vet school interviews. Depending on the interview format, your resume can serve you well. Faculty members or admissions officers may reference what you included during your time with them. They may also be more likely to ask you about topics you enjoy discussing and arenas where you most easily shine.

4. Resume maintenance is a best-practice skill that you should develop each year. You never know when you will need a current resume.

5. Consider your resume one of your indispensable tools of success. Even thriving veterinarians with no plans to make a professional move will benefit from regular updates to their resumes.

6. Milestones and continuing education components of a career are tough to remember if not recorded frequently. You do not need to update your resume every time you complete a class, but you should make a note about any developments or additions to your body of knowledge.

7. Keep those events in a folder, digital or otherwise. Then wait until a convenient time to assess the value of your entries and decide if each deserves a portion of your valuable CV real estate.

8. Let's face it, vet school is a tough academic journey. Vet schools cannot afford to lose any more students to attrition than necessary. They look very closely at your projected ability to stick with the program and do well. Less than half a percent of entering vet school students ultimately drop out for academic reasons. The desire to retain students and pull together a dedicated class is one of the main reasons why supplementary questions ask if you are committed to attending.

9. You will use your compiled lists to write your activity statements, describing what motivated you to pursue that activity, the meaning it has for you, and what you learned from your experiences.

10. Finally, you will be given the opportunity to describe a few activities that are the most meaningful to you. Describing these with fuller detail, you might include a relatable, profound, or significant anecdote that resonates with you and may more clearly show the admissions committee your more personal side.

Word to the wise: Be careful not to include fluff on your resume-- activities or accomplishments about which you are not particularly enthusiastic. Examples of fluff, or filler, material are one-and-done community service experiences, clubs for which you did not provide meaningful service or anything that could invite a negative line of questioning.

Most vet schools want to extend offers of admission to students who will accept those offers and attend their school. They need to fill their classes fully with dedicated students who want to live and support animals in that state.

Prepare your materials in a timely manner.

WHAT SHOULD YOU INCLUDE?

Aside from your name, address, contact information, and the basic information regarding your undergraduate experience, your resume should illustrate where and how you spend your time. For this reason, no particular layout or specific sections are recommended. The layout and organization of the resume are a function of your life and experiences.

A strong pre-vet resume includes evidence of the following:

- Demonstrate your persistent effort to stick to a sport, hobby, service activity by including those that show your long-term commitment.
- Be mindful to include any honors earned (academic or otherwise) as well as any details which underscore your strong academic ability.
- Animal experience should be a highlight of your resume. Since you have spent considerable time around veterinarians and vet offices, be sure to include and describe those areas where you solidified your decision to pursue a DVM.
- You should highlight your compassion for and commitment to animal health through your service activities and work experience.
- Show your diverse experiences and commitment to diversity through your action. Also, demonstrate that your uniqueness offers diversity to the entering class.

DESIGNING YOUR RESUME

Now, how do you display this information in written words?

Thank you, technology!

As you may know, almost all word processing software provides free resume templates. Look through the templates on Microsoft Word or other sites to see which one fits your experiences or best highlights your strengths.

Websites like Canva offer hundreds of formatting options, including many at no charge to the user.

Rule of Thumb: Focus on substance without forsaking style. A visual display of your qualifications is easy to read and clearly laid out.

Exert your brainpower on articulating and clarifying your resume's content. However, all that work should be easily digestible from the document itself. It should be well-organized and easy to read and understand. If you are not proficient at design or word processing, find a friend with a knack for resume design and ask them to give you a hand.

Important to Note: In this digital age, you may choose not to include your address.

It is not uncommon to take the address on your resume and put the information into Google to get details about your home that may prejudice the process. Demographic territories, socioeconomic background, and other information are readily available from an address.

Check it out on Zillow if you have not perused this before. Furthermore, that is not the only site that reveals more than you want others to know about you.

That is a note of caution from admissions, faculty, and students who have gleaned impressions – right and wrong - about students.

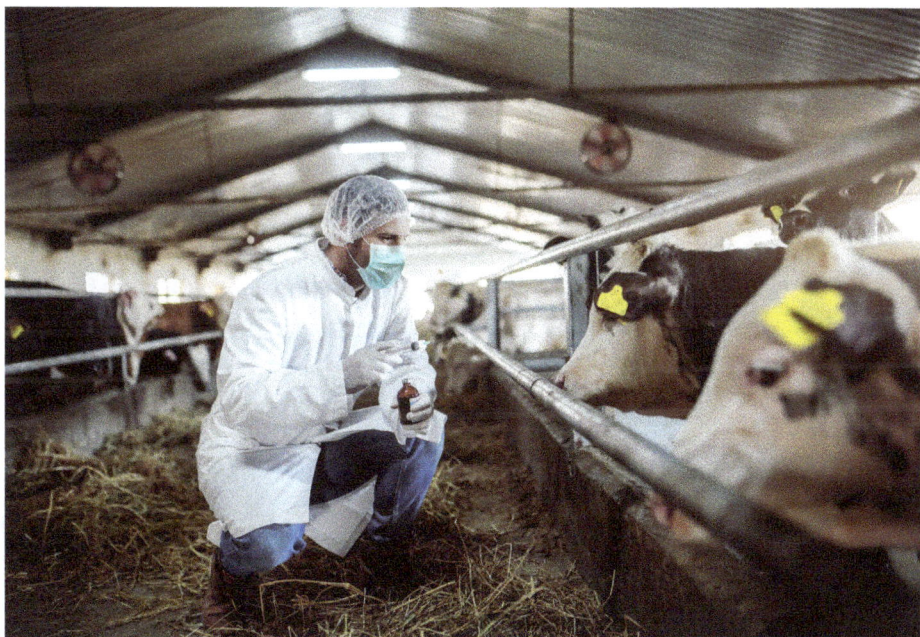

"If having a soul means being able to feel love and loyalty and gratitude, then animals are better off than a lot of humans."

– James Herriot

CHAPTER 33

SECONDARIES

M ost schools have additional essays specific to their school, called secondaries. Secondaries are a crucial part of the application process. These are tailored questions to the school which allows applicants to express why they are suitable for the program. Secondaries are similar to personal statements. However, they are comprised of a series of questions applicants are required to answer, just like questionnaires.

According to Vikki Cannon, the head of admissions and recruitment at the Royal Veterinary College, these questions ensure that students meet the minimum work experience requirements and clarify their experiences.

Be specific. Generic answers are those that any applicant could write and do not reveal anything about you. What is specific to you?

Also, the school may ask why you chose to apply to their school. Do your research. Look up information about the vet school to demonstrate why that vet school is a perfect fit for you and why you are a perfect fit for them. Using college buzzwords is not enough. Not only that, but every other busy pre-vet student hones in on the same buzzwords without doing adequate research.

Imagine if the tables were turned and you were to read a dozen essays from students who "BS-ed" their way through the question. Remember that you need to stand out from thousands of other applicants. Writing what you think the school wants to hear or some mash of buzzwords will not get you to your goal.

How you respond is a determining factor as to whether you get an interview. Keep your eye on the prize. Your goal is to get the interview, receive an acceptance letter, and complete vet school.

MANAGING NUMEROUS ESSAYS

You need to be highly organized. One way of managing the time crunch between school, activities, and essays is to research the vet schools ahead of time and make a chart of specific institutional philosophy, programs, classes, lectures, examinations, vet boards, clinical opportunities, organizations, and community-building activities.

Beware that online forums may be biased or even untrue. Read information from the vet school and talk to students who attend if that is possible. Especially now, with the changes in vet student education during the pandemic, a current representative's take on education is better than five-year-old forum responses. If you cannot find a current student or cannot visit in person to meet students, the next best option is through the alumni network. Some of these are even published online, or you can locate people through LinkedIn.

Secondaries can be difficult. Applicants can find the questions strange. Some secondary applications contain short questions, while others ask candidates to submit up to four full-length essays.

Remember, only a few essays are truly "Optional".

COMMON SECONDARY QUESTIONS

Secondary applications vary from one vet school to another. They require students to answer a series of questions regarding their interest in the vet profession.

Some common secondary questions include:

1. Why are you interested in veterinary medicine?
2. What self-education, research, or independent work have you done, and what do you feel you have accomplished in this work?
3. Briefly describe a situation where you had to overcome adversity; state the lessons learned and how you think it will impact your career as a veterinarian.
4. Select one non-academic experience and describe in a brief essay how it impacted your decision to enter vet school.

5. How would you add to the diversity of our school?[1]

6. Discuss a time when you did something out of your comfort zone. What were the challenges? What did you learn?

7. Describe a challenging situation you have had to overcome?

8. If you could tell the admission committee one thing about you, what would you want to make sure they knew?

9. If you previously applied, what have you done since the last cycle?

10. If you have already graduated, what have you done since then?

FIVE SIMPLE TIPS FOR COMPLETING SECONDARY APPLICATIONS

1. Study Ahead.

A vet student shared his experience about how he finally gained admission into vet school. He said that he boosted his chances of getting accepted through reading over the essays of admitted applicants.

2. Briefness and Accuracy

Applicants must be succinct in their secondaries. Although most vet schools limit students to a word or character limit for the secondary essay questions, applicants must ensure the answers are accurate, straightforward, and brief. Questions can be controversial and may require more time for applicants to answer.

3. Organization

Organization is a critical component of writing secondaries.

4. Prioritize Secondaries.

Applicants need to recognize the importance of secondary applications and why they should be among the highest priorities. Applicants must understand that their chances of getting an interview invitation are slim without carefully constructed secondary essays.

5. Get Feedback

Getting valuable feedback can help you produce better essays. Have your pre-

---

1   Ali Lotfi, "3 Med School Secondary Application Questions," *U.S. News & World Report*, August 25, 2020, https://www.usnews.com/education/blogs/medical-school-admissions-doctor/articles/2018-07-17/how-to-answer-3-medical-school-secondary-application-questions

vet advisor look over your essays or go to your school's writing center. A second proofreader is invaluable. Clarity is vital as it reflects good communication skills.

6. Practice

Applicants should go over essays of people already in vet school, reviewing these to contemplate their vet school journey.

THE DIVERSITY ESSAY

Almost all institutions of higher learning value and prioritize diversity. From promotional materials to admissions practices, from the racial distribution of the faculty to the religious organizations on campus, colleges aim to be melting pots, welcoming communities in which students and professors from all walks of life can learn from one another. Vet schools are no exception.

TYPES OF DIVERSITY

Gender

Student veterinarians, as a group, look much different than they did fifty years ago. So do vet school faculty members. Most notable has been the increased presence of women and LGBTQ+ within vet school classes. DVM faculties are slower to change, of course, but are moving in the same direction nonetheless.

Racial/Ethnic

Racial and ethnic diversity tracks more slowly than gender diversity, but vet admissions personnel see pluralism as a critically important institutional objective. Along with the traditional vet school admissions metrics, like average GREs and GPAs, annual results are broken down by ethnic and racial groups. Not only is it important to a university to draw more applicants from diverse backgrounds, but it is also a matter of progress to see how those groups fare in admissions and vet school studies.

Age

Another kind of diversity is age. It is not unusual for someone to discover a passion for veterinary medicine in their thirties or after earning their bachelor's degree.

Citizenship

Many U.S. vet schools include a percentage of international students from across the world. People from other countries introduce differences to the cohort. Language, religion, foods, traditions add variety to the group.

Socioeconomic

A very tough kind of diversity to add is socioeconomic diversity. Because of the costs associated with a vet school degree, DVM-granting institutions face an uphill climb when it comes to diversifying their classes along socioeconomic lines. That said, the veterinary medicine community understands the importance of considering an applicant in the context of their environment and associated challenges.

The VMCAS incorporates opportunities for students to tell their stories. These narratives are appreciated and considered during the evaluation process. The categories above do not cover every kind of diversity among either the public in general or even among vet students. Rather, they are provided to give the applicant a broad lens through which to view the ideal.

WHAT DIVERSITY WILL YOU BRING?

Efforts to diversity higher education are more noticeable on some college campuses than on others. However, it is safe to say that all accredited colleges and universities articulate a commitment to students of all colors, beliefs, and backgrounds. As a part of that shared mission, most prospective vet students will have addressed diversity multiple times during their academic careers.

At some point during the vet school admissions process, the topic will arise. You will either write about it within your secondary essays or you will be asked about it during your individual interviews.

You should consider how you will talk or write about diversity as an applicant to vet school.

Here are a few topics to get you started.

- Consider the "why." What is it about diversity, of any type, which makes it inherently valuable within a community? Give this question some deep thought if you have not encountered it previously. Of course, diversity is beneficial and you should be able to demonstrate your "why".

- Think about how the experiences of the past few years have shaped your thoughts about or appreciation of diversity. What did you think or write about diversity as a high school student applying to college? How have your ideas evolved or matured?

- What makes you diverse? Of course, you are special and wonderful. However, in this context, we mean something different. What about you makes you feel uncomfortably different from your peers, either sometimes or always?

- Have you ever been marginalized by others? When? How? How did you cope with it? How does this part of your story inform your beliefs today?
- List anything tangible you have done to welcome diversity into your community. Were any clubs or groups more "in tune" with diversity?
- Why is diversity important within the field of veterinary medicine?
- Have you participated in any diversity initiatives related to veterinary medicine? If so, list them. Grab a pen and paper or a Word doc.

Write your thoughts about each of the above. Then, sleep on it and return to the questions on a different day, adding more thoughts that have come to mind in the meantime.

What you have to say about diversity is sure to depend on the specific question(s) you encounter along the way and the format in which you can express yourself.

In preparation, do the significant work of self-reflection. Contemplate the hardest questions faced by society. Where do you see yourself within the community? What ideas do you have about how you might improve your environment? Your thoughts about diversity will be valuable to the reader or interviewer.

THE COVID-19 ESSAY

In a perfect world, every vet school applicant applies ahead of time. No students encounter an error message associated with their account and everyone's documents are quickly moved through the verification process. Moreover, vet schools have plenty of time to evaluate their applicants thoroughly.

In that world, the playing field is reasonably flat. Vet schools would not have to worry about inequities or special circumstances surrounding anyone's applications. Also, in a perfect world, there are no pandemics.

Enter 2020. Everything changed as chaos ensued.

For most people in the United States, the wheels came off of our life's vehicles during the second week in March 2020. No one needs a lecture about the deep, wide, and ongoing impact of the COVID-19 emergency, least of all prospective vet students.

First Things First

The value of human and animal life elevated in importance as people died and others suffered.

NOT OPTIONAL!

Every vet school applicant was affected by COVID-19, and it is the right of each applicant to tell their story. The VMCAS offers an "optional" opportunity to contextualize your application in light of the pandemic. In my opinion, it would be a big mistake to skip this opportunity to provide more information about pitfalls along with the good preparation you have planned and/or executed.

Will a lot of applicants tell similar stories?

Sure. But the objective here is not so much being different as it is to make your case and show the reader even more about yourself. You faced and overcame challenges. You have tales to recount.

I promise. Get started! Begin by brainstorming all the ways your vet school plans were threatened by the many changes of 2020 and 2021.

Think categorically, first about the challenges you encountered:

Academic

- How and when did your coursework resume once you were off campus?
- Has your planned coursework been affected?
- How about labs?
- Were your grades affected adversely?
- How did remote learning affect the way teaching and learning happened for you?
- Was your class standing weakened as a function of Pass/Fail policies?
- How did your relationships with faculty mentors change?
- Were you able to prep for the GRE as planned?
- Was/is your exam date unchanged from that which you had anticipated?
- Were you able to study efficiently from your home (or other lodging during the pandemic)?
- Was your research project canceled?

Veterinary Medicine Experiences

- Which vet shadowing or work opportunities were impacted?
- Did you lose a position or were you unable to take advantage of plans for vet experiences?
- Were any other vet-related hands-on experiences postponed or canceled?
- What were telemedicine or tele-vet appointments like?

Environmental

- What were your stressors?
- Did anyone in your life die of COVID-19?
- Did you suffer from the disease?
- Were you quarantined? Did you miss something important like a class or project?
- Did you or your family lose a job or a significant amount of expected income?
- Were your professors unable to keep a stable internet connection or did Zoom cut out?
- Did you face internet problems at home?
- Were your books on campus while you went home?
- Is your family's long-term financial security at risk because of COVID-19?
- Did you have trouble traveling home or returning to school due to financial or other complications?
- Were any family responsibilities at home delegated to you? E.g., care of younger siblings? Cooking? Cleaning?
- Was there a quiet place to study?

Now, reflect on all you have done to prevail, to recover lost time or experiences. Organize your notes into the narrative you want to tell, being mindful to write about your challenges in a matter-of-fact way.

More bluntly: don't whine.

Over and Above

If you provided any solution, hope, or service for your friends, family, community, or neighborhood amidst the COVID-19 quarantines, be sure to include some notes about your efforts and any outcomes.

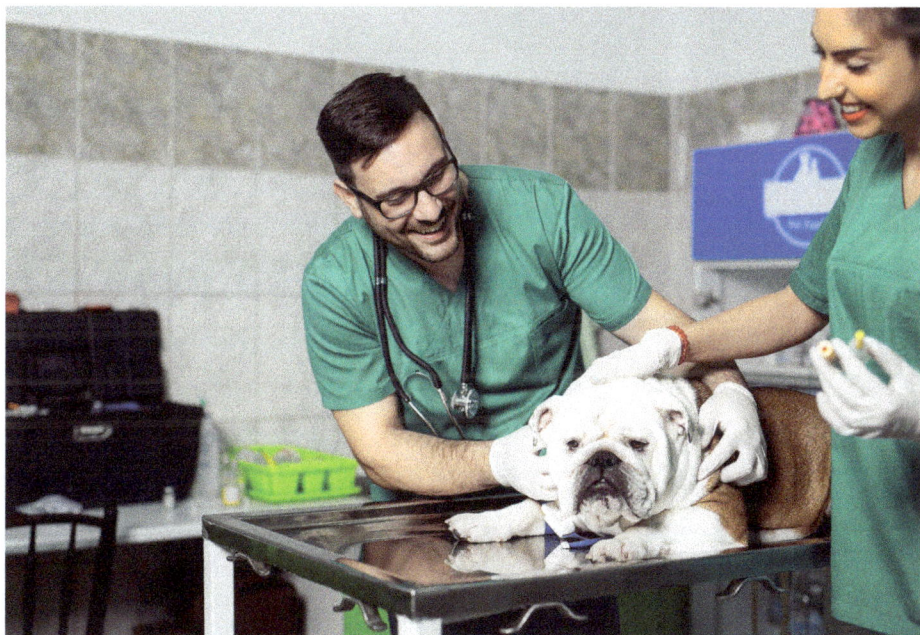

"An expert at anything was once a beginner."

— Helen Hayes

CHAPTER 34

THE INTERVIEW: TYPES, PREPARATION, AND EXECUTION

After investing hundreds of hours preparing your VMCAS, writing and revising essays, and gently reminding veterinarian mentors about submitting recommendation letters, interviews are the next step. It seemed like a full-time job simply to apply to veterinary school. Yet, once everything is submitted, you need to wait.

Every veterinary school has a slightly distinct interview procedure and timeline. Fortunately, many schools describe their interview process on their websites. Begin here to discover what to expect and how to prepare for your next steps. You might also gain interview tips is to ask other students who have successfully interviewed before.

Review popular interview questions in this chapter and consider your responses. Some vet schools have blog entries or articles that answer frequently asked questions.

Know why you want to work as a veterinarian. Admissions representatives seek to discover those who want to go into veterinary medicine versus those who just like animals and are not prepared for the challenges. A love for animals is essential, but the interviewer's job is to ensure that applicants know the harsh realities of both the training and the numerous personal and ethical problems you may confront. Vet schools aim to admit applicants who will be excellent veterinary students and veterinarians.

Some institutions use a panel interview, although more are moving to the Multiple Mini Interview (MMI). Each school conducts the interview process differently. Some have two faculty members interview you, while others have a larger panel consisting of an admissions representative, a faculty member, and a current veterinary student. From school to school, the focus of the interview may differ. Some of your interviewers will concentrate on your experiences, while others will focus on your qualifications.

THE NEXT BIG STEP TOWARD YOUR ADMISSION

Interviews are a big step – one step away from the university's determination about your admissions. However, after you submit your application, by September 15th, your chance for an interview is just around the corner.

What do you want vet schools to know about you? Which of your life experiences are the most relevant?

Determining your fit among their incoming class, admissions committees want to meet you in person. Even so, you may have a virtual 'Zoom' interview. While the essay portion of the application process is very helpful, an in-person meeting is very different in assessing a student's interest in veterinary medicine, experiences that led them to this juncture, and commitment to both attend and persist.

Your character and personality will show through in the interview. This demonstration is critical to the university's professional environment, where you will represent the school and eventually work with their patients. Experienced interviewers use this time to determine your communication style and effectiveness in a professional setting.

PREPARATION

You followed all of the steps, completed the coursework, took your tests, received glowing recommendations, wrote your essays, and applied. Now, it is time to finish off the process with a live or virtual personal demonstration of who you are and why you would be a good candidate for that vet school.

To be prepared for your interviews, you should practice. Get a list of practice questions that might be available online. These will differ by school. However, at first, they may ask basic questions about your interest, drive, intention, motivations, vision, and future.

Since most schools will have multiple mini interviews, read through some practice scenarios. Think through your responses. Calmly think through emergencies and how you would handle them. You might find a partner to bounce ideas off of or to ask you questions.

Make sure you know about that school, their curriculum, the patients they most likely see, and what they value. Read their mission statement. Get there early to ask random people what they think about the school. Know something about that state, the types of animals they typically see, and the caseload. Basically, know why you want to attend that school over all other schools.

Reduce your anxiety by reviewing questions, practicing with someone, and considering what you want to say. Mock interviews are very helpful.

Take the time to practice. This interview is your golden opportunity to achieve what you have worked so hard to accomplish.

- If you are in school, inquire if your school offers practice interviews. Some universities even have career services specialists knowledgeable with medical and veterinary school interviews and can assist you in your preparation.

- Get feedback on how you respond and keep practicing to improve your delivery.

- Get in the habit of answering basic questions. "Tell me about yourself" is notoriously tough for interviewees. Having a prepared response will help you start on the right foot and feel more confident during your interview.

- Recording and playing back your voice can help you hear things like "like" or "uh," as well as give you an idea of how fast or slow you speak.

- Investigate current events and issues in the field to determine your position. Questions about euthanasia ethics, for example, are frequently asked in interviews. When it comes to figuring how to respond to these questions, have a sense of what you would feel comfortable doing ethically as a veterinarian.

- Determine your response to the cost of care, offering life-saving surgeries to clients who cannot afford them, and animal welfare difficulties.

- Prepare a list of what you believe are the most pressing issues in veterinary medicine.

- Finally, familiarize yourself with your own application. What did you say months ago? While this may seem obvious (after all, you were the one who completed those internships and worked those jobs), refreshing your memory is very helpful. The interview can be tense. It is easy to lose track of time or become tongue-tied. You can more successfully explain those aspects during the interview if you read your essay questions immediately before your meeting and remember why they were important to you and your experiences.

QUESTIONS TO PREPARE

It is critical to demonstrate your significant commitment to veterinary medicine. Here are some of the questions your vet school might ask to gauge your comprehension:

- What draws you to a career as a veterinarian?
- What are your experiences with animals?
- What impact do you believe you can have in this field?
- What aspects of veterinary medicine do you find the most fascinating, and why?
- How do you envision your work after graduation?
- What difficulties do you believe veterinarians face?
- What are the advantages and disadvantages of working as a veterinarian?
- How do you envision a typical day in the life of a private practice veterinarian?
- Studying at veterinary school is not simple. How will you manage the workload?
- What, in your opinion, makes a great veterinarian?
- Why did you choose our school instead of another institution?
- What makes our vet school uniquely tailored to your interests?
- Is your academic record a true reflection of your abilities?
- What do you want to be ten years from now?
- Tell me about a period when you had to work closely with your coworkers to keep them engaged. What was the significance, and how well did it work?
- Do you want to work as a veterinarian in a specific field?
- Do you have any ambitions to work in a setting that is atypical?
- Give an example of a time when you were forced to follow a policy in which you disagreed. What happened, and what was the outcome?
- What qualities do you believe a competent veterinarian should possess? When have you exemplified these abilities?
- How well do you work in a group, and can you confidently lead?
- Everyone cares about their pet. How will you demonstrate compassionate care while maintaining a busy practice?

- How would you break the news to an owner regarding a pet's health?
- You want to help everyone, but you do not have the time. What are your priorities?
- What's the most significant distinction between animal welfare and animal rights?
- How do you make sure that your subordinates follow all veterinary practice's legal and clinical protocols?
- What is your organization and time management system?

VET SCHOOL INTERVIEW QUESTIONS - ETHICS

Veterinary medicine has numerous ethical concerns. Thus, working as a veterinarian sometimes necessitates making less-than-ideal concessions. You may be asked a variety of uncomfortable questions in your vet school interview. Respond as honestly and ethically as possible:

- How would you handle a situation when you feel a pet is being mistreated?
- What would you do if you made a mistake that resulted in the death of an animal in your care?
- Would you euthanize a healthy animal if the owners no longer wanted to keep the pet?
- What are your thoughts on euthanasia as a cost-cutting measure?
- Are pedigree breeds' nips and tucks justified?
- Is it moral to kill badgers if it prevents bovine tuberculosis?
- What would you do if someone brought in a sick or injured animal but was unable to pay for treatment?
- What are your thoughts on laws requiring pet owners to spay or neuter their animals?
- Should animal welfare take a back seat to business considerations?
- Would you refuse to treat a sick or injured animal whose owner could not afford it?
- What are your thoughts on live animals being used in veterinary research?
- Exotic animals as pets: Is it a good idea? What do you see as the dangers?
- A client brings a grossly fat dog to your practice. You had previously discussed their pet's nutrition, but the dog is even more obese. What is your communication plan? What will you say to the client?

- Stephanie, your best friend, calls to inform you that she has been rejected for the second time by all of the vet schools to which she applied during the previous application cycle. She invites you to her home to talk about her plans for the future. What would you say in a conversation with Stephanie?

- A fresh theory has been proposed by scientists about cancer treatment. However, they must first conduct clinical trials on 50,000 rats and other animals, many of whom will perish in the process, before moving on to clinical trials with existing cancer patients—assuming the animal trials are successful. How do you feel about this concept? Is it necessary to continue the trials?

WHAT IS THE PROCESS?

You will receive a letter or a call from the vet school letting you know that they think you were worthy enough to get one of their few interviews. This moment is both exciting and uncertain at the same time. Remember, they must have been impressed by something they read or saw in your application. Now they just want to learn a little bit more.

They are inviting you to their campus to get to know you in person. If there is another pandemic outbreak or societal interruption, you may be invited to attend a virtual interview. Respond to the interview request as soon as possible. Pull out your calendar and schedule a time. Do not wait. There are often limited openings. You want a choice of slots.

You might feel nervous. However, you've got this!

Besides, you know you. Be able to answer why you want to attend vet school. The interview gives you the chance to explain your reasons to the committee.

WHO INTERVIEWS YOU?

Your interviewers are either admissions team members or professors in the department who have agreed to participate in the interview process. Vet school professors have a vested interest in ensuring that the class is composed of a collegial body of students who will work well with the other students and, of course, the faculty.

Often alumni or current vet students are available during the interview process to answer your questions as well. The admissions officers may also ask them about their impression of candidates. These responses may or may not be used in the decision-making process.

TYPES OF INTERVIEWS

Each school has a different process. Traditionally, interviews were always on the campus so the college admissions team could see you, greet you, and get to know you more personally. For student interviewees, it was the chance to walk around the campus, get a sense of the environment, meet students more personally, and see the facilities.

However, during COVID-19, few schools had on-campus interviews. Thus, most of the interviews were in a virtual format.

Here are some of the different types of interviews.

Open File Format

As the name implies, your file is open, and the interviewer knows what you submitted in your VMCAS. Often the grades, GRE scores, CASPer results are omitted so that the interviewer is not prejudiced by knowing your admissibility based on the school's quantitative assessment. The interviewer, in this case, is likely to ask questions based upon your application, clarifying what you wrote and getting to know your story in your words.

Closed File Format

In this case, your file is closed. The interviewer does not know what you put on your initial application or your secondaries. You are a blank slate to them. They are likely to explore your interests by asking you general questions and leading to more specific ones. Occasionally, the interviewer will be able to see your file after the interview.

Traditional Interview

In this interview, the interviewer asks the candidate a fixed set of questions decided upon ahead of time. These questions are standardized so that all interviewers will ask the same questions and be consistent. As a result, all interviewers ask the same questions. Thus, while the interviewers might change, the answers can be, in some way, compared to other candidates.

Panel Interview

This type of interview is a typical format whereby a committee of two or three people interview you simultaneously. In this way, they can meet afterward to confer about each candidate and score, rank, or evaluate the interview in some substantive way to provide a recommendation to move forward with the candidacy. One or more interviewers may have seen your file, but the questions are typically from a set of questions defined before the process starts and will not be unique to your application.

Multiple Mini Interviews (MMI)

More colleges are going to the Multiple Mini Interview (MMI) style, though not all schools use this format. In this process, you will proceed from station to station. You will be asked a short format question for that station, or you will be given a scenario, photo, or a case to evaluate and provide a response. Occasionally, you will be asked a follow-up question.

Here are some problem-solving examples:

- Experiments on animals
- Bovine tuberculosis
- Prices of milk
- The fox hunting
- Obesity in pets
- Animal hoarding
- Horse and dog racing
- Camel and elephant riding
- Animals kept under inhumane conditions (e.g., SeaWorld)
- Canine training (Caesar Milan, etc.)
- Dogfighting in a controlled environment
- Race laws and specific legislation on dangerous dogs
- Puppy reproduction
- Breeding goals (e.g., brachycephalic dogs)
- Remedial surgery
- Declawing and docking of the tail and ears
- Control of cats and dogs
- The killing of sharks for their fins

In the Multiple Mini Interview (MMI) process, short, structured interviews provide a robust idea of the student. Schools gain additional information about students' viewpoints, traits, qualities, teamwork, communication skills, and decision-making to quickly assess situations and handle difficult interactions. While not all schools will use the MMI process, and their questions and scenarios will be different, admissions teams are likely to want to get to know students on multiple levels.

In this format, you will be sent to stations whether your interview is in person or virtual. The stations are not long, usually 7 – 10 minutes. Each station will be different.

In one station, the interviewer may ask you why you want to become a veterinarian. This question is fairly typical, and you should be very clear why you have chosen vet school. You might also be asked what skills you have that make you an excellent vet or what skills you are missing?

Time yourself as you prepare to answer the question with time to spare for the interviewer to ask a follow-up question.

In the next station, you might be asked how COVID-19 impacted your education. You know some reasons, but you want to be succinct. Prepare by picking out a few examples that you can explain in a couple of sentences.

You might be asked an ethical question, like, "If your classmate cheated on an exam and you knew about it, what would you do?"

Brainstorm four or five scenarios. For instance, what if you were asked to perform a procedure in an emergency that you studied but never practiced?

What if you knew that the medicine a patient needed was unavailable, and your mentor gave the patient a placebo to reassure them?

What would you say and do if you were treating a patient and you accidentally damaged a body part?

At the next station, you might be given a photo of a veterinarian, climbers on a rugged mountainside, skiers in an avalanche, friends at a beach campfire, or students in a university lecture.

You may be asked what you see, what people are experiencing, or what you think happens next. The answer you give tells quite a bit about how you see the world and its people.

The next station might present you with a video. This station is much like the picture type. You will watch the short video and then be asked by the interviewer to discuss what you saw and what the situation means. The situation may relate to animal care or not.

Next, you might be given a card or be shown a slide with a scenario or vignette with one to two minutes to formulate how you would handle the situation presented before entering the room and sitting down or having the interviewer show up on the screen to hear your answer.

In a similar role evaluation station, you will be asked to play a role. A person will enter the room acting out a part. The person may be confrontational or attitudinal. You must interact with the individual while the 'interviewer' watches your actions and reactions. This exercise aims to see if you can be calm in your communication and handle the situation with a professional demeanor.

The University of Arizona uses the Multiple Mini Interview (MMI). Afterward, students are notified by e-mail whether they are accepted, placed on an alternate list, or not accepted.

UC Davis also uses the MMI. Candidates will have short interviews with dialogue with the interviewer or assessor. UC Davis has a 10-station circuit. The questions are not designed to test the student's knowledge but to understand the student better and determine whether they would be a valuable, contributing member of the UC Davis team. With approximately 240 interviewees who come to the campus in early December, UC Davis seeks to find students who present the qualities of empathy, honesty, and reliability. UC Davis does not have remote interviews.

RIGHT BEFORE THE INTERVIEW

Keep to the schedule.

Try to adhere to your routines on your interview day. If you are a coffee drinker, ensure that you have additional time to have coffee before your interview. If you usually miss breakfast, this moment may not be the best time to decide that breakfast should be your main meal. The same goes for the opposite way around: if you generally eat a large breakfast, allow ample time in the morning to let your food digest.

- Dress to Impress
- For many pre-vet students, getting ready for the interview induces anxiety. Relax. Exhibit your natural professionalism.
- Carefully read the information over regarding the interview. Universities often provide information about the interview style and structure. Read it attentively.
- When you speak, note that any point you make should be backed up with real-life examples. Instead of simply saying, "I have excellent communication skills," give an example of your effective communication in a clinical context.
- Don't overthink what you plan to say!

- Although you should practice questions, and it might be tempting to craft "perfect" responses based on what you believe the interviewer wants to hear, these responses sound contrived and unauthentic. Remember that the interviewer wants to learn more about you, hear about your experiences, and better understand why you chose to pursue a career in veterinary medicine. If you are applying because you have a real interest in the field and have engaged with your work, your responses will be more unique.

- Concentrate on topics or examples that make you feel more comfortable.

- Prepare by reading current news in veterinary and scientific communities. Also, know two research areas that interest you – a disease, cure, or diagnostic methods might be good places to start. Again, this demonstrates your interest beyond your work experience and schoolwork.

DURING THE INTERVIEWS

- Steer the conversation to areas where you are comfortable. You can answer MMI questions to highlight your strengths. Extend your responses to include relevant situations and real-life examples, emphasizing your participation in work experience placements. Avoid bringing up issues about which you have little expertise, and avoid conversational pitfalls.

- Do not be afraid to say you do not know. There's a good chance you will be asked a question in which you do not know the answer. If this happens, admit that you do not know the answer but are willing to offer an educated guess. Interviewers care just as much about how you think as they do about your knowledge.

- Allow enough time for the interviewer to ask questions. While it is essential to consider your answers, do not just keep talking to the interviewer. Interviewers frequently have a list of questions they must ask.

- Prepare questions to ask during the interview process. You will most likely be asked if you have any questions at the end of the interview. Think of at least one question that follows up on what was said or that relates to their specific institution.

VIRTUAL INTERVIEW – 20 POINTS TO CONSIDER

1. **Be Prepared** – Be prompt and seated in front of your webcam 15 minutes before the scheduled interview.

2. **Know the School's Mission** – Read the vet school's website ahead of time.

3. **Quiet and Isolated** – Interruptions can create anxiety. Furthermore, you do not want to be interrupted during your interview. Find a quiet and

private place free from distractions.

4. **Clean and Well-Lit Environment** – The background can be distracting. Construct your environment so that it is clean, neat, and well-lit. A neutral background is best.

5. **Re-Read the Instructions** – Information in the interview invitation may remind you what they require. Prepare for the type of interview (traditional, panel, MMI) they offer and follow their instructions.

6. **Research the Curriculum and Focus** – Prepare for the interview by researching the vet school, know their animal focus, consider current faculty research, understand their philosophy, and get a sense of their academic environment.

7. **Check Your Equipment** – Sound – Camera – Lighting – Background - Make sure your computer, webcam, and Wi-fi are operational. If you choose a background, test how it looks. Ensure that your screen name is your first and last name.

8. **Be Professional** – Your attire should fit a professional job interview- simple, tasteful, and modest.

9. **Time Zone Check** – Since vet schools exist in multiple time zones, match the appointment time to the correct time zone.

10. **Get Enough Sleep** – You are expected to be clear-headed, quick-minded, and at the top of your game. Make sure you have a good night's sleep before the interview.

11. **Remind Roommates or Family of Your Interview** – Share your interview schedule with your roommates or family to avoid issues of someone coming into the room or overloading the Wi-fi.

12. **Mock Interview Practice** – Schedule and participate in a mock interview with your pre-vet advisor or career center staff. Use the feedback to adapt your body language and get suggestions on improving your responses.

13. **Turn Cell Phone Off** – Make sure your cell phone is off or on silent.

14. **Photo ID** – You may be asked to show a photo ID at the interview. Put it next to your computer before you begin.

15. **Smile and Relax** – Sit up straight in the center of the camera's frame and smile. Be calm and speak slowly while making eye contact.

16. **Listen Carefully and Speak Genuinely** – Listen to the interviewer's questions and take your time to answer with an honest, genuine response.

17. **Notetaking and Questions** – If you take notes, write them on a pad next to your computer. The noise of the keyboard and the distraction of typing can be disruptive. Prepare thoughtful questions ahead of time and put them on the pad.

18. **Be Humble, Courteous, and Polite** – Both during the interview and with any communications afterward, be respectful, thoughtful, and responsible. If you promised to follow up, do so shortly after the interview.

19. **Thank You E-Mail** – After the interview, send a thank-you note telling the interviewer(s) that you appreciated their time. If possible, reference something from the interview to jog their memory. With hundreds of interviews, it is hard for the interviewer to remember you. You might put your picture in the signature section of your e-mail to jog their memory.

20. **Be Patient** - You have done your job and sent a thank you. Unfortunately, you now have to wait. However, it is not disrespectful for you to reach out to admissions representatives in a couple of weeks if you have not heard anything.

A FINAL NOTE

Be yourself. Relax. Enjoy the experience. They chose you over other candidates. It's yours if you exude confidence, commitment, and desire.

Know why you want that school.

Go for it!

"You don't have to see the whole staircase, just take the first step."

– Martin Luther King, Jr.

CHAPTER 35

THE HOME STRETCH: UPDATING YOUR APPLICATION

Updates are optional, but they may provide important information.

After you submit your vet school application, you may have updates. For example, you may receive grades from summer or fall classes after your application has been verified, or you might decide to enroll in additional classes in the fall. Note that you cannot change your personal statement or college selections.

However, you might accept a position as a scribe or get a job in a veterinary hospital. On the other hand, an international service organization might contact you with a chance to work in a foreign country for part of the year.

Either way, after you submit your application, your life will continue, and you will have new and meaningful experiences to add to your application.

You do not want to contact admissions repeatedly, but you do want to include any relevant changes or additions to the university's portal. If you have interviewed, provide a monthly update with your status and any new information. This effort shows your continued interest.

Typically, vet schools are more worried that you committed to taking a class and either dropped the course or earned a D or F grade. Make sure you contact the school immediately. Most vet schools will not hold it against you if you take the class again and do well, but they can be unforgiving if you do not inform them of what happened.

Monitor your "Check Status" tab to determine your application status. You want to ensure that your application is up to date with the correct information about how you are progressing academically and what you are taking. Frequently, classes you expected to take are canceled, changed, overlapped, or you chose new courses due to your new interests. Either way, it is helpful to update your application.

One is updating your individual schools with information that is pertinent to your application for admission. The other is updating your schools with a note of your continued interest.

An important note of caution.

Many students are anxious about the application process. Vet school admissions officers could be annoyed by aggressive students. They often have hundreds of candidates they are evaluating and do not have the time for students who repeatedly contact them.

Use your communications sparingly. You want to make sure your schools are aware of anything new and that you are highly interested in their program, but you do not want to contact them every time you start a new activity, win a new award, or get a new certification.

Thus, you want to hold off until you have new activities set.

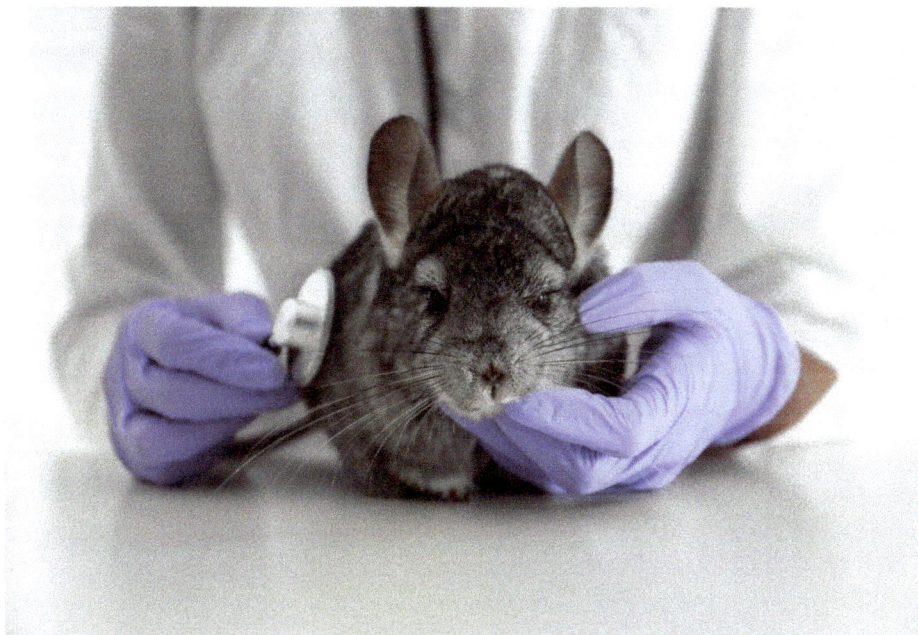

"Wisdom is not a product of schooling but of the lifelong attempt to acquire it."

— Albert Einstein

CHAPTER 36

FINANCIAL AID & SCHOLARSHIPS

Take a look at how much your undergraduate education will cost you. The cost of veterinary medical school varies based on whether you attend a private or public school and if you live in the state. Vet school costs have risen many times faster than the cost of living over the last three decades, as is the case with all higher education costs.

HOW MUCH DOES VETERINARY SCHOOL COST?

In-state vet schools charge less for in-state residents. However, on average, a DVM costs more than $200,000. The anticipated total cost of attendance (tuition + fees + average living expenses) for students attending veterinary school in the United States ranges from $150,000 to $420,000 over four years. The cost of education varies depending on the state or country of residence. Public versus private veterinary school costs can differ widely too. While scholarships can help, most veterinary medical students must borrow money to pay for their education. Furthermore, with student loans, interest ultimately adds to the overall cost of attendance.[1]

Data from the VIN Foundation, a nonprofit that supports veterinary students and veterinarians, suggests that a four-year veterinary school

---

1   VIN Foundation, "Blog | How Much Does it Cost to Attend Veterinary School?," *VIN Foundation*, n.d., https://iwanttobeaveterinarian.org/how-much-does-it-cost-to-attend-veterinary-school/

education costs more than $200,000 for in-state students and $275,000 for out-of-state students. The Association of American Veterinary Colleges tracks resident/nonresident tuition and living expenditures at all recognized veterinary schools.

The following provides the costs at a few in-state and out-of-state U.S. vet schools where the class of 2019 spent the most and least for those expenditures.

These are the most and least expensive vet schools offering a DVM.

Most Expensive Vet Schools Tuition/Living Expenses (2015-2019)

- University of California, Davis - $247,455
- Midwestern University - $402,136
- Ohio State University - $246,885
- University of Pennsylvania - $335,662
- University of Minnesota - $330,642
- University of Florida - $215,400
- Western University of Health Sciences - $326,453
- Michigan State University - $212,923

For the 2026 class, the tuition and living costs for a couple of schools are approximately

Cornell In-State $240,000; Out-of-State $315,000

UPenn In-State $350,000; Out-of-State $390,000

Virginia-Maryland Vet School $180,000 (VA/MD residents); Out-of-State $350,000

Least Expensive Vet School Tuition/Living Expenses (2015-2019)

- Purdue University - $146,815
- North Carolina State University - $194,440
- University of Georgia - $156,971
- University of Missouri - $208,144
- Iowa State University - $158,966
- Washington State University - $218,464
- Oklahoma State University - $163,130
- Texas A&M University - $229,674
- Mississippi State University - $163,341

The AAVMC Cost Comparison Tool compares costs at all 33 recognized veterinary schools in the United States.[2] The cost of the 12 authorized overseas vet school programs is also listed for tuition and living fees. The University of Guelph in Canada is the least expensive

Keeping Vet School Expenses Under Control

Attending veterinary medical school at a public university in your home state is generally the most cost-effective option. Public schools are typically less expensive than private schools, even if students are out-of-state.

If your native state lacks an authorized veterinary program or you wish to attend school somewhere else, you can establish residency, but it is likely to take a full year of receipts and taxes to do so. In addition, the state wants you to demonstrate your intent to stay and ensure that you will contribute to their communities. Still, the money you save may be worth the effort.

Because in-state programs still cost more than $200,000 on average for four years, take the following steps to keep veterinary school costs under control, regardless of where you enroll:

- Look for ways to get free cash like grants, scholarships, and fellowships
- TA or research positions may take too much time and not fit into your schedule. Students in veterinary medicine can get these. For more information, contact your university's financial aid office.
- Save money from summer jobs or income from a business.

According to the Bureau of Labor Statistics, a veterinarian is likely to make almost $100,000 per year.[3] This amount gives you an idea of what you can borrow and how you might pay back the loan. Most U.S. students will use federal loans to finance the costs of a DVM which include income-driven repayment plans.

The following scholarships represent only a small portion of the total number of scholarships available to veterinary school students. Many scholarships are offered by reputable institutions like schools, foundations, or state veterinary associations. Furthermore, for most of the scholarships on this list, a specific scholarship application is required, which is usually submitted through an organization, association, school, or foundation. Details about an applicant's

---

2   AAVMC, "Cost Comparison Tool," *AAVMC*, n.d., https://www.aavmc.org/students-applicants-and-advisors/exploring-the-cost-of-a-veterinary-medical-education

3   U.S. Bureau of Labor Statistics, *"Veterinarians," U.S. Bureau of Labor Statistics*, n.d., https://www.bls.gov/ooh/healthcare/veterinarians.htm

veterinary interests, extracurricular activities, and/or GPA may be required as part of the scholarship requirements.

VETERINARY STUDENTS' SCHOLARSHIPS AND FINANCIAL AID

American Association of Bovine Practitioners

Each year, the AABP offers Bovine Veterinary Student Recognition Awards with $1,500 grants available for a second or third year of study.[4] Academic excellence is used to choose award recipients, interest in bovine medicine, work experience, career ambitions, and recommendations. The deadline for applications is March 15.

American Association of Equine Practitioners & Zoetis Scholarship

Veterinary students planning to work in equine medicine can apply for a $4,000 scholarship from the AAEP and Zoetis. Students apply in their fourth year of study.[5]

American Association of Swine Veterinarians (AASV)

AASV student members may qualify for a $5,000 veterinary school award if they attend the annual symposium's student seminar and deliver a paper.[6]

American Kennel Club

The American Kennel Club offers scholarships to veterinary medical students. In the United States, each AVMA-accredited veterinary school nominates four candidates. Awards are based on academic achievement, enthusiasm in purebred dogs, and financial need. Awards vary from $2,000 to $7,000.[7]

American Veterinary Medical Foundation (AVMF) Scholarships

These scholarships are available to veterinary students in their first three years of education, including a $500 women's award and a $2,500 feline grant. The application deadline is May 15. Additional AVMF scholarships include Zoetis and

---

4   AABP, "AABP Bovine Veterinary Student Recognition Award," *AABP*, n.d., http://www.aabp.org/students/stud_rec_award.asp

5   American Association of Equine Practitioners, "Zoetis Scholarship," *American Association of Equine Practitioners,* n.d., https://aaep.org/scholarships/zoetis-scholarship

6   AASV, "Student AASV Membership Benefits," *AASV,* n.d., https://www.aasv.org/students/

7   American Kennel Club, "AKC Veterinary Network," American Kennel Club, n.d., https://webapps.akc.org/vetnet/#/

Merck.[8]

Bayer Healthcare, LLC

Veterinary students must demonstrate excellent and successful client communication skills by providing video clips of themselves discussing an interaction with a customer. Applicants are eligible for Bayer Excellence in Communication scholarships. More than $70,000 in scholarships were awarded to students at 27 veterinary schools, with regional winners receiving $2,500 apiece.[9]

Cornell University College of Veterinary Medicine

More than 100 scholarships are offered to students attending Cornell's vet school. These opportunities range widely, may be gender-specific, and may apply equally to practicing veterinarians interested in horse science or sheep. Endowments from past veterinary school graduates support Cornell students.

Health Professions Scholarship Program (HPSP) of the United States Army Veterinary Corps

The U.S. Army HPSP offers full-tuition scholarships and monthly stipends to veterinary students who commit to three years of active duty. Applicants must be U.S. citizens and retain full-time status in an accredited vet school. In addition, students must complete other requirements to become a commissioned officer in the United States Army Reserve, including graduation from a U.S. veterinary college and meeting all other requirements.[10]

Merck and The Foundation for the Horse Scholarship

Merck Animal Health and The Foundation for the Horse teamed up to improve the health and well-being of equines by honoring exceptional veterinary students dedicated to equine practice. Five scholarships of $5,000 are awarded based on academic excellence, leadership, and a commitment to equine veterinary medicine.[11]

---

8   American Veterinary Medical Foundation, "Student Scholarships," *American Veterinary Medical Foundation,* n.d., https://www.avmf.org/programs/student-scholarships/

9   AGWeb, "Bayer Launches Bayer Plus Rewards 2021 Program," *AGWeb,* September 28, 2020, https://www.agweb.com/scoop-news/new-products/bayer-launches-bayer-plus-rewards-2021-program?videoId=6265275566001

10 U.S. Army, "Army Medicine," *U.S. Army,* n.d., https://www.goarmy.com/amedd/education/hpsp.html

11 American Association of Equine Practitioners, "Merck Animal Health Scholarship," *American Association of Equine Practitioners,* n.d., https://aaep.org/scholarships/merck-animal-health-scholarship

Morris Animal Foundation Scholarships

The Morris Animal Foundation has created the Veterinary Student Scholars program for veterinary medical students interested in clinical research. Stipends of up to $4,000 may be awarded for original research projects.[12]

Nebraska Veterinary Medical Association (NVMA)

The NVMA awards several scholarships for full-time students who have graduated from a Nebraska high school. Students in their second, third, or fourth year can apply for the scholarship, ranging in amounts.[13]

Ocean State Veterinary Specialists in East Greenwich, Rhode Island

A Compassionate Care award is offered to a first-, second-, or third-year veterinary student who demonstrates an interest in animal welfare, protection, or rights. Rhode Island residents are given priority - college or high school.[14]

Oxbow Animal Health Scholarships

Two $500 scholarships are available from Oxbow Animal Health to study small animal and exotic animal medicine. Veterinary students interested in exotic animal medicine can apply for a $1,000 scholarship. Applications must be postmarked by March 1; winners are announced on May 1.[15]

Pennsylvania Veterinary Foundation

The Pennsylvania Veterinary Foundation awards scholarships to students who are Pennsylvania residents based on demonstrated financial need and expected graduation year. Recipients can attend any vet school in the U.S. Deans of veterinary colleges nominate eligible students.[16]

Race for Education & American Association of Equine Practitioners (AAEP) Scholarships

The Winner's Circle scholarship is offered by the Race for Education in

12 Morris Animal Foundation, "Research Grants," Morris Animal Foundation, n.d., https://www.morrisanimalfoundation.org/grants

13 NVMA, "Scholarship Opportunities and Guidelines," *NVMA*, n.d., https://nvma.org/page/Scholarships

14 Ocean State Veterinary Specialists, "Home," *Ocean State Veterinary Specialists*, n.d., https://osvs.net/

15 Oxbow Animal Health, "Academic Scholarships," *Oxbow Animal Health*, n.d., http://www.oxbowanimalhealth.com/the-oxbow-way/education/academic-scholarships/

16 Animal Care, "Animal Care PA's Veterinary Student Scholarship," *Animal Care*, n.d., https://www.animalcarepa.org/programs/veterinary-scholarship-program/pvf-scholarship.html

collaboration with the AAEP. Third-year veterinary students interested in equine veterinary medicine may apply to pay for fourth-year vet school fees.[17] The amounts range from $1,500 to $5,000. Students must apply to their local Student Chapter of the American Association of Equine Practitioners (SCAAEP). One scholarship will be awarded to each of the 36 SCAAEP jurisdictions.[18]

Rhode Island Veterinary Medical Association (RIVMA)

Veterinary students can apply for a $1,000 grant from the RIVMA to help them finish their final year of vet school. Applicants must have completed high school in Rhode Island.

Saul T. William Veterinary Scholarship

The University of Maryland awards the Saul T. William Veterinary Scholarship for up to $10,000 per year to graduate students. Recipients agree to work for the USDA's Animal and Plant Health Inspection Service.[19]

Simmons Educational Fund Business Aptitude Award

The SEF provides a $3,000 stipend to a third-year veterinary student from each veterinary school in the U.S. Students must submit an original essay about the challenges of running a private practice. One top winner will get a $15,000 prize and a free trip to the North American Veterinary Conference if their essay is considered the best overall.[20]

The Association for Women Veterinarians

This organization awards scholarships from $1,000 to $1,500 to second, or third-year vet students enrolled in a U.S. or Canadian vet school.

Veterinary Scholarship Trust of New England

VSTONE offers scholarships and incentives to students pursuing veterinary medicine in New England. The organization has supported over 500 scholars,

17 Mary Hope Kramer, "Learn About Being an Equine Veterinarian," *The Balance Careers,* Updated December 30, 2018, https://www.thebalancecareers.com/equine-veterinarian-125796

18 The Race for Education, "2021 Scholarships," *The Race for Education,* n.d., http://www.raceforeducation.org/programs/scholarships

19 College of Agriculture & Natural Resources, "Scholarships," *College of Agriculture & Natural Resources,* n.d., https://agnr.umd.edu/admissions/scholarships

20 Simmons Educational Fund, "Making Business Education a Priority," *Simmons Educational Fund,* n.d., https://www.simmonsedfund.org/about-awards

offering $5,000 scholarships to third- and fourth-year veterinary students. One winner will be awarded the scholarship from each of the six New England states.[21]

Western Veterinary Conference (WVC)

The WVC offers 33 scholarships through its Dr. Jack Walther award to DVM students who demonstrate leadership abilities, active involvement, and long-term promise.[22]

A FEW OF THE MANY OTHER SCHOLARSHIPS INCLUDE

Iowa State University Academic Excellence Awards - Nearly $400,000 in awards are given out.

New Jersey Federation of Dog Clubs - New Jersey residents can apply for these veterinary school scholarships.

The North Dakota Veterinary Medical Association offers scholarships to students accepted or are currently enrolled in accredited U.S. vet schools. Applicants must be North Dakota high school graduates or have lived in the state for at least two years prior to admission.

Ross University Dean's Scholarships - $3,000 for first-year veterinary students.

---

21 VStone, "Veterinary Scholarship Trust of New England," *VStone*, n.d., https://www.veterinaryscholarshiptrust.org/

22 Viticus Group, "Home," *Viticus Group*, n.d., https://www.viticusgroup.org/splash

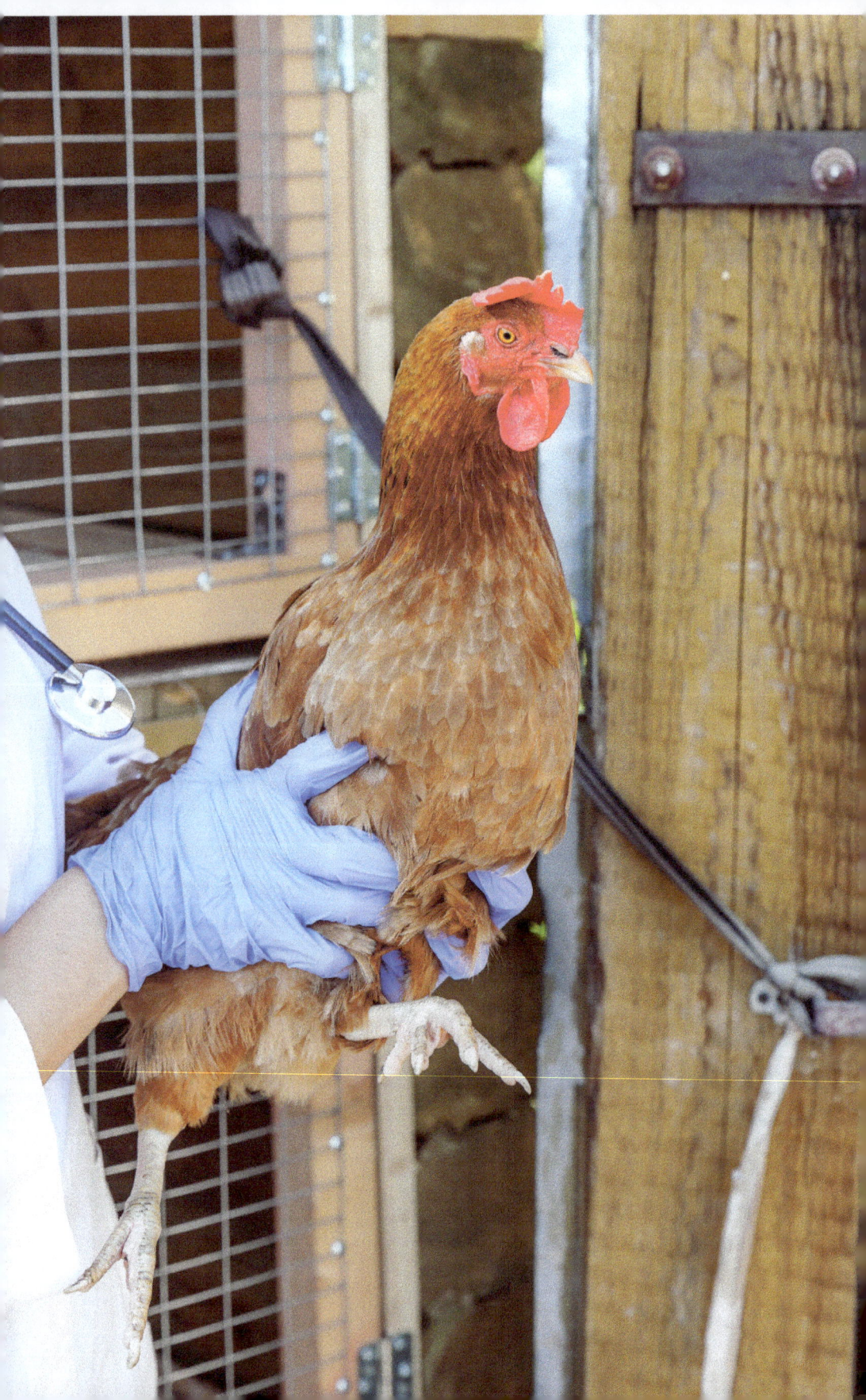

PART 7

DECISIONS, DECISIONS

"The place between your comfort zone and your dream is where life takes place."

– Helen Keller

CHAPTER 37

"DECISION DAY" – ACCEPTANCES & DECISIONS

I t would be great if you knew you were accepted to vet school by the winter holidays. However, applications are on a rolling basis for most schools, and the dates on which you will get an interview and hear back vary widely.

With rolling admissions, the dates may seem rather arbitrary. Whichever date is given will be for 2022 or 2023 admissions. It is often just the first date when colleges respond with acceptances. There is plenty of time during the next few months in which you could be accepted. On the positive side, interviews will be scattered between different months. If you are not accepted in December, there is still January, February, March, and April.

Rolling admissions means that colleges continue to admit students during the process. Thus, the application review, interview, and admissions process will continue until all of the seats in that year's class are filled.

Think of it this way. Students accepted in December tend to be the top students a college wants to enroll in and ensure they get a spot. Even so, some of those admits will get multiple offers. There is no real guarantee that they will go to College X, when College Y and College Z are vying for the same student. The student can only accept one of these schools.

April 15th -The Candidate Reply Date

All candidates accepted to vet school must respond whether or not they will accept a spot in a school's class. The candidate must also reply to the schools to which they will not attend. This frees up a spot for students put on a waitlist.

Some waitlisted students will not hear back about their admissions status until May or June.

Walk back your timeline of where you want to be so that you are not disappointed. Remember, your goal is to get to an interview and show the side of you that can shine brilliantly in a personal, professional, and intellectual way. The application is important, but the interview is the essential next step.

Your interview is crucial.

If you are in the planning stages now, the goal is to apply early enough so that your application can be verified. You want to make sure there are no missteps with recommenders, transcripts, GRE scores, or any other missing part of the application.

As you are aware, the process of getting accepted to vet school is arduous and stressful. However, it is also competitive and uncertain. Vet school admissions rates are low. There are no easy-admit schools like there were when you applied to undergraduate schools.

Everyone who applies to attend vet school did well in college. They took tough classes and scored well on the GREs. A very few get accepted without mostly A's in the hardest classes. Almost all vet schools reject three-fourths of their applicants.

Give yourself that early edge and show that you are truly committed by planning and applying early. Take the tests early. Start working on essays and secondaries as soon as you can. If you are offered an interview, respond ASAP so that you have the best shot at a convenient time.

Also, remember that more schools are signing on to require the CASPer test. This test is just one more requirement to add to a very busy year. It is also why taking a gap year to strengthen your profile might be better than writing weak essays.

There is nothing wrong with a gap year if it strengthens your skills, allows you to take more classes, gives you more experience, and leads you to your desired program.

Besides, you want to make sure VMCAS has all of your documents, that you correct any errors, and you have plenty of time to think about what you want to say in your secondaries. In the end, you will get your decision. Hopefully, you are accepted to your top choice school. Victory is around the corner. You worked hard. Check everything to make sure you are prepared. Hopefully, you will be holding celebrations during the winter holidays.

Good Luck!

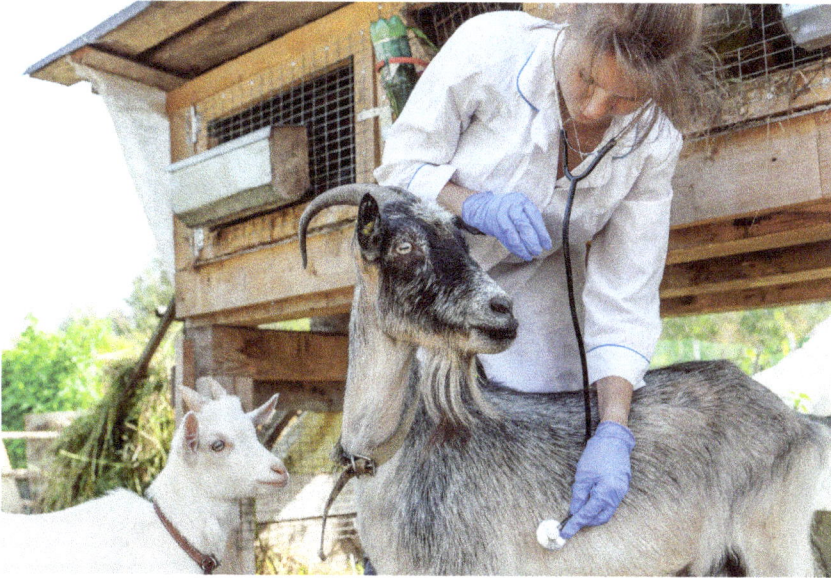

"Whatever the mind of man can conceive and believe, it can achieve."

– Napoleon Hill

CHAPTER 38

VET SCHOOL RESIDENCIES

VETERINARY RESIDENT

Students who want to gain additional training and specialize continue after vet school for an extended period that varies depending upon the specialization. Licensed veterinarians must graduate from an accredited veterinary school, pass state and national exams, and apply to these programs.

Residencies offer veterinarians supervised clinical experience, training, and educational enhancement to prepare for board certification. Most residents have completed a one-year general internship, including supervised experience in medicine and surgery, though some veterinary residents have completed additional training.[1]

Board-certified veterinarians monitor residents in their specialization, subject to regulations. Only the top vet students are chosen for veterinary residencies; most specialties are highly competitive. Residents work at approved veterinary hospitals that meet the highest requirements. The Veterinary Internship and Residency Matching Program (VIRMP), promoted by the American Association of Veterinary Clinicians, oversees the selection

---

1   AVMA, "Internships and Residency Programs," *AVMA*, n.d., https://www.avma.org/resources-tools/avma-policies/internships-and-residency-programs

of residents for member veterinary schools, colleges, institutes, and private practices.[2]

Residents must attend and present at journal clubs, daily clinical rounds, and formal rounds. They are required to manage emergency medical and surgical cases and consult with specialists. Residents must also conduct research to further their knowledge of veterinary medicine and publish their findings in peer-reviewed journals. In addition, due to their current, cutting-edge knowledge in their expertise, they are frequently called upon to give continuing education lectures to veterinarians and veterinary students and supervise interns and veterinary students.[3]

Finally, they must pass a comprehensive examination and fulfill practical experience criteria to become a board-certified veterinary specialist after completing their residency term.

International opportunities include Small Animal Teaching Hospital (SATH), which offers three-year residency programs for veterinarians interested in specializing in small animal medicine with a world-renowned veterinary practice.[4] Residents are enrolled in the proper European Board of Veterinary Specialization (EBVS) linked program.

While the training received during veterinary internships and residencies is highly regarded for enhancing a veterinarian's experience, successful interns and residents also profit from completing these programs in a variety of ways. The additional time, respect, building contacts, and networking with individuals is a significant benefit. Another advantage, as noted in a 2013 edition of the Journal of the American Veterinary Medical Association, is the increased earning potential (JAMVA).[5] Private practitioners who finished a residency often earn double the income of those who complete an internship or a basic DVM degree.

2   Veterinary Internship & Residency Matching Program, "2021-2022 Veterinary Internship & Residency Matching Program," *Veterinary Internship & Residency Matching Program,* 2021, https://www.virmp.org/

3   Tufts Pre-Veterinary Society, "Becoming a Specialist: Internships and Residencies," *Tufts Pre-Veterinary Society,* n.d., https://sites.tufts.edu/tuftsprevetsociety/careers-in-veterinary-medicine/specializing/becoming-a-specialist-internships-and-residencies/

4   University of Liverpool, "Residencies," *University of Liverpool,* n.d., https://www.liverpool.ac.uk/sath/teaching/postgraduates/residencies/

5   Malinda Larkin, "Pluses and Minuses," *AVMA,* June 19, 2013, https://www.avma.org/javma-news/2013-07-01/pluses-and-minuses

RESIDENCY PROGRAMS [6]

Veterinary Biosciences[7]

- Anatomic Pathology[8]
- Clinical Pathology

Veterinary Clinical Sciences

- Anesthesia
- Behavior Medicine
- Cardiology
- Dermatology
- Diagnostic Imaging & Radiology
- Equine Emergency and Critical Care
- Equine Field Service/Ambulatory Medicine
- Equine Medicine
- Equine Surgery
- Food Animal Medicine and Surgery
- Neurology/Neurosurgery
- Oncology
- Ophthalmology
- Radiation Oncology
- Small Animal Emergency/Critical Care
- Small Animal Internal Medicine
- Small Animal Surgery
- Theriogenology

Veterinary Preventive Medicine

- Lab Animal Medicine
- Conservation Medicine and Ecosystem Health in Zoos and Wildlife

6   Cornell University College of Veterinary Medicine, "Residencies & Internships," *Cornell University College of Veterinary Medicine*, n.d., https://www.vet.cornell.edu/education/residencies-internships

7   The Ohio State University College of Veterinary Medicine, "Veterinary Biosciences Residency/Post-Doc Programs," *The Ohio State University College of Veterinary Medicine*, n.d., https://vet.osu.edu/biosciences/pathology-residencyphd-graduate-program

8   College of Veterinary Medicine University of Illinois at Urbana-Champaign, "Pathobiology Graduate Study," *College of Veterinary Medicine University of Illinois at Urbana-Champaign*, n.d., https://vetmed.illinois.edu/college-organization/pathobiology/graduate-study/

Anatomic Pathology

Anatomic pathology is a specialty concerned with illness diagnosis based on macroscopic, microscopic, biochemical, immunologic, and molecular study of organs and tissues. Discoveries in surgical pathology, from examinations of entire bodies during autopsy to more sophisticated approaches focused on cancer diagnosis and prognosis, aid in the decision-making and treatment in oncology.

Surgical pathology, autopsy, and clinical pathology laboratories are included in the anatomic pathology residency. Anatomic pathology residents also gain training in molecular biology, virology, oncology, biochemistry, immunohistochemistry, gnotobiology, cell culture, and quantitative histomorphometry.

The Ohio State University, for example, offers laboratories for autopsy, surgical pathology, and clinical pathology services. Experiential work is conducted at the Veterinary Medical Center, the Columbus Zoo, the Capital Areawide Humane Society, and the University Comparative Pathology & Mouse Phenotyping Shared Resource.[9] Additionally, diagnostic pathology support assists the Veterinary Medical Center's large caseload.

A National Institute of Health (NIH) training grant funds a study of genetically engineered mice based on submissions to the Phenotyping Shared Resource. Trainees also contact pathologists from the Ohio Department of Agriculture. Ph.D. research options range from infectious disease research to oncology and drug development. This training includes work within the college and with partners across the OSU health sciences community and Nationwide Children's Hospital. Anatomical pathology is one of two divisions of pathology. Pathologists frequently practice both anatomical and clinical pathology.

Clinical Pathology

Clinical pathology is a medical specialty concerned with diagnosing disease utilizing the techniques of chemistry, microbiology, hematology, and molecular pathology to analyze physiological fluids such as blood, urine, and tissue homogenates or extracts.

Clinical pathologists are typically responsible for blood banks, as well as areas surrounding clinical chemistry, toxicology, hematology, immunology, serology,

---

9   The Ohio State University College of Veterinary Medicine, "Comparative Pathology and Mouse Phenotyping Shared Resource/Histology & Immunohistochemistry," *The Ohio State University College of Veterinary Medicine,* n.d., http://vet.osu.edu/biosciences/comparative-pathology-and-mouse-phenotyping-shared-resource-histology-immunohistochemist

and microbiology. Maintenance of laboratory information systems, research, and quality control are all part of clinical pathology. According to the American Society for Clinical Pathology (ASCP), "pathologists are problem solvers, fascinated by the process of disease and eager to unlock medical mysteries, such as AIDS and diabetes, using the tools of laboratory medicine and its sophisticated instruments and methods…Pathologists enable scientific advances to be applied to improve the accuracy and efficiency of medical diagnosis and treatment."[10]

Anesthesia

A residency program in anesthesia incorporates advanced clinical training in applied veterinary pharmacology, anesthesia, and perioperative pain management. The regular curriculum is a three-year residency and graduate studies program resulting in a Certificate of Residency and a Master of Science degree.

A few of the schools that offer this residency include Tufts, UC Davis, University of Georgia, University of Guelph, University of Illinois, University of Melbourne, University of Montreal, UPenn, University of Prince Edward Island, and Virginia-Maryland Regional College of Veterinary Medicine.[11]

Behavioral Medicine[12]

The focus of behavioral medicine is the integration of knowledge from the behavioral, biological, psychological, and social disciplines relevant to health and illness. Epidemiology, anthropology, sociology, psychology, physiology, pharmacology, nutrition, neuroanatomy, endocrinology, and immunology are among these disciplines.

In addition, applied psychophysiological therapies such as biofeedback, hypnosis, and bio-behavioral therapy are applied to the treatment of animals' physical illnesses, occupational therapy, rehabilitation medicine, physiatry, and preventive medicine. The objectives of behavioral medicine are:[13]

- offer residents with the chance to learn diagnostic and therapeutic procedures in behavioral medicine

---

10 The Dark Report, "TAG: Clinical Pathology," *The Dark Report,* n.d., https://www.darkintelligencegroup.com/tag/clinical-pathology/

11 ACVAA, "List of ACVAA Approved Residency Programs," *ACVAA,* n.d., https://acvaa.org/wp-content/uploads/2020/04/List-of-ACVAA-residency-Programs-copy-updated-final-copy.pdf

12 Medical College of Wisconsin, "Psychiatry and Behavioral Medicine," *Medical College of Wisconsin,* n.d., https://www.mcw.edu/departments/psychiatry-and-behavioral-medicine/education/residency-programs

13 The Ohio State University College of Veterinary Medicine, "Behavior Medicine Residency," *The Ohio State University College of Veterinary Medicine,* n.d., https://vet.osu.edu/education/behavior-medicine

- give clinical teaching experience to veterinary students engaging in the clinical behavior rotation
- contribute to the didactic instruction of pre-clinical veterinary students
- provide opportunities to create and implement one or more research projects in clinical animal behavior
- provide opportunities for members of the veterinary profession to share clinical results through case reports, scholarly publications, seminars, or lectures

A few of the residency programs approved by the American College of Veterinary Behaviorists include North Carolina State, Purdue University, The Ohio State University, UC Davis, University of Montreal (Canada), UPenn, and University of Prince Edward Island (Canada).[14]

Cardiology

Cardiologists are internal medical specialists focused on heart and circulatory system problems. Training includes medical diagnosis and treatment of congenital heart defects, coronary artery disease, heart failure, valvular heart disease, and electrophysiology.

Residents must understand the fundamental causes and mechanisms of cardiovascular (CV) illness and gain expertise in the diagnosis and therapy of cardiovascular disorders in domesticated animals along with:[15]

- Competence in performing and evaluating noninvasive and invasive diagnostic heart and circulation procedures
- Competence in standard catheter-based interventional CV techniques like catheterization and pacing
- Improvement of clinical and didactic teaching abilities
- Skill development in clinical research skills
- Published contribution to veterinary literature

Additionally, at the end of the residency, training, and testing process, you will earn your MS in Veterinary Clinical Science.

A few of the 3-4 year residency programs in cardiology approved by the American College of Veterinary Internal Medicine include Colorado State, Cornell,

---

14 American College of Veterinary Behaviorists, "Certification," *American College of Veterinary Behaviorists,* n.d., https://www.dacvb.org/page/Certification

15 The Ohio State University College of Veterinary Medicine, "Cardiology Residency," *The Ohio State University College of Veterinary Medicine,* n.d., https://vet.osu.edu/education/clinical-cardiology

Iowa State, Purdue, Texas A&M, Royal Veterinary College (UK), University of Bristol (UK), the University of Guelph (Canada), UPenn, Virginia-Maryland College of Veterinary Medicine, and Washington State University.[16]

Dermatology

Training is intended to provide extensive clinical specialization under the supervision of board-certified specialists. Residents learn methods to diagnose and treat the skin and ear disorders of small and large animals, ensuring clinical competence in dermatology by encouraging the development of clinical competency, skills, and knowledge of dermatology through exposure to situations of varying complexity.

For example, The Ohio State University Veterinary Medical Center's location in a major metropolitan area with a population of over 1.5 million provides a diverse range of cases and a referral base that spans Ohio, Indiana, Pennsylvania, Kentucky, West Virginia, and Michigan. In addition, OSU provides state-of-the-art equipment and facilities to acquire technical expertise in diagnostic and treatment operations.[17]

A few of the many established programs include Cornell, Iowa State, Louisiana State, Michigan State, UC Davis, University of Florida, University of Minnesota, UPenn, University of Tennessee, and the University of Wisconsin-Madison.[18]

Diagnostic Imaging & Radiology

The radiology residency program provides postdoctoral clinical experience intended to satisfy the standards of the American College of Veterinary Radiology (ACVR). The culminating goal of this program that requires a minimum of three years is to apply for the ACVR's preliminary and certification tests.

Subspecialties in veterinary radiology include standard and special procedures in small and large animal diagnostic radiology in five core areas: Roentgen diagnosis; diagnostic ultrasound; computed tomography (CT); magnetic resonance imaging (MRI), and diagnostic nuclear medicine. Graduates of the program are prepared to work in either an academic or specialty practice setting.

A few universities that offer this residency include Auburn, Colorado State,

---

16 ACVIM, "2021-2022 Cardiology Approve Residency Training Programs," *ACVIM*, n.d., https://www.acvim.org/certification/approved-residency-training-programs/cardiology-approved-residency-training-programs

17 The Ohio State University College of Veterinary Medicine, "Dermatology Residency," *The Ohio State University College of Veterinary Medicine*, n.d., https://vet.osu.edu/education/dermatology

18 ACVID, "Training Program," *ACVID*, n.d., http://www.acvd.org/pages/category.asp?ids=34_Training_Program

Cornell, Kansas State, Purdue University, Texas A&M, Tufts, UC Davis, University of Florida, and the University of Wisconsin-Madison.[19]

Equine Emergency and Critical Care

Residencies in Equine Emergency and Critical Care focus on increasing the chances of survival for horses in emergency situations. Equine veterinarians monitor and support horses from birth to death, assisting mares in reproduction from conception to delivery. Many give immunizations and advice on nutrition and maintenance. As the horses mature, equine veterinarians treat horses for a range of diseases, disorders, illnesses, and infections.

Horses are susceptible to the following diseases and viruses:

- Clostridial Diarrhea
- Botulism
- Equine Coronavirus
- Encephalomyelitis
- Equine Herpesvirus (EHV)
- Equine Encephalitis
- Equine Protozoal Myeloencephalitis (EPM)
- Equine Infectious Anemia
- Influenza
- Viral Arteritis
- Lyme Disease
- Pigeon Fever
- Potomac Horse Sickness
- Rabies

A few of the large animal residencies approved by the American College of Veterinary Surgeons include Colorado State, Cornell, Iowa State, Kansas State, Louisiana State, Virginia Tech, Michigan State, Mississippi State, Murdoch University (Australia), University of Guelph (Canada), Oregon State, Texas A&M, University of Florida, and Tufts University.[20]

Lab Animal Medicine

---

19 American College of Veterinary Radiology, "Diagnostic Imaging Residency Programs," *American College of Veterinary Radiology,* n.d., https://acvr.org/veterinary-professionals/residents/radiology-residency-programs/

20 ACVS, "Registered Residency Training Programs in Large Animal Surgery," *ACVS,* 2021, https://www.acvs.org/residents/registered-programs#LA

Residency training in this area focuses on lab animals, surgery, and care. The objectives of the training program and expectations include the following:

- Be familiar with biomedical research regulations and guidelines and develop a preventive medicine program for a laboratory animal population.
- Participate in a research project that leads to the creation of a first-author paper and submission to a peer-reviewed journal.
- Understand the requirements of researchers in terms of animal models.
- Recognize the clinical and pathologic changes that occur in common laboratory animal diseases.
- Have a grasp of personnel management issues relevant to laboratory animal medicine.

The American Society of Laboratory Animal Practitioners offers residencies in a few dozen locations, including Baylor, CDC, Colorado State, Columbia, Cornell, Emory, MIT, USC, Stanford, UCSD, the University of Chicago. Vanderbilt, Wake Forest, and Yale.[21]

Radiation Oncology

Radiation oncology uses ionizing radiation to treat cancer patients and resolve the problems of other diseases. Radiation oncologists work closely with physicians from different disciplines in the multidisciplinary management of cancer patients. The residency prepares trainees for ionizing radiation, clinical management, radiotherapy, basic surgical oncology, cancer biology, state-of-the-art assessment strategies, and treatment plans.

Residency programs in radiation oncology approved by the American College of Veterinary Radiology include Texas A&M, Tufts, UC Davis, University of Georgia, University of Minnesota, University of Missouri, and the University of Wisconsin.[22]

Theriogenology

Theriogenology studies the physiology and disease of male and female reproductive systems of animals. Reproduction is considered from conception and birth to reproduction planning, including veterinary obstetrics, gynecology, and andrology. Veterinary surgeons that specialize in animal reproduction

---

21 ASLAP, "Current Residencies," *ASLAP*, n.d., https://www.aslap.org/career-development/current-residencies

22 American College of Veterinary Radiology, "Radiation Oncology Residency Programs," *American College of Veterinary Radiology,* n.d., https://acvr.org/veterinary-professionals/residents/radiation-oncology-residency-programs/

and obstetrics are known as thieriogenologists. The American College of Theriogenologists certifies most theriogenologists in the United States.

A few of the residency programs in theriogenology include Auburn, Colorado State, Cornell, University of Florida, University of Guelph (Canada), Hebrew University (Israel), University of Illinois, Iowa State, Kansas State, University of Liverpool (UK), UPenn, and University of Queensland (Australia).[23]

Ophthalmology

Ophthalmology is a medical specialty that is concerned with the diagnosis and treatment of vision. Under the supervision of board-certified specialists, residency programs in ophthalmology provide extensive clinical training and specialization in diagnosing and treating ocular problems in small and large animals, often resulting in a Master of Science. This residency aims to ensure the development of clinical competence in ophthalmology through exposure to cases of varying degrees of complexity.

Subspecialties of ophthalmology are:

- glaucoma
- the cornea
- the retina
- uveitis
- refractive surgery
- pediatrics
- neuro-ophthalmology
- plastic and reconstructive surgery
- ocular oncology

Residency programs and certifications by the American Board of Veterinary Ophthalmology and American College of Veterinary Ophthalmologists are available from schools including UC Davis, University of Florida, Texas A&M, The Ohio Staten University, and North Carolina State.

---

23 American College of Theriogenologists, "List of Current Residency Programs," *American College of Theriogenologists,* n.d., https://www.theriogenology.org/page/ResidencyProgramList

"There are no secrets to success. It is the result of preparation, hard work, and learning from failure."

— Colin Powell

CHAPTER 39

WAITLIST, REJECTION, APPEAL

DECISION DAY!

Congratulations to those who were accepted. Patience to those who have not yet heard.

Due to COVID-19, there were changes in some admissions processes and decisions. This may not be true for Fall 2021 or 2022. Check the school's websites for specific dates.

Typically, candidates hear back from a college with a phone call from an admissions committee member. An official letter from the admissions committee is also mailed to the address on the application. Students can be accepted to multiple schools since admissions processes are independent.

With your call, admissions officers or deans will enthusiastically welcome you to next year's class.

This call, letter, and acceptance is an important milestone since vet schools have now selected their best candidates from the pool. Congratulations if you are one of those selected.

Some students will be put on a waitlist. This means you are still in the running, but you did not yet make it over the threshold to the accepted group. You may not hear whether you are off the waitlist for four months.

However, you may have only thirty days to decide on whether to accept an offer or offers. You will need to decide which school you will choose from the offers you are given.

Note: Respond to all schools that offer you a spot as to whether or not you will attend. This response allows schools to extend admission to worthy candidates who were put on the waitlist. You should do some research to consider where you want to attend.

First, you will spend four years there. You may want to talk with your family members or others very close to you to get second or third opinions. They may be more candid if you are unsure.

Second, since your time will be consumed with vet school, you may be mulling over multiple factors to determine which school you choose. Family and personal reasons might influence your decision based upon proximity, spouse's job, or family responsibilities.

Third, finances might also play into which school you will attend. You could ask any of the schools to which you were accepted if they have scholarships, fellowships, or other financial aid opportunities. If you are not accepted, your pathway is not at its end.

Decisions roll in over the next few months. Be patient. There are a few online discussion boards where students post their angst about being on a waitlist and when they hear. This community makes applicants feel as if they are not alone.

You are not alone.

There are many others who are trying to be patient throughout the process while their future is on the line. Vet schools update your status when it changes. Do not call the admissions offices. Vet schools are flooded with calls. Applications are often still being reviewed.

On the other hand, you do want to update your file with a letter of continued interest and possibly any new information about courses, grades, research, service, clinical experiences, or other activities. Vet school committees would not know your true interest otherwise.

If you are no longer interested, please tell them. Lots of anxious students would love to know that there is one more spot available.

If you are rejected, you have lots of options.

You could explore alternate career paths. You could reapply next year. You could also pursue a master's degree. This is not the end of the road.

The next chapter of this book discusses some of your options. While it is possible to appeal a decision, with so many students on the waitlist, appeals are less likely to succeed. On the other hand, if you have a compelling reason and you are confident that veterinary medicine is the field you want to pursue, then you could appeal the decision.

Good luck in your pursuit!

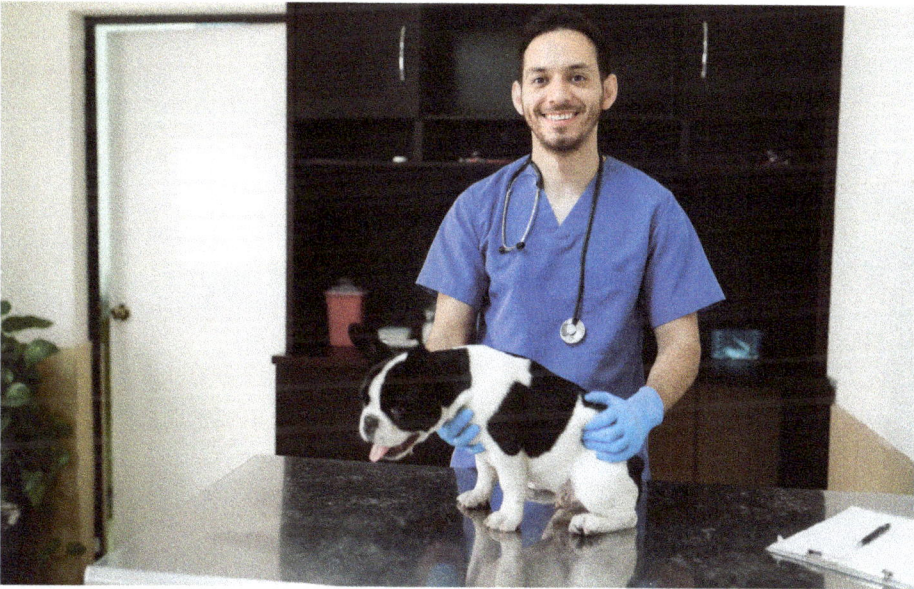

"

"*People may doubt what you say, but they will believe what you do.*"

— *Louis Cass*

CHAPTER 40

REAPPLICATION, CONSIDERATION, & PLAN

D eciding to reapply is the first step toward your goal of becoming a veterinarian. Reapplying is a big decision and shows a genuine commitment to the field. You could have easily quit and gone another direction. Some people do because they are not completely committed to this career. Now, you need to determine what you will do differently this time.

WHY WAS I NOT ACCEPTED?

There are numerous reasons why you were not accepted that may not be on your radar. Some of those include institutional priorities. You might have been a highly desirable candidate. Still, the university may have needed to accept a student of a particular type to ensure that they were fair in their admissions process. Colleges must accept students from diverse backgrounds.

The vet school may have had an applicant who completely wowed the committee in the interview that was not as high on the list beforehand.

You can contact the school after the admissions cycle and ask them to provide you with a post-rejection interview with one of their admissions staff members. Many vet schools offer this option. You should ask and not just assume that you know why. Admissions committee members can tell you the weaknesses you had in your application and what you can do to improve. This call may be the key to success in your reapplication and admissions process.

Maybe you did not show enough experience in veterinary medicine as other candidates or did not appear to be as committed to the field. In your secondaries, you may not have shown an understanding of the particular institution, program, or student body.

Maybe you picked the wrong schools. Last year, one of my students applied to top schools that did not require the tests since she did not have a score. Her grades were good, but she had little experience in veterinary medicine. When she called a vet school admissions staff member, the representative explained that her background did not show significant commitment to veterinary medicine.

You need to be brutally honest and figure out what you need to do to improve your application. Realistically assess your situation, consider what you plan to passionately pursue, and determine if vet school is truly your path.

Review your application.

Be critical.

You are a year older and a year wiser.

This review opportunity offers you a sobering maturity about how you consider the activities, interests, academics, letters of recommendation, GRE, essays, and even the schools you chose. You will need to strengthen areas where you are weak and add to those areas where you are stronger.

YOU HAVE A YEAR. THE LOOMING QUESTION IS, WHAT WILL YOU DO WITH THAT TIME?

If your GPA is lower than the average, particularly your science GPA, enroll in classes to lay a stronger foundation in biochemistry, immunology, human physiology, microbiology, or genetics. There is always more to learn in any field of your interest.

Another option is to pursue a post-baccalaureate program specifically for vet school applicants that possibly has a summer GRE prep option. The challenge is that many of these programs have deadlines from December to March, and you may not hear until May 1. This timing is quite late, so you may have to convince a school to let you apply past the deadline.

Whether you take science classes to learn and improve your science GPA or pursue a post-bacc vet program to strengthen your science foundation and prepare anew for the GRE, you should consider alternatives if your grades are low.

Though some people will dissuade you about retaking the GRE, this test is one of the critical components of your application. Carefully evaluate whether this is the right decision and do not rush to take the test. An improvement in your score by fifty points can make a significant difference and put your test results closer to the range of applicants.

Retaking the GRE will take some time since you want to be sure you are prepared. After all, you are eight months to two years away from when you took the test. You may need to relearn the material covered on the test if you are not enrolled in school.

If you did not have much in the way of veterinary medical experiences, you would want to build on that area and learn more about the field you intend to enter. Apply for positions in vet offices. Any chance to learn more about the vet office experience, lifestyle, terminology, acronyms, procedures, referrals, emergencies, and outcomes would be valuable.

Clinical exposure is often difficult to manage while in college, though with additional time, more healthcare settings may be available. Vet schools want to ensure that you are committed and you know what to expect.

Some students drop out of vet school because they cannot take some of the heartbreaking pressures of working with sick animals. Some actually do not like the sight of blood.

Even if you previously volunteered, shadowed, or worked in a clinic or vet office, additional experiences show that you are committed to making veterinary medicine your career.

Write a new personal statement. First, you will be different a year later. Second, you will have new activities to describe. Third, your frame of mind is in a different place. With your commitment and personal growth, you will see the world in a different light. This light will shine through in your personal statement.

Finally, demonstrate what you did over this period that reawakened your commitment to veterinary medicine and made you feel that you are more prepared than ever to pursue your chosen field of study. Finally, write an entirely new personal statement and incorporate elements and experiences learned during that additional year.

Do whatever you can to strengthen your application since this will help demonstrate your commitment to becoming a veterinarian.

YOUR GAP YEAR

This time between the end of school and the beginning of vet school is crucial. Think of this year as a "growth" year. Besides, about half of all vet school applicants take a gap year. Do not consider this year a detriment to your application. In many ways, it is an enhancement.

How can you grow to be a more competitive applicant?

- Clinical Experiences
- Coursework and Science Knowledge
- Retake the GRE
- Research Projects
- Develop Interview Skills
- Improve Your Health
- Lead a Service Project
- Fulbright Scholar
- Peace Corps
- Overseas Animal Support Teams
- Develop Greater Self-Awareness

Consider the possibility of gaining certifications in areas around the healthcare field to learn more about medicine, emergency care, and patient support. These include Basic Life Support (BLS), Lifesaving, Phlebotomy, Cardiopulmonary Resuscitation (CPR), Automated External Defibrillator (AED), Emergency Medical Technician (EMT), Certified Medical Assistant, Certified Nursing Assistant (CNA), Certified Veterinary Assistant.

Jobs in the healthcare industry allow prospective applicants the chance to experience veterinary medicine with and without certifications like working as a medical scribe, phlebotomist, clinical research assistant, hospital administration staff member, or clinic assistant.

Volunteer or paid work with the community may be of interest to you with local or national organizations like The Red Cross, Muscular Dystrophy Association, United Cerebral Palsy, March of Dimes, Alzheimer's Association, Autism Speaks, and the American Association of People with Disabilities.

Some specific animal service groups include

- Christian Veterinary Mission
- Equitarian Initiative
- International Veterinary Students' Association exchange programs
- Mazunte Project
- Project Samaná
- Remote Area Medical Veterinary Program
- Rural Area Veterinary Services (RAVS)
- Silent Heroes Foundation
- South Pacific Animal Welfare
- Vet Treks Foundation
- Veterinarians Without Borders U.S.
- ViDAS
- World Vets

Although you will take an additional year, you may need this time to be better prepared and truly know this is the direction you want to head. Seek out your pre-vet advisor for more information. Add letters to the list and ensure that you have updated transcripts or revised documents. If not, organize your files so that you have everything ready for your application when it opens again.

Good luck!

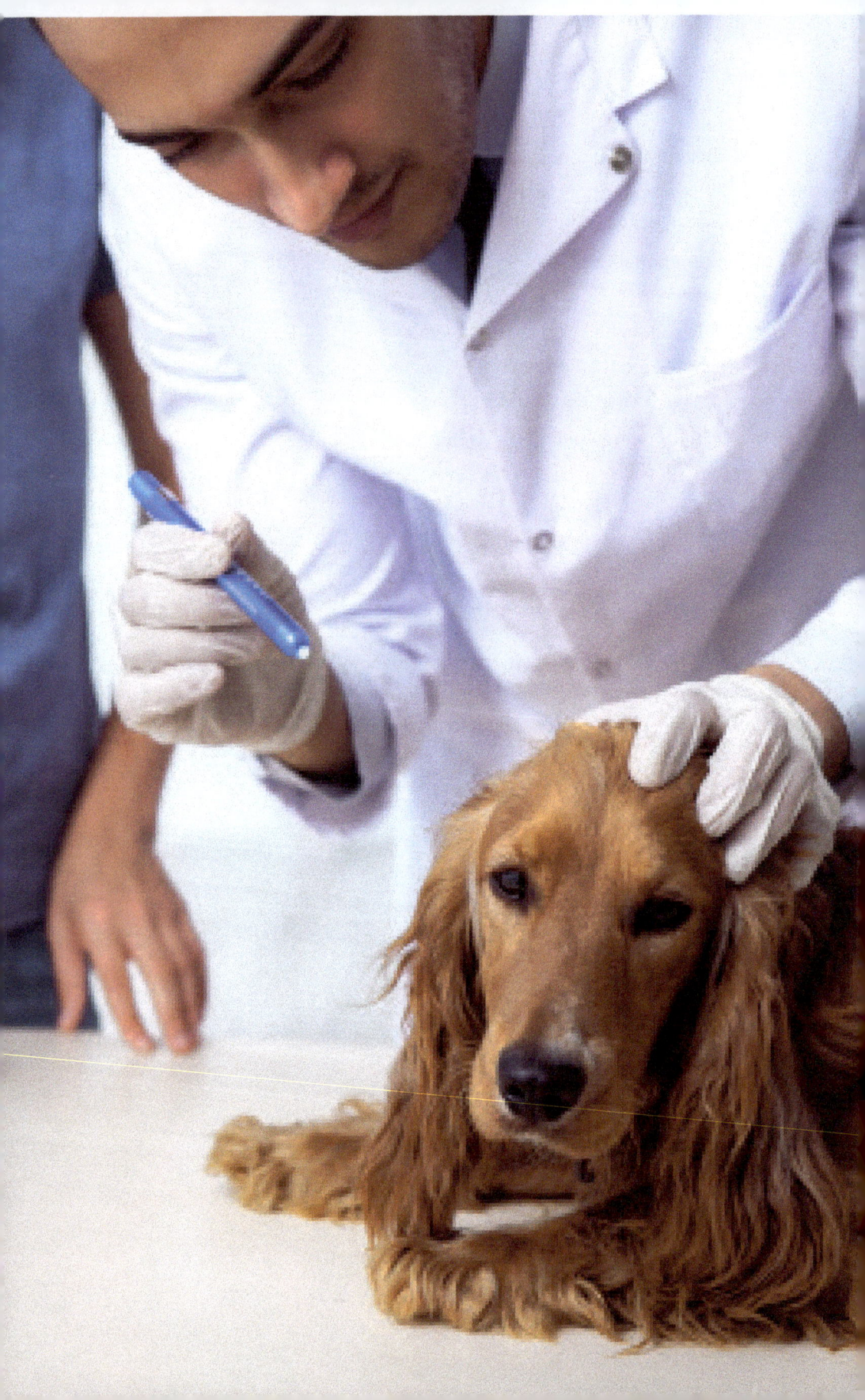

PART 8

VETERINARY MEDICAL SCHOOL LISTS

CHAPTER 41

VET SCHOOLS BY CITY/STATE

Vet Schools	City	State	Region	Website
Auburn University College of Veterinary Medicine	Auburn	AL	3	https://www.vetmed.auburn.edu/
Tuskegee University School of Veterinary Medicine	Tuskegee	AL	3	https://www.tuskegee.edu/programs-courses/colleges-schools/cvm
Midwestern University College of Veterinary Medicine	Glendale	AZ	4	https://www.midwestern.edu/academics/our-colleges/college-of-veterinary-medicine.xml
University of Arizona College of Veterinary Medicine	Oro Valley	AZ	4	https://vetmed.arizona.edu/
University of California, Davis School of Veterinary Medicine	Davis	CA	4	https://www.vetmed.ucdavis.edu/
Western University of Health Sciences College of Veterinary Medicine	Pomona	CA	4	https://www.westernu.edu/veterinary/
Colorado State University College of Veterinary Medicine and Biomedical Sciences	Fort Collins	CO	4	https://vetmedbiosci.colostate.edu/dvm/
University of Florida College of Veterinary Medicine	Gainesville	FL	3	https://education.vetmed.ufl.edu/
University of Georgia College of Veterinary Medicine	Athens	GA	3	https://vet.uga.edu/
Iowa State University College of Veterinary Medicine	Ames	IA	2	https://vetmed.iastate.edu/
University of Illinois College of Veterinary Medicine	Urbana	IL	2	https://vetmed.illinois.edu/
Purdue University College of Veterinary Medicine	West Lafayette	IN	2	https://www.purdue.edu/vet/
Kansas State University College of Veterinary Medicine	Manhattan	KS	2	https://www.vet.k-state.edu/

Louisiana State University School of Veterinary Medicine	Baton Rouge	LA	3	https://www.lsu.edu/vetmed/
Tufts University School of Veterinary Medicine	North Grafton	MA	1	https://vet.tufts.edu/
Michigan State University College of Veterinary Medicine	East Lansing	MI	2	https://cvm.msu.edu/
University of Minnesota College of Veterinary Medicine	St. Paul	MN	2	https://vetmed.umn.edu/
University of Missouri - Columbia College of Veterinary Medicine	Columbia	MO	2	https://cvm.missouri.edu/
Mississippi State University College of Veterinary Medicine	Mississippi State	MS	3	https://www.vetmed.msstate.edu/
North Carolina State University College of Veterinary Medicine	Raleigh	NC	3	https://cvm.ncsu.edu/
Cornell University College of Veterinary Medicine	Ithica	NY	1	https://www.vet.cornell.edu/
Long Island University School of Veterinary Medicine	Brookville	NY	1	https://liu.edu/vetmed
Ohio State University College of Veterinary Medicine	Columbus	OH	2	https://vet.osu.edu/
Oklahoma State University College of Veterinary Medicine	Stillwater	OK	3	https://vetmed.okstate.edu/
Oregon State University College of Veterinary Medicine	Corvallis	OR	4	https://vetmed.oregonstate.edu/
University of Pennsylvania School of Veterinary Medicine	Philadelphia	PA	1	https://www.vet.upenn.edu/
Lincoln Memorial University College of Veterinary Medicine	Harrogate	TN	3	https://www.lmunet.edu/college-of-veterinary-medicine/index.php
University of Tennessee College of Veterinary Medicine	Knoxville	TN	3	https://vetmed.tennessee.edu/

Texas A&M University College of Veterinary Medicine & Biomedical Sciences	College Station	TX	3	https://vetmed.tamu.edu/
Texas Tech University School of Veterinary Medicine	Amarillo	TX	3	https://www.depts.ttu.edu/vetschool/
Virginia Tech Virginia-Maryland College of Veterinary Medicine	Blacksburg	VA	3	http://www.vetmed.vt.edu/
Washington State University College of Veterinary Medicine	Pullman	WA	4	https://www.vetmed.wsu.edu/
University of Wisconsin-Madison School of Veterinary Medicine	Madison	WI	2	https://www.vetmed.wisc.edu/

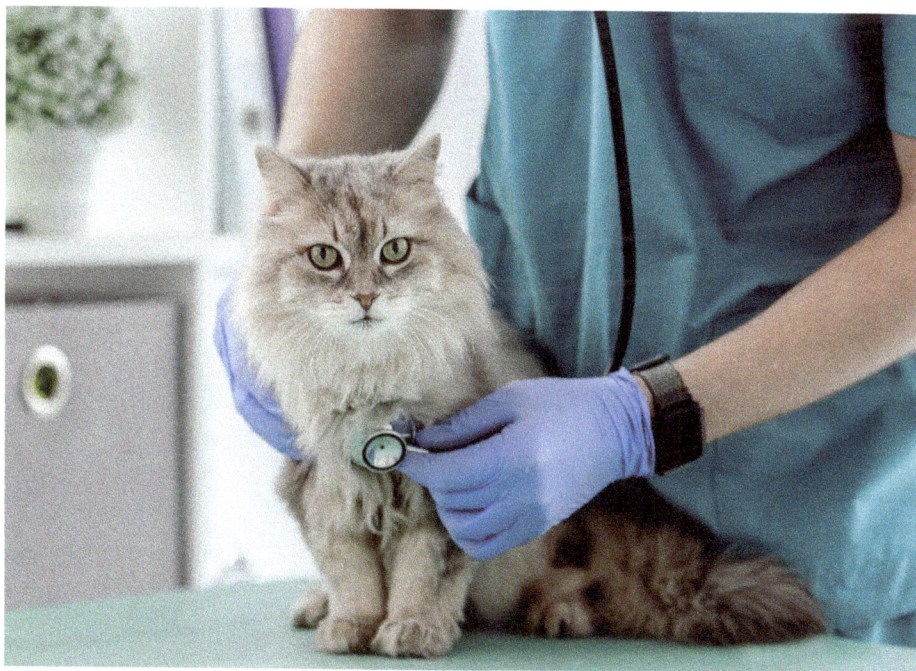

CHAPTER 42

VET SCHOOL PREREQUISITES

ALABAMA

School	Required	Recommended	Notes
Auburn University College of Veterinary Medicine	Written Comp., Literature, Fine Arts, Humanities, History, Social &Behav. Science Electives, Pre-Calc/Trig or higher, Biology w/Lab, Chem. w/ Lab, OChemw/ Lab, Physics, Cell Biology (see notes), Biochem., Animal Nutrition (see notes), Science Electives (see recommended).	Science electives must include 2+ of the following: comparative anatomy, genetics, embryology, mammalian or animal physiology, microbiology, physics 2, histology, reproductive physiology, parasitology, or immunology	Microbiology or genetics cannot be used to fulfill Cell Biology requirement. Animal nutrition may be taken online.
Tuskegee University School of Veterinary Medicine	English or Written Comp., Humanities & Social Studies, Liberal Arts, Math, Medical Terminology, Advanced Biol. Coursework, Biochem. w/Lab, Chem. w/Lab, OChemw/Lab, Physics 1 and 2 w/Labs, Science Electives, Intro to Animal Science, Physical Education (if no B.S. degree).	N/A	No listed information on AP credits. Contact admissions.

For the number of hours required for prerequisite courses, and for the most up-to-date information, please refer to the individual school websites.
*A.P. credit satisfies the requirement.
** When A.P. credit is awarded, upper-level coursework in the same subject area is required.
*** A.P. credit may satisfy the requirement on a case by case basis

ARIZONA

School	Required	Recommended	Notes
Midwestern University College of Veterinary Medicine	Biochem., Biol., Chem. w/Lab, OChemw/Lab, Math (College Algebra or higher), Physics w/ Lab, Engl. Comp. Science Electives (see recommended).	Science electives: cell biology, microbio., genetics, animal nutrition, etc.	No listed information on AP credits. Contact admissions.
University Of Arizona College of Veterinary Medicine	Biol., Chem., OChem., Physics, Math (Algebra, Trig., Pre-Calc., Calc., or Stats.), English Comp. (writing intensive), Arts & Humanities, and Social Sciences.	Labs not required, but strongly encouraged.	AP credits accepted as long as they are listed on undergraduate transcript. Online and community college courses are acceptable. No more than half of a student's pre-requisites can be Pass/Fail.

CALIFORNIA

School	Required	Recommended	Notes
University Of California, Davis School of Veterinary Medicine	Physics*, Biol., w/ Lab*, Chem. w/Lab*, OChemw/Lab*, Biochem., Genetics, Systemic Physiology, Stats.*	N/A	AP credits accepted as long as they are listed on undergraduate transcript. AP credits may fulfill certain courses if applicant receives "3" or higher. Official score report from CollegeBoard also required upon admission.

For the number of hours required for prerequisite courses, and for the most up-to-date information, please refer to the individual school websites.
*A.P. credit satisfies the requirement.
** When A.P. credit is awarded, upper-level coursework in the same subject area is required.
*** A.P. credit may satisfy the requirement on a case by case basis

School	Required	Recommended	Notes
Western University of Health Sciences College Of Veterinary Medicine	OChemw/Lab, Biochem. or Physiological Chem., Stats., Microbio., Upper Div. Physiology, Genetics or Molecular Bio., Upper Div/ Bio and Life Sciences w/Lab, Humanities/ Social Sciences, Physics w/ Lab, Engl. Comp.	Biochem/ or Physiological Chem. preferably with lab.	AP credits accepted as long as they are listed on undergraduate transcript. Virtual labs not accepted. Biostatistics may be accepted in lieu of Statistics on case-by-case basis.

COLORADO

School	Required	Recommended	Notes
Colorado State University College of Veterinary Medicine And Biomedical Sciences	Biol. w/Lab, Genetics (see notes), Chem. w/Lab, Biochem. (see notes), Physics, Stats., Engl., Comp., Humanities/ Behavioral & Social Sciences, Electives.	Upper division statistics preferred.	Genetics must have biology as prerequisite. Biochem. must have OChem as prerequisite. AP English Composition will fulfill prerequisite, not AP English Literature. AP credit accepted as long as it is listed on undergraduate transcript.

For the number of hours required for prerequisite courses, and for the most up-to-date information, please refer to the individual school websites.
*A.P. credit satisfies the requirement.
** When A.P. credit is awarded, upper-level coursework in the same subject area is required.
*** A.P. credit may satisfy the requirement on a case by case basis

FLORIDA

School	Required	Recommended	Notes
University of Florida College Of Veterinary Medicine	Biol. w/Lab, Microbio. w/Lab, Genetics, Chem. w/Lab, OChemw/Lab, Biochem., Physics w/Lab, Stats., Advanced Electives (see recommended), Engl., Humanities & Social Science.	Microbiology intended for Nursing programs will not be accepted. 9+ credits of Advanced Electives, recommended: Animal Nutrition, Biol. Sciences (Physiology, Human Physiology, Molecular Physiology, Histology, Molecular Biology, Bacterial Pathogens, Parasitology), Advanced Communications, Advanced Psychology, Advanced Business.	AP credits accepted by rules put forth by University of Florida. A maximum of 45 credit hours may be granted by combining AICE, AP, CLEP, and IB credit.

GEORGIA

School	Required	Recommended	Notes
University Of Georgia College of Veterinary Medicine	Engl., Humanities or Social Studies, Biol. w/Lab, Chem. w/Lab, OChemw/Lab, Physics, Biochem., Advanced Biol. Courses (see recommended). Online courses not accepted for General Biol., General Chem., Organic Chem., or Physics.	Advanced Biol. recommended: Comparative Anatomy, Physiology, Microbio., Cell Bio. or Genetics.	AP credits accepted as long as they are listed on undergraduate transcript.

For the number of hours required for prerequisite courses, and for the most up-to-date information, please refer to the individual school websites.

*A.P. credit satisfies the requirement.

** When A.P. credit is awarded, upper-level coursework in the same subject area is required.

*** A.P. credit may satisfy the requirement on a case by case basis

ILLINOIS

School	Required	Recommended	Notes
University Of Illinois College of Veterinary Medicine	Biol. w/Lab**, Chem. w/Lab, OChemw/ Lab, Biochem, Physics w/Lab*.	N/A	AP credits accepted as long as they are listed on undergraduate transcript. More pre-requisite requirements for individuals applying without an undergraduate degree. See admissions for more details.

IOWA

School	Required	Recommended	Notes
Purdue University College of Veterinary Medicine	Chem. w/Lab 1 & 2, OChemw/Lab 1 & 2, Biochem (upper div), Biol. w/Lab 1 & 2, Genetics, Microbio. w/Lab, Physics w/Lab 1 & 2, Stats, Engl. Comp., Communication, Humanities.	Careers in Vet. Medicine (if available)	AP credits accepted as long as they are listed on undergraduate transcript. Online lecture courses accepted, however lab courses must be taken in-person.

KENSAS

School	Required	Recommended	Notes
Kansas State University College of Veterinary Medicine	Chem., OChemw/ Lab, Biochem., Physics, Biology or Zoology, Microbio. w/Lab, Genetics, Expository Writing, Public Speaking, Social Sciences/ Humanities, Electives.	Anatomy and Physiology, Business, Immunology, Animal Sciences.	AP credits accepted as long as they are listed on undergraduate transcript.

For the number of hours required for prerequisite courses, and for the most up-to-date information, please refer to the individual school websites.
*A.P. credit satisfies the requirement.
** When A.P. credit is awarded, upper-level coursework in the same subject area is required.
*** A.P. credit may satisfy the requirement on a case by case basis

LOUISIANA

School	Required	Recommended	Notes
Louisiana State University School of Veterinary Medicine	Biol. w/Lab, Microbio., Chem. w/Lab, OChem, Biochem., College-level Math, Physics, Engl. Comp., Electives.	N/A	AP credit accepted but not used in computation of GPA. Students using AP credits are expected to take higher level university courses.

MASSACHUSETTS

School	Required	Recommended	Notes
Tufts University School of Veterinary Medicine	Bio w/Lab, Chem w/Lab, OChemw/ Lab, Physics, Genetics, Biochem, Math, Engl., Social/ Behavioral Science, Humanities/Fine Arts.	N/A	AP credits accepted as long as they are listed on undergraduate transcript.

MICHIGAN

School	Required	Recommended	Notes
Michigan State University College of Veterinary Medicine	Math* (College Algebra & Trig. or Pre-Calc or Calc.), Physics w/Lab*, Chem w/Lab*, OChem w/Lab, Biochem., Biology w/Lab*, Upper Level Biol. (see notes)	N/A	Upper Level Biol. includes Cell Biology, Physiology, Neurobiology, Immunology, Genetics, Microbiology, or Histology.

For the number of hours required for prerequisite courses, and for the most up-to-date information, please refer to the individual school websites.

*A.P. credit satisfies the requirement.

** When A.P. credit is awarded, upper-level coursework in the same subject area is required.

*** A.P. credit may satisfy the requirement on a case by case basis

MINNESOTA

School	Required	Recommended	Notes
University of Minnesota College of Veterinary Medicine	Writing, Math (see notes), Stats, General Chem w/Lab, OChem, Biochem, Biology w/Lab, Zoology w/Lab, Genetics, Microbiology w/ Lab, Physics, Liberal Education.	N/A	Math: College Algebra, Pre-Calculus, or Calculus. AP credits accepted as long as they are listed on undergraduate transcript.

MISSOURI

School	Required	Recommended	Notes
University of Missouri - Columbia College Of Veterinary Medicine	Composition/ Communications, College Algebra/ Advanced Math; Biochem, Physics 1 and 2, Biol (see notes), Social Science/Humanistic Studies (see notes).	N/A	Biol: Animal Sciences courses do not qualify towards Biol requirement. Examples of courses to fulfill Biol req. include Genetics, Microbiology, Anatomy, or Physiology. Social Science/Humanistic Studies examples include Economics, History, Political Science, Literature, Mythology, etc.

For the number of hours required for prerequisite courses, and for the most up-to-date information, please refer to the individual school websites.

*A.P. credit satisfies the requirement.

** When A.P. credit is awarded, upper-level coursework in the same subject area is required.

*** A.P. credit may satisfy the requirement on a case by case basis

MISSISSIPPI

School	Required	Recommended	Notes
Mississippi State University College of Veterinary Medicine	Engl. Comp, Speech/Technical Writing, Fundamentals of Public Speaking or junior/senior level technical writing, Humanities/Social Sciences, Math (minimum college alg.), Biol. w/Lab, Microbio. w/Lab, Chem. w/Lab, OChemw/Lab, Biochemistry, Physics, Advanced Science Electives (see recommended).	Advanced science elective examples: animal physiology, histology, immunology, nutrition, zoology, genetics, embryology, etc.	AP credits accepted as long as they are listed on undergraduate transcript.

NORTH CAROLINA

School	Required	Recommended	Notes
North Carolina State University College of Veterinary Medicine	Animal Nutrition, Biochem, Biol. w/Lab, Chem. w/Lab, OChemw/Lab, Genetics, Humanities/Social Sciences, Microbio. w/Lab, Physics w/Lab, Stats., Composition & Writing or Public Speaking or Communications.	N/A	AP credits accepted as long as they are listed on undergraduate transcript.

For the number of hours required for prerequisite courses, and for the most up-to-date information, please refer to the individual school websites.

*A.P. credit satisfies the requirement.

** When A.P. credit is awarded, upper-level coursework in the same subject area is required.

*** A.P. credit may satisfy the requirement on a case by case basis

NEW YORK

School	Required	Recommended	Notes
Cornell University College of Veterinary Medicine	English Comp./ Writing (see notes), Biol. w/Lab**, Chem. w/Lab** (see notes), OChem, Advanced Life Science, Biochem., Physics w/Lab*.	Biochem Lab	Engl. req. can be satisfied with GRE V score of 163. AP credits with grade of 4+ are accepted.
Long Island University School of Veterinary Medicine	Biol. 1 or Zoology, Biol. 2 or Zoology, Chem. w/Lab, OChem. w/Lab, Biochem., Math or Stats., Genetics, Engl. Comp., and Public Speaking.	Cellular Biol., Sociology, Psych., and Medical Terminology.	No information listed on AP credits.

OHIO

School	Required	Recommended	Notes
The Ohio State University College of Veterinary Medicine	Biochem, Microbiology w/ Lab, Physiology, Communication, Science Electives, Humanities/Social Science Electives.	Communication course should be Public Speaking	AP credits accepted as long as they are listed on undergraduate transcript.

For the number of hours required for prerequisite courses, and for the most up-to-date information, please refer to the individual school websites.
*A.P. credit satisfies the requirement.
** When A.P. credit is awarded, upper-level coursework in the same subject area is required.
*** A.P. credit may satisfy the requirement on a case by case basis

OKLAHOMA

School	Required	Recommended	Notes
Oklahoma State University College of Veterinary Medicine	Engl., Chem. w/ Lab, OChem w/Lab, Biochem., Stats., Physics w/Lab, Animal Nutrition, General Zoology or equivalent w/ Lab, Bio. for Science Majors, Microbiology w/Lab, Genetics, Humanities/Social Sciences, Science and/or Business Elective (see recommended).	Business and commerce courses encouraged.	AP credits accepted as long as they are listed on undergraduate transcript. Nutrition course must cover digestion, absorption, and metabolism.

Animal Breeding courses will not cover genetics requirement. Animal Nutrition, Biochemistry, Animal Genetics, and OChem 1 & 2 w/Labs must be taken at a 4-year institution. |

OREGON

School	Required	Recommended	Notes
Oregon State University College of Veterinary Medicine	Biol., Upper-Division Biol. w/ Lab, Physics, Chem., w/Lab, OChem, Biochem., Genetics, Math, Physiology, Stats., Engl., Public Speaking, Humanities/Social Sciences.	Additional biochemistry (especially encouraged), additional physiology and/or anatomy, animal reproduction, cell bio., cell physio., epidemiology, histology, immunology, microbio., parasitology, and virology.	AP credits for lower division courses accepted as long as they are listed on undergraduate transcript.

For the number of hours required for prerequisite courses, and for the most up-to-date information, please refer to the individual school websites.
*A.P. credit satisfies the requirement.
** When A.P. credit is awarded, upper-level coursework in the same subject area is required.
*** A.P. credit may satisfy the requirement on a case by case basis

PENNSYLVANIA

School	Required	Recommended	Notes
University Of Pennsylvania School of Veterinary Medicine	Engl., Social Sciences/ Humanities, Physics, Chem., Biol. or Zoology, Microbiology, Biochem, Calc., Stats.	As many science-based courses as possible, especially in Biology. Most applicants have minimum 15 semester hours in biology.	AP credits accepted as long as they are listed on undergraduate transcript.

TENNESSEE

School	Required	Recommended	Notes
Lincoln Memorial University College of Veterinary Medicine	Biol. w/Lab, Genetics (Animal Breeding/Reproduction), Biochem., Adv. Science Electives (upper-level), OChem w/Lab, Chem. w/Lab, Physics, Engl., Social Sciences.	N/A	AP credits accepted as long as they are listed on undergraduate transcript.
University Of Tennessee College of Veterinary Medicine	Engl. Comp, Social Sciences/Humanities, General Biol./Zoology w/Lab, Cellular Biology, Genetics, Chem. w/Lab, OChem w/Lab, Physics w/Lab, Biochem.	Applicants strongly encouraged to take comparative anatomy, mammalian physiology, and microbiology w/ lab.	No mention of AP credits. Contact admissions for information.

For the number of hours required for prerequisite courses, and for the most up-to-date information, please refer to the individual school websites.

*A.P. credit satisfies the requirement.

** When A.P. credit is awarded, upper-level coursework in the same subject area is required.

*** A.P. credit may satisfy the requirement on a case by case basis

TEXAS

School	Required	Recommended	Notes
Texas A&M University College of Veterinary Medicine & Biomedical Sciences	Biol. w/Lab, Microbio. w/Lab, Genetics, Animal Nutrition or Feeds & Feeding, Chem. w/Lab, OChem w/Lab, Biochem., Stats., Physics w/Lab, Engl., Speech Communication.	N/A	AP credits accepted as long as they are listed on undergraduate transcript. Applicants must complete 53 hours of pre-requisite coursework by the end of spring semester prior to matriculation. In addition, applicants must have completed or be enrolled in OChem 1, Physics 1, and Biochem. 1, prior to Fall Semester of their application.
Texas Tech University School of Veterinary Medicine	Animal Nutrition, Biochem., Engl., Bio. w/Lab, Microbio. w/Lab, Genetics, Chem. w/Lab, OChem. w/Lab, Stats., and Physics.	N/A	AP credits accepted as long as they are listed on undergraduate transcript.

For the number of hours required for prerequisite courses, and for the most up-to-date information, please refer to the individual school websites.

*A.P. credit satisfies the requirement.

** When A.P. credit is awarded, upper-level coursework in the same subject area is required.

*** A.P. credit may satisfy the requirement on a case by case basis

VIRGINIA

School	Required	Recommended	Notes
Virginia Tech Virginia-Maryland College of Veterinary Medicine	Biol. w/Lab, OChem w/Lab, Physics w/Lab, Biochem., Engl., Math, Humanities/Social Sciences, Medical Terminology.	Suggested elective courses in liberal arts.	AP credits accepted as long as they are listed on undergraduate transcript. AP credit for one semester of Engl. will be accepted as long as student takes additional Engl. requirements at a college or university.

WASHINGTON

School	Required	Recommended	Notes
Washington State University College of Veterinary Medicine	Biol. w/Lab, Chem. w/Lab, OChem w/Lab, Genetics, Biochem., Physics w/Lab, Stats., Algebra/Pre-Calc or higher, Engl. Comp/Communications, Arts & Humanities/Social Sciences.	Applicants should take higher level courses even if AP credits satisfy prerequisites.	AP credits accepted. Refer to WSU AP Credit Chartfor which courses may be satisfied. If applicant receives bachelor's degree prior to matriculation, then general ed. prerequisites are considered fulfilled regardless of credit hours.

For the number of hours required for prerequisite courses, and for the most up-to-date information, please refer to the individual school websites.

*A.P. credit satisfies the requirement.

** When A.P. credit is awarded, upper-level coursework in the same subject area is required.

*** A.P. credit may satisfy the requirement on a case by case basis

WISCONSIN

School	Required	Recommended	Notes
University of Wisconsin-Madison School of Veterinary Medicine	Biol. or Zoology, Genetics or Animal Breeding; Chem. and Qualitative Chem. w/Lab, OChem., Biochem., Physics, Stats., Engl. Comp. or Journalism, Social Sciences or Humanities.	N/A	AP credits accepted as long as they are listed on undergraduate transcript.

For the number of hours required for prerequisite courses, and for the most up-to-date information, please refer to the individual school websites.
*A.P. credit satisfies the requirement.
** When A.P. credit is awarded, upper-level coursework in the same subject area is required.
*** A.P. credit may satisfy the requirement on a case by case basis

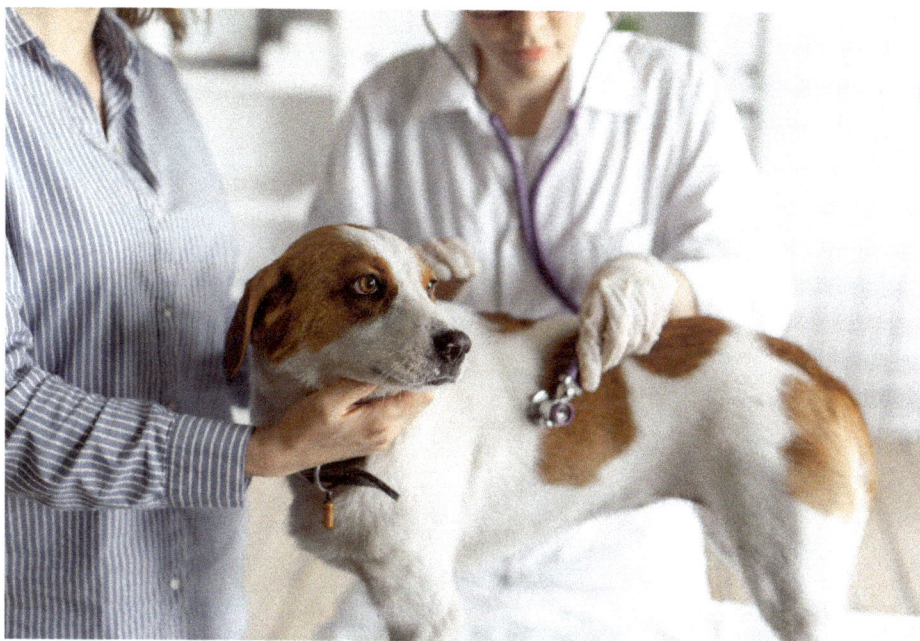

CHAPTER 43

TOP 10 VETERINARY MEDICAL SCHOOLS

Ranking	Vet School
#1	University of California, Davis School of Veterinary Medicine
#2	Cornell University College of Veterinary Medicine
#3	Colorado State University College of Veterinary Medicine and Biomedical Sciences
#4	North Carolina State University College of Veterinary Medicine
#4	Ohio State University College of Veterinary Medicine
#4	Texas A&M University College of Veterinary Medicine & Biomedical Sciences
#4	University of Pennsylvania School of Veterinary Medicine
#8	University of Wisconsin-Madison School of Veterinary Medicine
#9	University of Florida College of Veterinary Medicine
#10	University of Georgia College of Veterinary Medicine

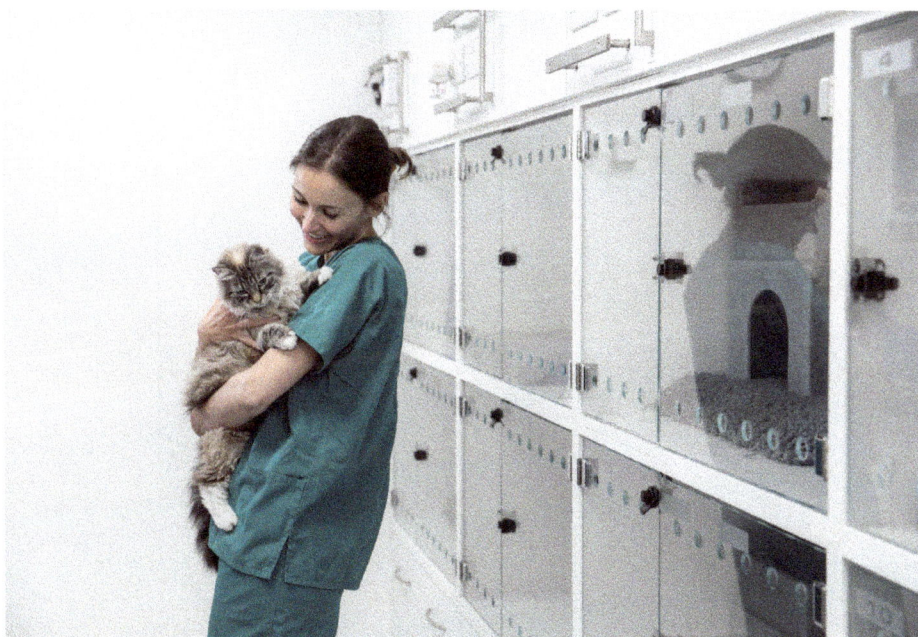

CHAPTER 44

VET SCHOOLS BY COST OF ATTENDANCE

Vet Schools	Tuition (Out-of-State)	COA (Out-of-State)
Texas Tech University School of Veterinary Medicine	$32,800.00	$52,590.00
Tuskegee University School of Veterinary Medicine	$41,170.00	$44,190.00
Texas A&M University College of Veterinary Medicine & Biomedical Sciences	$42,022.00	$63,582.00
University of California, Davis School of Veterinary Medicine	$44,406.00	$73,876.00
Purdue University College of Veterinary Medicine	$44,746.00	$61,556.00
University of Florida College of Veterinary Medicine	$45,500.00	$65,062.00
Oklahoma State University College of Veterinary Medicine	$46,795.00	$74,730.00
University of Georgia College of Veterinary Medicine	$47,176.00	$67,698.00
Michigan State University College of Veterinary Medicine	$47,436.00	$68,468.00
North Carolina State University College of Veterinary Medicine	$47,657.00	$67,610.00
Mississippi State University College of Veterinary Medicine	$48,448.00	$69,418.00
Auburn University College of Veterinary Medicine	$49,040.00	$72,051.00
Lincoln Memorial University College of Veterinary Medicine	$50,500.00	$71,614.00
Oregon State University College of Veterinary Medicine	$51,375.00	$71,331.00
University of Illinois College of Veterinary Medicine	$51,398.00	$74,364.00
Virginia Tech Virginia-Maryland College of Veterinary Medicine	$51,900.00	$77,520.00
University of Wisconsin-Madison School of Veterinary Medicine	$52,150.00	$74,022.00
Louisiana State University School of Veterinary Medicine	$53,227.85	$82,743.00
Iowa State University College of Veterinary Medicine	$53,304.00	$136,732.00
Western University of Health Sciences College of Veterinary Medicine	$55,575.00	$77,435.00
Kansas State University College of Veterinary Medicine	$55,742.00	$75,470.00

Long Island University School of Veterinary Medicine	$56,100.00	$87,597.00
University of Tennessee College of Veterinary Medicine	$56,602.00	$79,688.00
University of Minnesota College of Veterinary Medicine	$57,948.00	$76,650.00
Cornell University College of Veterinary Medicine	$58,244.00	$77,744.00
Tufts University School of Veterinary Medicine	$60,694.00	$109,858.00
Washington State University College of Veterinary Medicine	$61,714.00	$80,460.00
Colorado State University College of Veterinary Medicine and Biomedical Sciences	$62,660.00	$83,464.00
University of Missouri - Columbia College of Veterinary Medicine	$65,170.00	$86,602.00
Midwestern University College of Veterinary Medicine	$67,354.00	$101,871.00
University of Pennsylvania School of Veterinary Medicine	$69,278.00	$94,312.00
University of Arizona College of Veterinary Medicine	$72,719.00	$106,292.00
Ohio State University College of Veterinary Medicine	$72,923.00	$95,056.00

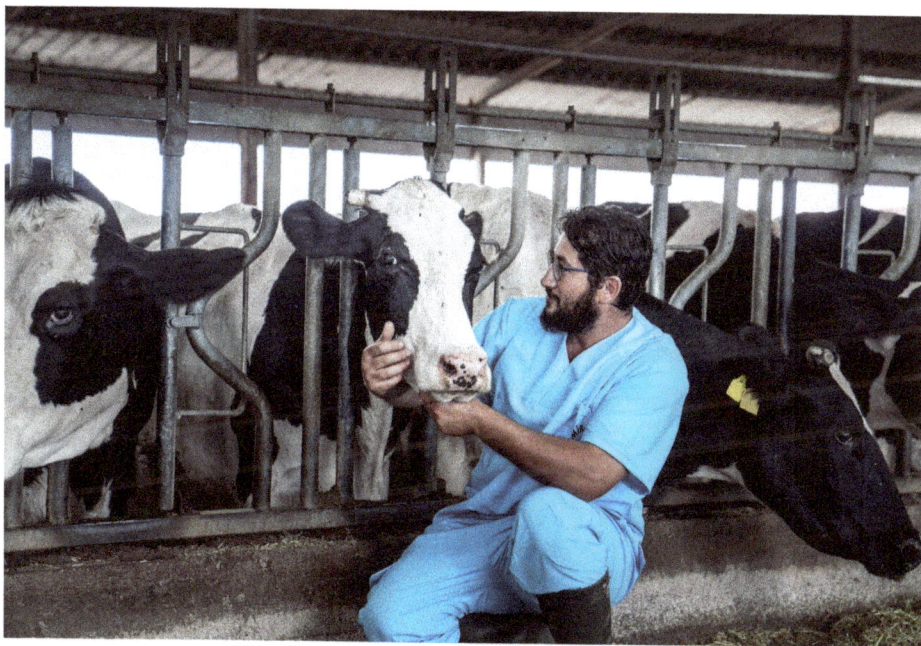

CHAPTER 45

VET SCHOOLS BY # OF INCOMING STUDENTS

School	# Enrolled in 2020
Tuskegee University School of Veterinary Medicine	56
Oregon State University College of Veterinary Medicine	72
Virginia Tech Virginia-Maryland College of Veterinary Medicine	80
Purdue University College of Veterinary Medicine	84
University of Tennessee College of Veterinary Medicine	85
University of Wisconsin-Madison School of Veterinary Medicine	96
Mississippi State University College of Veterinary Medicine	97
Long Island University School of Veterinary Medicine	100
North Carolina State University College of Veterinary Medicine	100
University of Arizona College of Veterinary Medicine	100
Tufts University School of Veterinary Medicine	105
University of Minnesota College of Veterinary Medicine	105
Western University of Health Sciences College of Veterinary Medicine	105
Oklahoma State University College of Veterinary Medicine	106
Louisiana State University School of Veterinary Medicine	115
Michigan State University College of Veterinary Medicine	116
Cornell University College of Veterinary Medicine	120
University of Florida College of Veterinary Medicine	121
Kansas State University College of Veterinary Medicine	124
University of Missouri - Columbia College of Veterinary Medicine	124
Lincoln Memorial University College of Veterinary Medicine	125
Midwestern University College of Veterinary Medicine	125
University of Georgia College of Veterinary Medicine	125
University of Pennsylvania School of Veterinary Medicine	127
Auburn University College of Veterinary Medicine	130
University of Illinois College of Veterinary Medicine	130
Washington State University College of Veterinary Medicine	138
Colorado State University College of Veterinary Medicine and Biomedical Sciences	150
University of California, Davis School of Veterinary Medicine	150
Iowa State University College of Veterinary Medicine	157
Ohio State University College of Veterinary Medicine	162
Texas A&M University College of Veterinary Medicine & Biomedical Sciences	162
Texas Tech University School of Veterinary Medicine	N/A

COMPREHENSIVE HEALTH CARE SERIES

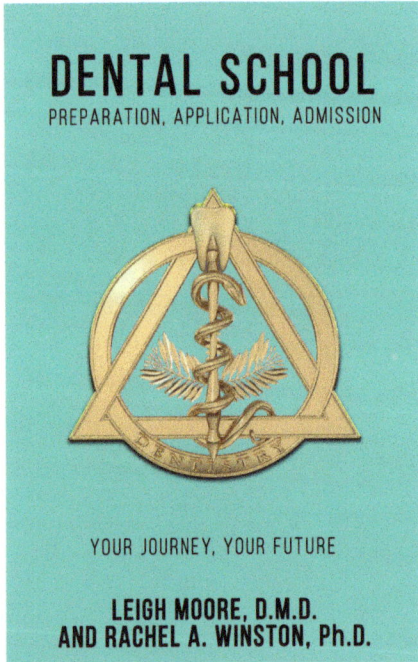

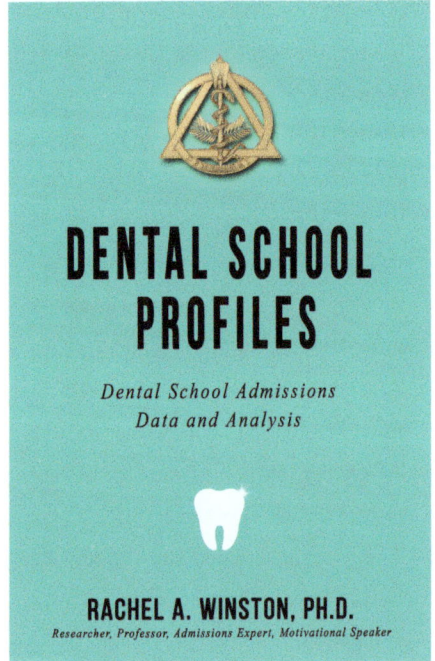

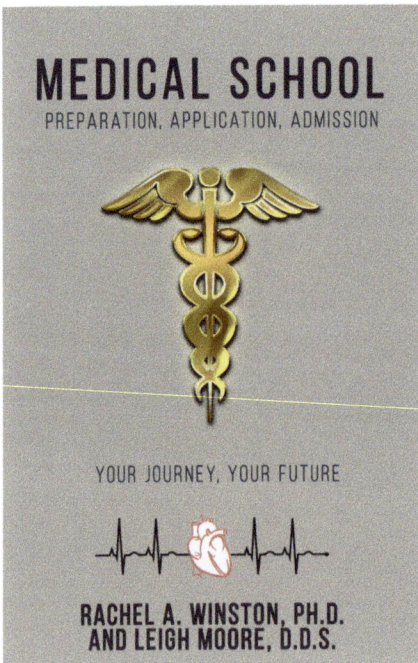

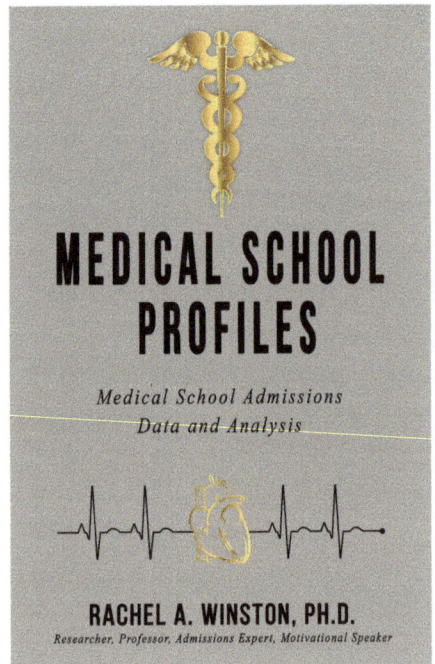

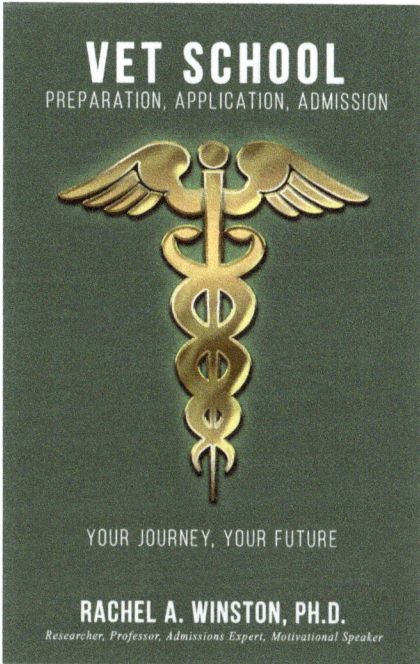

VET SCHOOL
PREPARATION, APPLICATION, ADMISSION

YOUR JOURNEY, YOUR FUTURE

RACHEL A. WINSTON, PH.D.
Researcher, Professor, Admissions Expert, Motivational Speaker

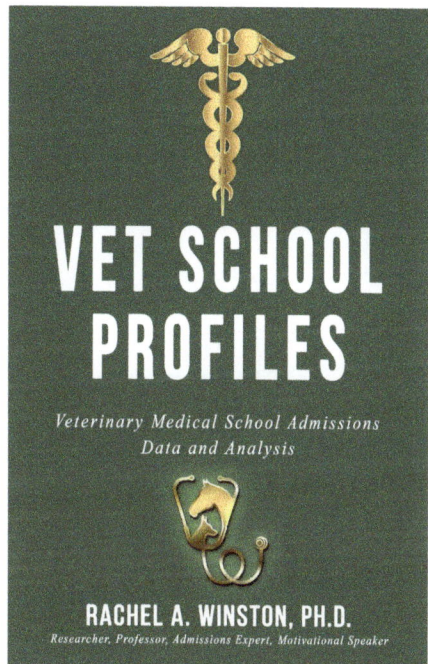

VET SCHOOL PROFILES

Veterinary Medical School Admissions Data and Analysis

RACHEL A. WINSTON, PH.D.
Researcher, Professor, Admissions Expert, Motivational Speaker

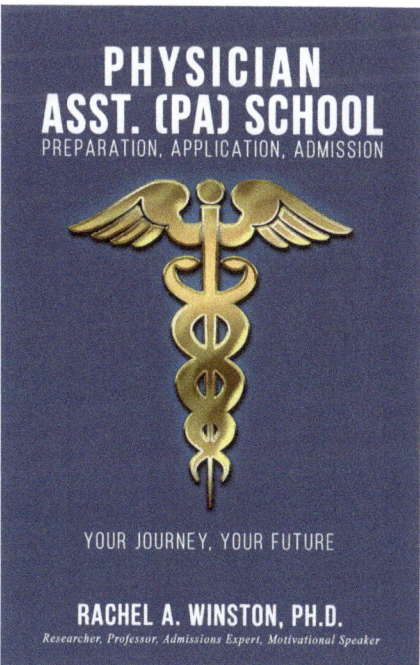

PHYSICIAN ASST. (PA) SCHOOL
PREPARATION, APPLICATION, ADMISSION

YOUR JOURNEY, YOUR FUTURE

RACHEL A. WINSTON, PH.D.
Researcher, Professor, Admissions Expert, Motivational Speaker

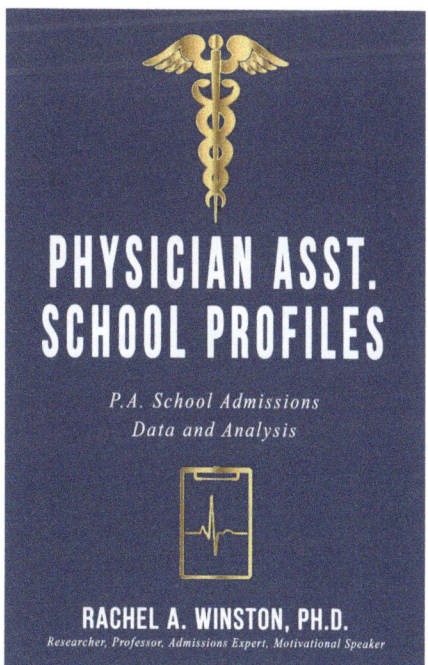

PHYSICIAN ASST. SCHOOL PROFILES

P.A. School Admissions Data and Analysis

RACHEL A. WINSTON, PH.D.
Researcher, Professor, Admissions Expert, Motivational Speaker

PHARM.D. SCHOOL
PREPARATION, APPLICATION, ADMISSION

YOUR JOURNEY, YOUR FUTURE

RACHEL A. WINSTON, PH.D.
Researcher, Professor, Admissions Expert, Motivational Speaker

PHARM.D. SCHOOL PROFILES

Pharmacy School Admissions Data and Analysis

RACHEL A. WINSTON, PH.D.
Researcher, Professor, Admissions Expert, Motivational Speaker

OSTEOPATHIC MEDICAL SCHOOL
PREPARATION, APPLICATION, ADMISSION

YOUR JOURNEY, YOUR FUTURE

RACHEL A. WINSTON, PH.D.
Researcher, Professor, Admissions Expert, Motivational Speaker

OSTEO SCHOOL PROFILES

Osteopathic Medical School Admissions Data and Analysis

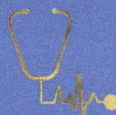

RACHEL A. WINSTON, PH.D.
Researcher, Professor, Admissions Expert, Motivational Speaker

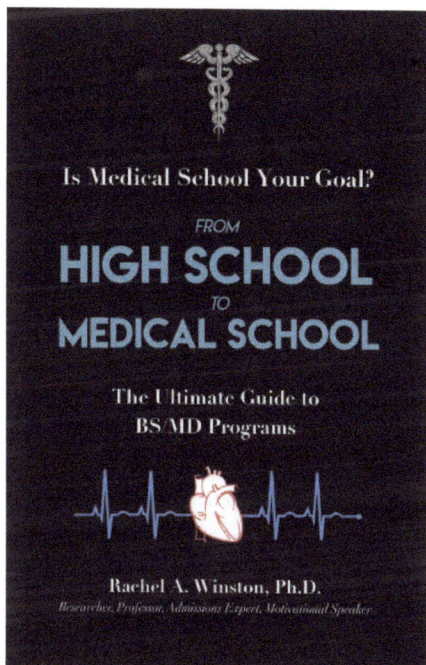

INDEX

Symbols

A

B

C

M

N

O

P

Q

R

S

T

U

V

W

Z

www.ingramcontent.com/pod-product-compliance
Lightning Source LLC
Chambersburg PA
CBHW052014030426
42335CB00026B/3146